AF531574

Come up to Success in Education

Edited by

Dr. S.K. PANNER SELVAM

Assistant Professor, Department of Education

Bharathidasan University, T.N

and

Dr. R. SUMATHI

Principal,

Cheran College of Education,

Karur, Tamil Nadu.

RANDOM PUBLICATIONS

NEW DELHI (INDIA)

Come up to Success in Education

ISBN 978-93-5111-889-3

Published in 2016 in India by
RANDOM PUBLICATIONS
4376-A/4B, Gali Murari Lal, Ansari Road
New Delhi-110 002
Phone : +9111-43580356, 011-43142548, 011-23289044
e-mail : sales@randompublications.com
info@randompublications.com
randomexports@gmail.com

Reprinted 2024

Type Setting by : Shah Computer Graphics, Delhi-110094
Digitally Printed at: Replika Press Pvt. Ltd.

Contents

Chapter I

Education Achievement Through 3D Approach

Introduction

This chapter reveals, origin of the research topic arise and introducing the problem of the present study. The investigator selected this topic and framed his work in a systematic manner with sound scientific background and interest.

Definition of Education

According to J.C.AGGARWAL (1987), Education aims to seek and cultivate new knowledge, to engage vigorously and fearlessly in the pursuit of truth and to interpret old knowledge and benefits in the light of new needs and discoveries.

John Dewey writes the Education is the process of living through a continuous reconstruction of experience. It is the development of all these capacities in the individual, which will enable him to control his environment and fulfil his responsibilities. Education meets the immediate needs of a child and also prepares him for his future life. It develops all his intellectual and emotional powers, so that he is able to meet the problems of life squarely and solve them successfully. It also develops the social qualities of service, tolerance, co-operation and fellow feeling. "Education is a key that open the eyes of a person towards the brightness of the world"-**Dr. Radhakrishnan**.

One of the most popular definitions, given by our ancient Indian Educational thinker Rabindranath Tagore is given below:

"Education means enabling the mind to find out the ultimate truth which emancipates us form the bondage of the lust and gives us the wealth, not of things but of inner light, not power but of love, making this truth of its own and living expression to it".

"The Central task of education is to implant a will and facility for learning; it should produce not learned but learning people. The truly human society is a learning society, where grandparents, parents and children are students together - **Eric Hoffer.**

No one has yet realized the wealth of sympathy, the kindness and generosity hidden in the soul of a child. The effort of every true education should be to unlock that treasure - **Emma Goldman.**

"The only purpose of education is to teach a student how to live his life-by developing his mind and equipping him to deal with reality. The training he needs is theoretical, i.e., conceptual. He has to be taught to think, to understand, to integrate, to provide. He has to be taught the essentials of the knowledge discovered in the past and he has to be equipped to acquire further knowledge by his own effort" - **Ayn Rand.**

Aristotle: "Education is the creation of sound mind in a sound body. It develops man's faculty, especially his mind so that he may be able to enjoy the contemplation of supreme truth, goodness and beauty of which perfect happiness essentially consists".

Meaning of Education

The act or process of education and the result of education, as determined by the knowledge, skill or discipline of character is acquired and the process is unending. The act or process or training by prescribed or customary course of study or discipline-as, an education for the bar or the pulpit-has a finishing point and we say the student has finished his education. The Destiny of India is now being shaped in her classrooms (Kothari-1966). Education is the most essential human value. Knowledge is developed through literacy education. Education being a most important social activity, its meanings has been changing through the ages due to changes in social and physical conditions as well as philosophical outlook of people towards life.

Need of Education

Across countries, education plays a vital role not only in acquiring knowledge but also inculcating social, ethical, moral and spiritual values. In our model, schooling teaches people to interact with others and raises the benefits of civic participation including voting and organizing. Education raises the benefits of civic participation. Education is able to in still in the child a sense of maturity and responsibility in bringing in him the desired changes. According to this needs and demands of ever changing society of which he is an integral part.

Importance of Education

The importance of education is quite clear. Education is the knowledge of putting one's potentials to maximum use. One can safely say that a human being is not in the proper sense complete till he is educated. The second reason for the importance of education is that only through the attainment of education, man is enabled to receive information from the external world; to acquaint him with past history and receive all necessary information regarding the present. Without education, main is as though in a closed room and with education he finds himself in room with all its windows open towards outside world.

A conceptual framework is used in a research to outline possible theoretical background of the study. This chapter mainly deals with topic such as effectiveness of 3D approach for showcasing the concepts of basic physics, advanced teaching techniques used in science and role of 3D Approach in AchievingCertain Competencies in Physics among IX standard students.

Importance of 3d Approach in Physics

Multimedia, is the combination of various digital media types such as text, images, audio and video, into an integrated multi-sensory interactive application or presentation to convey information to an audience.

Learning in conventional approach often use the whiteboard and textbook that only shows text and graphic to show certain concepts of physics by using 3D technology approach is possible to apply to assist learners for easy understanding of the physics competencies. This research addresses the impact of using 3D approach in teaching and its advantage over current approach. Besides, 3D model can be rotated around any axis, panned or zoomed in any direction. With this 3D viewing, students are able to position and recognize the object with relation to others scene, enabling a better and more complete visualization and interactive learning process in physics.

3D Approach in the Development of physics Subject

This research highlights the development of 3D approach in learning the physics subject. Throughout the years, various teaching methods have been adopted to assist students to better understand in learning physics subject. Current knowledge delivery system in education is dynamically changing to more flexible and reliable. This research attempt to present new ways of learning physics subject by using 3D approach to encounter the problems found from the survey and interview done.

Therefore, computer aided learning is up scaled to increase the efficiency of the student through augment the ability of visualization with the aid of multimedia elements. Beside, 3D model assists learners to gain more understanding in Thermal capacity, specific heat capacity and change of states.

Physics and Technology

Physics as a branch of science is highly important in modern societies because of its requirement as a pre-requisite to the study of many other science oriented courses. It thus appears that for a nation to develop in science and technology, the teaching and learning of chemistry need to be improved. It is therefore becomes pertinent that performances in physics and in science generally should be of high levels.

Prominent factors contributing to the persistence of students poor performance in physics are:

1. Ineffective teaching methods adopted by the physics teacher.
2. Lack of infrastructures and teaching materials.
3. Lack of organized strategies for problem solving and poor reasoning.
4. Poor mathematics background.

Physics is one of the fundamental ingredients of technology. It is a branch of science that deals with the practical and experimental understanding of natural phenomena. The study of physics follows from the simple to a more complex, hence physics is said to be more process than a product. A very important aspect in the delivery of physics is the methods and materials employed in transmitting knowledge. This implies that, like every other science subject, the teaching and learning of physics can only be effective by the use of instructional resources (instructional materials, teaching aids, audio – visuals). Instructional resources are aids employed by the teacher to enhance the effectiveness of instruction. They are information carries specifically designed to elicit desired behavioural change in the learners. Instructional resources include a wide variety of equipments and materials used for teaching and learning ranging from hardware to software.

Multimedia courseware is believed as the most appropriate way to encounter the problem of student in visualizing. 3D environments in a conventional academic course can be engaging and beneficial in improving learning capabilities. Traditional learning to 3D environments has improved the quality of student learning through effective integration of current module design. Beside that 3D model can be rotate around any axis, and panned or zoomed in any direction.

Motivation of Students to Learn Physics

Motivation to learn physics benefits all young students by fostering their physical literacy, which is the capability to recognize physics concepts as such, define some key-concepts, identify important scientific questions, use their understanding of physics concepts to explain phenomena, use their knowledge in physics to read a short article, or analyze information provided in commercial advertisements or internet resources. Physical literacy is considered as a component of scientific literacy and the importance of all students becoming scientifically literate is advocated internationally.

In general, motivation is the internal state that arouses, directs, and sustains goal-oriented behaviour. In particular, motivation to learn refers to the disposition of students to find academic activities relevant and worthwhile and to try and derive from them the intended benefits. Motivated students achieve academically by strategically engaging in behaviours such as class attendance, class participation, question asking, advice seeking, studying, and participating in study groups.

Motivation is a complex, multidimensional construct that interacts with cognition to influence learning. In the context of conceptual change theory of learning, Dole and Sinatra describe how both cognitive and motivational learner characteristics interact within a specific learning environment to support or hinder conceptual change. Social cognitive theory explains human learning and motivation in terms of reciprocal interactions involving personal characteristics (e.g., intrinsic motivation, self efficacy, and self-determination), environmental contexts (e.g., high school), and behaviour (e.g., enrolling in advanced science courses). In studying the motivation to learn science, researchers examine why students strive to learn science, how intensively they strive, and what beliefs, feelings, and emotions characterize them in this process.

Sanfeliz and Stalzer, like many high school science teachers, believe that one of their most important instructional responsibilities is to foster students motivation to learn. According to Sanfeliz and Stalzer, motivated students enjoy learning science, believe in their ability to learn, and take responsibility for their learning.

Competency of physics Teacher

The competence of a physics teacher can be judged by what goes on in the physics classroom. Ajaja (2005) indicated that science teachers continue to teach science using the lecture method despite the recommended guided discovery/inquiry methods. The inability of science teachers to apply guided discovery/inquiry approaches in their teaching is attributed to problems which include; lack of laboratories equipped with facilities in schools and competency problems arising from the training of science teachers.

Mostly, the teacher controls the instructional process, the content is delivered to the entire class and the teacher tends to emphasize factual knowledge. In other words, the teacher delivers the lecture content and the students listen to the lecture. Thus, the learning mode tends to be passive and the learners play little part in their learning process. Increasingly, scientific literacy is being described as the overall aim of science education (Bybee, 1997) the teaching of physics therefore, as a scientific discipline must help students gain scientific literacy abilities and to grow into scientific literate citizens.

Physics is a very important subject as its knowledge is required for the successful study n very many important professions. Because of this importance, physics is occupying a prime place in the senior secondary school curriculum. In is therefore necessary that students studying physics should understand the subject so that they can apply their knowledge to their everyday interaction with people and their ever changing environment.

Purpose of Teaching Science Curriculum

The purpose of teaching science curriculum is to give individuals a firm grasp of the concepts and processes of science and impart them the ability to use scientific method and develop scientific attitude and scientific temper, which are very valuable at the same time are transferable to other situations in life. So the purpose of teaching science curriculum should be placed in school curriculum at all levels and its teaching should be impressive in order to inculcate the ethics or values of science.

Role of Teacher and his Teaching Techniques in Science

Any technical procedure centre round the pivotal factors of the pupil, the teacher and the subject. When the teacher gain sufficient experiences he may lecture, demonstrate, organize laboratory work individually or in group. He may encourage the formation of societies and clubs provide film, lead to excursion and examination paper with questions of various types and recommend additional reading turn a class into a brain trust or into a committee to arrange and exhibition and so on.

When integrating science with other content matter, the teacher should give careful attention to designing "a logical and coherent structure" for ensuring that they clearly communicate and ensure contextual understanding of embedded scientific concepts, as recommended by Long Beach United School District (LBUSD).

Essentials of innovative approach needed in teaching physics

Nowadays, the students have diverse backgrounds, a variety of achievement levels and different learning styles which affects their ability to acquire knowledge. Teachers need to move away from the traditional methods of teaching and bring the new and innovative approaches to teach the content and lifelong skills. It is important to utilize a variety of techniques, way of teaching styles etc... for children to build their own understanding through real world applications and interactions with their peers in group activities.

At present, physics is taught in narrative form and the students are asked to memorize a vast amount of descriptive data and wider variety of apparently unconnected physical structure. It is not impressing that the subject is not favoured by students seeking intellectual contents. So as to improve the understanding capacity of the students through the innovative approach is paramount important. Not only physics, all the subjects must be taught through the innovative and ICT tools.

Physics is one of the science subjects easy to understand and play vital role in day to day life. If it is not teach properly in secondary level students, this subject is finding very difficult to understand and hinder the interest on science.

Science education and its importance in day to day life activities

Modern science and technology have changed our lives in many constructive ways. Aeroplanes, automobiles communications, satellites, computers, plastic and television are only a few of the scientific and technological inventions that have transformed human life. Research by nuclear physicist has led to the development of nuclear energy as a source of power. Agricultural scientists have developed better varieties in different crops to enhance production with high nutrient or fertilizer use efficiency. The development of antibiotics and other new drugs has helped to control many infectious diseases in the medical science. Studies in anatomy and physiology have led to amazing new surgical operations and to the invention of lifesaving machines that can do the work of such organs as the lungs, kidney and heart.

Some limitations which may prevail in traditional teaching method are

1. Teaching in classroom using chalk and talk is "one way flow" of information
2. Teachers often continuously talk for an hour without knowing students response and feedback.
3. The material presented is only based on lecture notes and textbooks.
4. Teaching and learning are concentrated on "plug and play" method rather than practical aspects.
5. The handwriting of the lecture decides the fate of the subject.
6. There is insufficient interaction with students in classroom.
7. More emphasis has been given on theory without any practical and real life time situations.
8. Learning from memorization but not understanding.
9. Marks rather than result oriented.

Students Learning Difficulties

Students are facing 3 types of difficulties in learning physical representations have been identified. First, a majority of students cannot appropriately interpret meanings of representations in the concepts of physics.

Second learning difficulty is students are less capable of providing equivalent representations for a given representation. Most of the students were unable to make translation among formula, and students performances on translations were correlated to their understanding of underlying concepts.

A third learning difficulty involves the mental transformation between two-dimensional (2-D) and three-dimensional (3-D) representations. Many students are not able to form 3-D mental images by viewing 2-D physical structures and to mentally rotate 3-D images.

Need and Significance of the Study

In this present context, most of the physics students learn the subject pass the examination and forget the concept, facts, terms and principles when they go out. Unless some intervention is made, the student cannot comprehend the concept in the physics. Hence it is the duty of the physics teacher to make an instructional design that would support them in realizing and envisaged instructional objectives. So the investigator felt a need to select this topic to improve the easy understanding capacity of the students.

At present, the teacher in Indian schools take more time to complete the classroom instructions by the traditional method of teaching due to over loaded syllabi and lack of time in the classroom situation. Further the teachers are not able to concentrate on the development of all the cognitive skills. The investigator felt that this kind of study is needed particularly for secondary students to improve better understanding and application of their mind in enhancing their knowledge.

Scope of the Study

The main purpose of the present investigation was to enhance the understanding level of the students in learning physics at secondary level particularly to IX standard students. The teaching strategy developed by the investigator can be followed by all Indian classroom situation, whether it is crowded or in multi-graded situation. It gives an opportunity for the teacher to motive the children. The teacher can identify the suitable method of teaching. The teaching strategy can be followed by analyzing the knowledge, understanding and application level competency and appropriate activities can be given to attain the competency in a joyful manner. This teaching approach used in schools to develop a positive attitude towards the physics subject and physics teachers, though the present study is to the class of IX standard, the strategy may be adopted to secondary and higher secondary level too. This strategy may be followed in teaching of other subject such as mathematics etc.

Statement of the Problem

Problem of the present research is to study the *"Effectiveness of 3D Approach in achieving certain competencies in physics Among IX Std Students".*

Operational Definition of the Key Terms

Effectiveness

Effectiveness means the impressive result produced in understanding the concept of physics through 3D approaches in accordance with teaching performance of the teacher.

3D Approach

Any object that can be represented on a three – axis system is 3D. Three dimensional models that display a picture or item in a form that appears to be physically present with a designated structure. Essentially, it allows items that appeared flat to the human eye to be display in a form that allows for various dimensions to be represented. These dimensions include width, depth, and height.

Objectives of the Study

1. To find out whether there is any significant difference between the mean sources of boys and girls in pre-test of control group in achieving certain competencies in physics among IX standard students.
2. To find out whether there is any significant difference between

the mean scores of boys and girls in pre-test of Experimental group in achieving certain competencies in physics among IX standard students.

3. To find out whether there is any significant difference between the mean scores of boys and girls in post-test of control group in achieving certain competencies in physics among IX standard students.
4. To find out whether there is any significant difference between the mean scores of boys and girls in post-test of Experimental group in achieving certain competencies in physics among IX standard students.
5. To find out whether there is any significant difference between the mean scores of boys in pre-test of Control and Experimental group in achieving certain competencies in physics among IX standard students.
6. To find out whether there is any significant difference between the mean scores of girls in pre-test of Control and Experimental group in achieving certain competencies in physics among IX standard students.
7. To find out whether there is any significant difference between the mean scores of Boys in post-test of Control and Experimental group in achieving certain competencies in physics among IX standard students.
8. To find out whether there is any significant difference between the mean scores of Girls in post-test of Control and Experimental group in achieving certain competencies in physics among IX standard students.
9. To find out whether there is any significant difference between the mean scores of Control and Experimental group students of pre-test performance in achieving certain competencies in physics among IX standard students.
10. To find out whether there is any significant difference between the mean scores of Control and Experimental group students in post-test performance in achieving certain competencies in physics among IX standard students.

11. To find out whether there is any significant difference between the mean scores of control group students of pre-test and post-test performance in achieving certain competencies in physics among IX standard students.

12. To find out whether there is any significant difference between the mean scores of Experimental group students of pre-test and post-test performance in achieving certain competencies in physics among IX standard students.

Hypothesis of the Study

1. There is no significant difference between the mean scores of boys and girls in pre-test of control group in achieving certain competencies in physics among IX standard students.
2. There is no significant difference between the mean scores of boys and girls in pre-test of Experimental group in achieving certain competencies in physics among IX standard students.
3. There is no significant difference between the mean scores of boys and girls in post-test of control group in achieving certain competencies in physics among IX standard students.
4. There is no significant difference between the mean scores of boys and girls in post-test of Experimental group in achieving certain competencies in physics among IX standard students.
5. There is no significant difference between the mean scores of boys in pre-test of Control and Experimental group in achieving certain competencies in physics among IX standard students.
6. There is no significant difference between the mean scores of Girls in pre-test of Control and Experimental group in achieving certain competencies in physics among IX standard students.
7. There is no significant difference between the mean scores of boys in post-test of Control group and Experimental group in achieving certain competencies in physics among IX standard students.
8. There is no significant difference between the mean scores of girls in post-test of Control group and Experimental group in

achieving certain competencies in physics among IX standard students.

9. There is no significant difference between the mean scores of Control and Experimental group students of pre-test performance in achieving certain competencies in physics among IX standard students.
10. There is no significant difference between the mean scores of Control and Experimental group students in post-test performance in achieving certain competencies in physics among IX standard students.
11. There is no significant difference between the mean scores of Control group students of pre-test and post-test performance in achieving certain competencies in physics among IX standard students.
12. There is no significant difference between the mean scores of Experimental group students of pre-test and post-test performance in achieving certain competencies in physics among IX standard students.

Limitation of the Study

1. The researcher conducted the experiment only in the school located in urban area
2. This study was conducted in only one chapter of the Physics syllabus for secondary school students
3. This study was conducted to IX standard students particularly in government Higher Secondary School, Pudukkottai, Tamilnadu.
4. The experimental treatment was given with duration of one month only the sample consist of 60 students

Conclusion

In the first chapter importance of 3D approach in Physics, scope of the study, Hypothesis of the present research are discussed. In the next chapter review of literature will be given.

Chapter II

Review of Related Literature

Introduction

The Review of related literature gives sufficient idea and information to the investigator. Since the problem under investigation is "Effectiveness of 3D Approach in Achieving Certain Competencies in Physics at secondary level" the investigator tried to collect studies related to 3D models and physics. After going through the profuse literature, the investigator has selected only those that are relevant for the present study.

According to Good, Barr and Scates, "The competent physician must keep abreast of the latest discoveries in the field of medicine. Obviously the careful student of education, the research worker and investigator should become familiar with location and use of sources of Educational information".

According to W.R. Borg, "The literature in any field forms the foundation upon which all future work will be built. If we fail to build the foundation of knowledge provided by the review of literature our work is likely to be shallow and naive and will often duplicate work that has already been done better by someone else".

According to charter V.Good, "The keys to the vast store house of published literature may open doors to sources of significant problems and explanatory hypothesis and provide helpful orientation for definition of the problem, background for selection of procedure, and comparative data for interpretation of results. In order to be creative and original, one must read extensively and critically as a stimulus to thinking".

According to Aggarwal J.C, "The state of related literature implies locating, speaking and evaluating reports of research as well as casual observation and opinions that are related to the individuals planned research project".

Importance of Related Literature

Survey of related literature provides valuable help in the development of knowledge in research work. It helps the investigator to gain insight into various aspects of the problem area that is in formulating a framework for the study, developing the methodology, constructing the tool for data collection and planning the analysis of data.

In general, the literature review should:

1. Provide a context for the research
2. Justify the research
3. Ensure the research hasn't been done before (or if it is repeated, that it is marked as a "replication study")
4. Show where the research fits into the existing body of knowledge
5. Enable the research to learn from previous theory on the subject
6. Illustrate how the subject has been studied previously
7. Highlight flaws in previous research
8. Outline gaps in previous research
9. Show that the work is adding to the understanding and knowledge of the field
10. Help refine, refocus or even change the topic

Significance of Literature Review

Review of the related literature besides, to allow the researcher to acquaint himself with current knowledge in the field or area in which he or she is going to conduct his or her research, serves the following significances.

1. The review of related literature enables the researcher to define the limits of his field. It helps the researcher to delimit and define his problem. The knowledge of related literature brings the researcher up to data on the work which others have done and them to state the objectives clearly and concisely.
2. By reviewing the related literature the researchers can avoid unfruitful and useless problem areas. He can select those areas in which positive findings are likely to result and his endeavours would be likely to add to the knowledge in a meaningful way.
3. Through the review of related literature the researcher can avoid unintentional duplication of well established findings. It is no use of replicate a study when the stability and validity of its result have been clearly established.
4. The review of related literature gives the researcher an understanding of the research methodology which refers to the way the study is to be conducted. It help the researcher to know about the tools and instruments which proved to be useful and promising the previous studies. The advantage of the related literature is also to provide insight into statistical methods through which validity of results is to be established.
5. The final and important specific reason for reviewing the related literature I to know about the recommendations of previous researcher for further research which they have listed in their studies.

Bruce W. Tuckman has enumerated the following significances of the review.

1. Discovering important variable.
2. Distinguishing what has done from what needs to be done.
3. Synthesizing the available studies to have perspective.

4. Determining meanings relevance of the study and relationship with the study and its deviation from the available studies.

Edward L. Vockell has pointed out the following two significances:

1. The main significance of this review is to put the hypothesis to be examined in the research report into its proper context.
2. Secondary significance of this part of the report are to provide readers with guidelines regarding where they can look find more information and to establish the author's credential by letting readers know that the researcher is aware of what has been giving on with regard to the current and related topics.

The review of literature provides some insight regarding strong points and limitations of the previous studies. It enables him to improve his own investigation.

Studies Conducted in India

Muthu (1978), conducted a study on "A study of the effectiveness of the use of motion pictures as Aids in the Teaching of Biological science as compared to the usual methods." This study revealed that, the sound pictures helped to a great extent the above average students to comprehend the subject matter in science. Instructional films stimulated the scientific Interest of the student.

Yadhav (1980), conducted a study on "Comparison between Lecture and discovery Methods in Teaching science" The finding of this study learning Situation according to the two methods may lead to the difference in academic development of the pupils. There was significant in mean achievement scores of the subject taught through lecture and discovery process for knowledge component.

Kumar (1981), conducted a study on" The Relative Effectiveness of Three Methods of Instruction-Exposition method, programmed learning method and multimedia method in Scientific Evaluation". This study revealed that, the multimedia, method was more effective than Expository method. Attention in learning by multi-media method was higher than by the other two methods.

Basu(1981), did a study on "effectiveness of multimedia programmed materials in teaching physics". In this study finding that the multimedia programmed instruction enables learner to reach mastery level. There was significant difference in achievement through different strategies due to different inability.

Anjaria(1984), conducted a study on "system approach in teaching of science-An Exploration". In this study, the experimental group scored high marks than the control group and the t-test was found to be significant. It could thus claim that the system approach to instruction was more effective than the traditional approach to education.

Desai(1985), conducted a study on "An investigation into the efficiency of different instructional media in the teaching of science to the pupils of class VII in relation to certain variables". The findings were studied with Discussion approach were more effective than traditional approach. The experimental approach was, more effective than traditional way of teaching science. The experimental approach was the most effective of all approaches.

Sivakumar (1994), conducted a study on "effectiveness of improvised aids in teaching science concepts at primary level". The findings of this study were the test performance revealed that the post-test performance is higher than the pre-test. This result might have arisen because of the effectiveness of the improvised aids.

Sinnathambi (1997), did a study on "Developing a video programme on Energetic in chemistry for Higher Secondary Students". The main Findings were the students improved their learning of concepts on energy after viewing the video programme. The student taught by video method learned more concepts on energy than the students taught by traditional classroom method.

Studies Conducted in Abroad

Festus, C (2012), conducted a detailed study on improving students' performance and attitude towards chemistry through problem-Based-Solving Techniques "The findings of this study had further established the fact that acceptable methods of instruction are capable of changing students' performance and attitude towards chemistry. The developed more positive performance and attitude after treatment. Based on the findings of the study, the following recommendations could be made.

Leopold et al (2012) did a study on Drawing, Main Idea Selection, and summarizing as learning strategies in science text comprehension". In this study, the results are consistent with the mental model approach to comprehension, showing advantages of drawing activity in fostering science text comprehension.

Cloonan et al (2011), conducted a study on "Understanding Chemical Reaction Kinetics and Equilibrium with Interlocking Building Blocks". This study revealed that, the flexible activity using building blocks is an appropriate activity for the both high school and under graduate general chemistry students and can be performed in a class room or laboratory.

Lee et al (2011), conduct study on "Visualizing chemical phenomena in micro droplets". In this study, the outcomes of various types of physical and chemistry phenomena including redo reaction, precipitation, interfacial extraction of metals, solubility of water in oils, and crystallization are illustrated.

Lee et al (2011), did a study on "Effectiveness of interactive multimedia module with pedagogical Agent (IMMPA) in the learning of electrochemistry-A preliminary Investigation". In this study results showed that, the students have higher scores on their post test as well as gained higher motivation level after learning with EC-Lab.

Rahaya et al (2011), conduct study on "Assessment of Electrochemical concepts: A comparative study involving high school students in Indonesia and Japan. This study had implications for teaching and learning, particularly in classroom discussions, using model and computer animations in order to reinforce understanding at the sub-microscopic level.

Cullen and Thomas (2011), did a study on "A Model Approach to the electrochemical cell-An Inquiry Activity". In this study the result pre and post testing and student comments, indicate that this Laboratory (EC) facilitates the student understanding of Electrochemical cells.

Lidan Fan and Youquan chen (2010), did a study "The combination of Network method and Traditional Model ". This study reveals the result of Traditional education to the net work aided education.

For this we should reasonably combine the network methods and traditional teaching according to the feature course.

Morris et al (2008), conduction a study on "Go Chemistry- A card game to help students Learn chemical formulas". This study finds that, the Difficulty of the Game can be easily adjusted to match the course objectives and the knowledge level of the students.

Sechmalz, M.S. (2008), conducted study on multimedia teaching aids and the finding revealed that teaching and learning based on computer had grown since forty years ago the latest innovation is multimedia field.

Paul warwick (2007), did a study on "Teaching and learning primary science with ICT". This study revealed that the teaching and learning primary science with ICT essential reading for students in science education and for teachers who want to use technology to improve learning in their science classrooms.

Nuraziera Mohd Hatta (2005), studied the topic on 3D Design of chemistry subject at UTEM: Atom Cubic" learning based computer is build to increase the efficiency. The student ability of visualization with the aid of multimedia elements. Beside, 3D model atom assists learners to gain more understanding in molecular structure.

Owolabi(2004) defined science as an integral part of human society. Its impact is felt in every sphere of human life, so much that it is intricately linked with a nation's development. Science as a field of study has done a lot for mankind. For instance, life has been made a lot easier for man as a result of the advancements in science. Through science, man has been able to better understand his environments and this has enabled him to manipulate the condition of his environment to suit his own benefit. Science has also made it possible for man to acquire his desired needs easily. It has reduced human needs to the barest minimum.

Ogunleye (2000) observed that science is a dynamic human activity concerned with understanding the workings of our world. This understanding helps man to know more about the universe. Without the applications of science, it would have been impossible for man to explore the other planets of the universe. Also, the awareness of the existence, of other planets would not have been realized without science.

Bassey (2002) opined that science is resource intensive. Furthermore, in a period of economic recession, it will be very difficult to adequately find some of the electronic gadgets and equipment for physics in schools. A situation that is further compounded by the galloping inflation in the country and often unrelatedness of some of the imported sophisticated materials and equipment; hence the need to produce materials locally.

Researches such as **Ogunleye (2000), Okonkwo (2000), Mkpanang (2005) and Obioha (2006)** reported that there were inadequate resources for the teaching of science subjects in secondary schools in Nigeria. They further stated that where there were little resources at all, they are not usually in good conditions, while the few that were in good conditions were not enough to go round those who needed them. Hence there is need for improvisation.

Omosewo (2008) and Akinsola (2000), considered the human factors as the teacher's professional commitment, creativity, mechanical skills, initiative and resourcefulness. They found that many of Nigerian science teachers were aware of possibility of improvisation but many exhibited poor attitudes towards improvisation. They also noted that very few teachers practice improvisation is time-consuming and fund depleting. The authors also noted that students too, possessed little or no interest in improvisation.

Conclusion

The summary of review of related literature reveals that there are adequate number of studies in this area of improving and developing the teaching methods in physics concepts. The researcher carefully searched how to improve the students understanding level in co-ordination physics.

Chapter III

Methodology

Introduction

This chapter deals with the methodological procedure used in this study. The methodological procedure includes Research methods, research tool, sampling, validity, Reliability, Data collection, Data analysis etc., adopted in the present study. The methodology considered as a "Blue print" for research. In this study the relevant data is collected by it investigator and analyzed by making appropriate statistical technique.

Research Design

In an experimental design, the researcher actively tries to change the situation, circumstances, or experience of participants (manipulation), which may lead to change in behaviour or outcomes of randomly assigned to different conditions and variables of interest are measured. The researcher tries to control the other variable in order to avoid confounds to causality. Therefore experiments are often highly fixed in the natural situation even before the data collection starts. It is also called "Empirical Research "or "Cause and effect Method". It is data based research. Coming up with conclusions which are capable of being verified with experiment. It is appropriate when proof is sought that certain variables affect other variables.

Selection of control and Experimental Group.

A control group in a scientific experiment is a group separated from the rest of the experiments where the independent variable being tested cannot influence the results. This isolates the independent variables effect on the experiment and it rules out the alternated explanation of the experimental results.

An experimental group is the group of scientific experiments where the experimental procedure is performed. This group is exposed to the independent variable being tested and the changes observed and recorded.

Steps involved in the Experimental process

1. Selecting the standard
2. Preferring 3D approach in physics subject
3. Developing the instructional material related to 3D approach in physics subject
4. Assessing the entry behaviour of the children by conducting a pre test
5. Selection of control and Experimental group based on the students marks
6. Teaching children through traditional method for control group
7. Teaching children through modern method of 3D method in teaching physics concepts
8. The treatment effect was given for four weeks
9. Administering the post-test for the children of control group and experimental group
10. Entering the scores of the post test of the students
11. Categorizing and analyzing the pre and post-test scores

12. Identifying the impact of the both traditional method and modern method of experimental group in teaching concepts of physics subject.

Variables controlled in the Experimental study

Researcher point out that certain intervening variable that appear in the experiment failure to control such variable may affect the outcome of the experiment. The following variables are controlled in the experimental study.

1. Time factor
2. Maturation
3. Pattern of the test.

Time factor

Time is one of the variables. It is controlled during the study. The time variable is controlled by prescribing equal time limit to the group in teaching the concept of physics as well as the duration of times of the test.

Maturation

Maturation means number of students in each group. In this study equal numbers of students are selected for the control and Experimental group. This study consist 30 students per in each group.

Conducting a criterion test for pre-test control and Experimental group

The criterion test was administrated and developed for collecting data in pre-test control and experimental group. This pre-test is used to assess the entry behaviour of the student. The criterion test score identified the basic knowledge of the students in the relevant field.

For the effective administration of the test following suggestions/ directions given by the **Dececco abd Crawford (1977) was carefully followed.**

1. Careful organization and efficient distribution of all the test material.

2. Brief directions and brief answers raised by students.
3. A record of time and chalk board to help the students pace their efforts.

Objectives of the Study

1. To find out whether there is any significant difference between the mean sources of boys and girls in pre-test of control group in achieving certain competencies in physics among IX standard students.
2. To find out whether there is any significant difference between the mean scores of boys and girls in pre-test of Experimental group in achieving certain competencies in physics among IX standard students.
3. To find out whether there is any significant difference between the mean scores of boys and girls in post-test of control group in achieving certain competencies in physics among IX standard students.
4. To find out whether there is any significant difference between the mean scores of boys and girls in post-test of Experimental group in achieving certain competencies in physics among IX standard students.
5. To find out whether there is any significant difference between the mean scores of boys in pre-test of Control and Experimental group in achieving certain competencies in physics among IX standard students.
6. To find out whether there is any significant difference between the mean scores of girls in pre-test of Control and Experimental group in achieving certain competencies in physics among IX standard students.
7. To find out whether there is any significant difference between the mean scores of Boys in post-test of Control and Experimental group in achieving certain competencies in physics among IX standard students.
8. To find out whether there is any significant difference between the mean scores of Girls in post-test of Control and Experimental

group in achieving certain competencies in physics among IX standard students.

9. To find out whether there is any significant difference between the mean scores of Control and Experimental group students of pre-test performance in achieving certain competencies in physics among IX standard students.

10. To find out whether there is any significant difference between the mean scores of Control and Experimental group students in post-test performance in achieving certain competencies in physics among IX standard students.

11. To find out whether there is any significant difference between the mean scores of control group students of pre-test and post-test performance in achieving certain competencies in physics among IX standard students.

4. To find out whether there is any significant difference between the mean scores of Experimental group students of pre-test and post-test performance in achieving certain competencies in physics among IX standard students.

Hypothesis of the Study

1. There is no significant difference between the mean scores of boys and girls in pre-test of control group in achieving certain competencies in physics among IX standard students.
2. There is no significant difference between the mean scores of boys and girls in pre-test of Experimental group in achieving certain competencies in physics among IX standard students.
3. There is no significant difference between the mean scores of boys and girls in post-test of control group in achieving certain competencies in physics among IX standard students.
4. There is no significant difference between the mean scores of boys and girls in post-test of Experimental group in achieving certain competencies in physics among IX standard students.
5. There is no significant difference between the mean scores of boys in pre-test of Control and Experimental group in achieving certain competencies in physics among IX standard students.

6. There is no significant difference between the mean scores of girls in pre-test of Control and Experimental group in achieving certain competencies in physics among IX standard students.
7. There is no significant difference between the mean scores of boys in post-test of Control group and Experimental group in achieving certain competencies in physics among IX standard students.
8. There is no significant difference between the mean scores of girls in post-test of Control group and Experimental group in achieving certain competencies in physics among IX standard students.
9. There is no significant difference between the mean scores of Control and Experimental group students of pre-test performance in achieving certain competencies in physics among IX standard students.
10. There is no significant difference between the mean scores of Control and Experimental group students in post-test performance in achieving certain competencies in physics among IX standard students.
11. There is no significant difference between the mean scores of Control group students of pre-test and post-test performance in achieving certain competencies in physics among IX standard students.
12. There is no significant difference between the mean scores of Experimental group students of pre-test and post-test performance in achieving certain competencies in physics among IX standard students.

Limitations of the Study

1. The researcher conducted the experiment only in the school located in urban area
2. This study was conducted in only one chapter of the Physics syllabus for secondary school students
3. This study was conducted to IX standard students particularly in government Higher Secondary School, Pudukkottai, Tamilnadu.

4. The experimental treatment was given with duration of one month only
5. The sample consist of 60 students

Research Methods

The researcher adopted Experimental method for this research. The researcher conducted the experiment for IX standard students in Government Higher Secondary School, Thirugokarnam, Pudukkottai.

Research Tool

The investigator himself developed a research tool which is indicated below. A questionnaire on co-ordination physics was taken by the researcher. The researcher conducted pre-test at the beginning of the study and Post-test after providing a suitable teaching learning experience.

Construction of Research Tool

The pattern of the test is same as the control and Experimental group. The test consists of fifty marks. All the Questions are objective type. The question paper consists of three levels. They are knowledge, understanding and application levels. In this study control and experimental group of the students are treated equally, without any partially based on the understanding the concept of the topic.

Samples of the study

60 students of male and female studying in class IX STD of Government Higher Secondary School, Thirugokarnam, Pudukkottai District were taken as the sample for analysis

Description of the research tool and scoring procedure

The researcher has taken only objective type questions. The test paper consist of choose, fill ups, match the following. Each question carries one mark. If the answer is correct one mark will be given if not zero.

Pilot Study

A pilot study is an initial investigation to give information that will be necessary when designing a future trial or study. For example a pilot may be used to:

1. Assess the time required to examine each patient,
2. To determine the quality of a proposed questionnaire
3. To estimate the variability of key variables.

Hence the investigator conducted the pilot study in the experiment to determine the quality of the question paper.

Validity of the Tool

Validity is the extent to which a test is measured what it claims to measure. It is vital for a test to be valid in order for the results to be accurately applied and interpreted. Validity is not determined by a single statistics, but by a body of research that demonstrates the relation between the test and the behaviour it is intended to measure.

There are three types of validity:

1. Content Validity
2. Criterion Validity
3. Construct Validity

In the present study Content Validity was used

Content validity

When a test has content validity, the items on the test represent the entire range of possible items the test should cover.

Reliability of the Tool

Reliability refers to the consistency of a measure. A test is considered reliable if we get the consistency of scores repeatedly. It can be estimated in a number of different ways.

1. Test – Retest Reliability
2. Inter – Rater Reliability

3. Parallel – Forms Reliability
4. Inter – Consistency Reliability

Test-Retest Reliability

To gauge test-retest reliability, the test is administrated twice at two different points in time. This kind of reliability is used to access the consistency of a test across time. This type of reliability assumes that there will be no change in the quality or construct being measured. Test-Retest reliability is the best method used for things that are stable over time. Generally, reliability will be higher when little time has passed between tests. In present study-Re-test method was used and the reliability value as follows.

$$R = \frac{2r}{1+r}$$

$$r = 0.65$$

$$= \frac{2x0.65}{1+0.65}$$

$$R = 0.79$$

Sampling Technique Used

60 students have been taken as sample for present study IX standard A section boys and girls are Control groups. And B section IX standard students boys and girls are Experimental groups. Each section consists of 30 students.

Collection of Data

The investigator collected the data from the selected control group and experimental group. The pre-test and post-test was conducted using the criterion test. The investigator himself taught physics to the control group by using traditional method. The experimental method was taught through the 3D approach in physics concepts in Govt. Hr. Sec.School, Thirugokarnam, Pudukkottai. After completion of the treatment the post-test was conducted to measure the understanding ability of learning in various concepts of the physics in both groups. Thus all the data were collected systematically for the analysis in the present study.

Analysis of the Data

In the present study, the relevant data obtained from the test scores in the pre-test and the post-test were analyzed using different statistical techniques.

Descriptive Analysis

It provides information about the nature of a particular group of individuals. Mean and standard deviation were calculated to determine the central tendencies and dispersion variables to describe the properties of the sample.

Differential Analysis

It provides inference involving determination of statistical significance of difference between groups with reference to the selected variables. To compare the difference between the mean scores of the sample can be calculated by using the T" test.

Relational Analysis

Correlation refers to the relationship between two or more paired variables or more sets of data. The degree of relationship is measured and represented by co-efficient of correlation. This coefficient may be identified either the letter.

Statistical Techniques Used

Standard Deviation

Standard deviation is the average or mean of all the averages for multiple sets of data. Scientists and statisticians use the standard deviation to determine how closely sets of data are to the mean of all the sets. Standard deviation is an easy calculation to perform.

"t" test

A ***'t'*-test** is any statistical hypothesis test in which the test statistic follows a student's **'t'** distribution if the null hypothesis is supported. It can be used to determine if two sets of data are significantly different from each other, and is most commonly applied when the test statistic would follow a normal distribution if the value of a scaling term in the test statistic were known. When the scaling term is unknown and is replaced by an estimate based on the data, the test statistic (under certain conditions) follows a Student's *t* distribution.

Conclusion

Selection of control group and experimental group, limitations of the study, research method and construction of research tool and technique of data analysis are discussed in this chapter. Data analysis and interpretation will be followed in the next chapter.

Chapter IV

Analysis and Interpretation of Data

Introduction

The chapter on analysis and Interpretation of Data deals with the application of statistical techniques such as mean, standard deviation, test of significance which is used to analyse the data and interpret the collected data in order to identify the Effectiveness of 3D Approach in Understanding the concept of Physics at Secondary level.

The findings are logically organized and interpreted in this chapter.

System of Data Analysis

The purpose of the present study is to find out the impact on 3D approach in teaching concepts of Physics at secondary level. In this Study, the test of significance (t-test) was used to test the Research Hypothesis and the computation of t-value was identified by the investigator using the Mean and Standard Deviation. Since the total number of students selected for the present study is sixty, the investigator used the formula of t-test related to correlated and un-correlated group.

Hypotheses Testing

Hypothesis – 1

There is no significant difference between the mean scores of boys and girls in pre-test of control group in achievingcertain competencies in physics among IX standard students.

Table 1

S. No	Gender	N	Mean	Standard Deviation	t–value	Level significance at 0.05 level
1	Boys	16	28.75	5.99	1.01	No significant
2	Girls	14	31.42	8.14		

Interpretation:

Since our obtained 't' – value (1.01) is less than the table value (2.05), with degree of freedom 28, there is no significance difference between the mean scores of boys and girls in pre-test of control group.

Finding

Hence the Null Hypothesis is **accepted**.

From the above figure it may be clear that boys and girls mean scores are 28.75 and 31.42 respectively. It may be observed that girls students show high mean than the boys students.

Hypothesis – 2

There is no significant difference between the mean scores of boys and girls in pre-test of Experimental group in achieving certain competencies in physics among IX standard students.

Table .2

S. No	Gender	N	Mean	Standard Deviation	t – value	Level of significance at 0.05 level
1	Boys	12	30.00	7.63	0.39	No significant
2	Girls	18	31.11	7.56		

Interpretation

Since our obtained 't' – value (0.39) is less than the table value (2.05), with degree of freedom 28, there is no significance difference between the mean scores of boys and girls in pre-test of Experimental group.

Finding

Hence the Null Hypothesis is **accepted**.

From the above figure it may be clear that boys and girls mean scores are 30 and 31.11 respectively. It may be observed that girls students show high mean than the boys students.

Hypothesis – 3

There is no significant difference between the mean scores of boys and girls in post-test of control group in achieving certain competencies in physics among IX standard students.

Table 3

S. No	Gender	N	Mean	Standard Deviation	t – value	Level of significance at 0.05 level
1	Boys	16	31.87	7.701	1.31	No significant
2	Girls	14	28.57	6.109		

Interpretation:

Since our obtained 't' – value (1.31) is less than the table value (2.05), with degree of freedom 28, there is no significance difference between the mean scores of boys and girls in post-test of control group.

Finding

Hence the Null Hypothesis is **accepted**.

From the above figure it may be clear that boys and girls mean scores are 31.87 and 28.57 respectively. It may be observed that boys students show high mean than the girls students.

Hypothesis – 4

There is no significant difference between the mean scores of boys and girls in post-test of Experimental group in achieving certain competencies in physics among IX standard students.

Table 4

S. No	Gender	N	Mean	Standard Deviation	t – value	Level of significance at 0.05 level
1	Boys	12	36.66	6.9	0.23	No significant
2	Girls	18	37.22	6.29		

Interpretation:

Since our obtained 't' – value (0.23) is less than the table value (2.05), with degree of freedom 28, there is no significance difference between the mean scores of boys and girls in post-test of experimental group.

Finding

Hence the Null Hypothesis is **accepted**.

From the above figure it may be clear that boys and girls mean scores are 36.66 and 37.22 respectively. It may be observed that girls students show high mean than the boys students.

Hypothesis – 5

There is no significant difference between the mean scores of boys in pre-test of Control and Experimental group in achieving certain competencies in physics among IX standard students.

Table 5

S. No	Gender	N	Mean	Standard Deviation	t – value	Level of significance at 0.05 level
1	Control Group	16	28.75	5.99	0.47	No significant
2	Experimental Group	12	30.00	7.63		

Interpretation

Since our obtained 't' - value (0.47) is less than the table value (2.06), with degree of freedom 26, there is no significance difference between the mean scores of boys in pre-test of control and experimental group.

Finding

Hence the Null Hypothesis is **accepted**.

From the above figure it may be clear that boys mean scores are 28.75 and 30 respectively. It may be observed that Experimental Group show high mean than the Control Group students.

Hypothesis – 6

There is no significant difference between the mean scores of girls in pre-test of Control and Experimental group in achieving certain competencies in physics among IX standard students.

Table 6

S. No	Gender	N	Mean	Standard Deviation	t – value	Level of significance at 0.05 level
1	Control Group	14	31.42	8.14	0.11	No significant
2	Experimental Group	18	31.11	7.56		

Interpretation:

Since our obtained 't' - value (0.11) is less than the table value (2.04), with degree of freedom 30, there is no significance difference between the mean scores of girls in pre-test of control and experimental group.

Finding

Hence the Null Hypothesis is **accepted**.

From the above figure it may be clear that girls mean scores are 31.42 and 31.11 respectively. It may be observed that Control Group show high mean than the Experimental Group students.

Hypothesis – 7

There is no significant difference between the mean scores of boys in post-test of Control group and Experimental group in achieving certain competencies in physics among IX standard students.

Table 7

S. No	Gender	N	Mean	Standard Deviation	t – value	Level of significance at 0.05 level
1	Control Group	16	31.87	7.701	1.73	No significant
2	Experimental Group	12	36.66	6.90		

Interpretation

Since our obtained 't' - value (1.73) is less than the table value (2.06) at with degree of freedom 26, there is no significance difference between the mean scores of boys in post-test of control and experimental group.

Finding

Hence the Null Hypothesis is **accepted**.

From the above figure it may be clear that boys mean scores are 31.87 and 36.66 respectively. It may be observed that Experimental Group show high mean than the Control Group students.

Hypothesis – 8

There is no significant difference between the mean scores of girls in post-test of Control group and Experimental group in achieving certain competencies in physics among IX standard students.

Table 8

S. No	Gender	N	Mean	Standard Deviation	t – value	Level of significance at 0.05 level
1	Control Group	14	28.57	6.109		
2	Experimental Group	18	37.22	6.29	3.92	significant

Interpretation:

Since our obtained 't' - value (3.92) is greater than the table value (2.04) with degree of freedom 30, Hence there is significance difference between the mean scores of girls in post-test of control and experimental group.

Finding

Hence the Null Hypothesis is **rejected**.

From the above figure it may be clear that girls mean scores are 28.57 and 37.22 respectively. It may be observed that Experimental Group show high mean than the Control Group students.

Hypothesis – 9

There is no significant difference between the mean scores of Control and Experimental group students of pre-test performance in achieving certain competencies in physics among IX standard students.

Table 9

S. No	Gender	N	Mean	Standard Deviation	t – value	Level of significance at 0.05 level
1	Control Group	30	30.085	7.065	0.25	No significant
2	Experimental Group	30	30.555	7.595		

Interpretation

Since our obtained 't' - value (0.25) is less than the table value (2.01) with degree of freedom 58, there is no significance difference between the mean scores of pre-test performance in control and experimental group.

Finding

Hence the Null Hypothesis is **accepted**.

From the above figure it may be clear that boys and girls mean scores are 30.085 and 30.555 respectively. It may be observed that

Experimental Group show high mean than the Control Group students.

Hypothesis – 10

There is no significant difference between the mean scores of Control and Experimental group students in post-test performance in achieving certain competencies in physics among IX standard students.

Table 10

S. No	Gender	N	Mean	Standard Deviation	t – value	Level of significance at 0.05 level
1	Control Group	30	30.22	6.095	3.85	significant
2	Experimental Group	30	36.94	6.595		

Interpretation

Since our obtained 't' - value (3.85) is greater than the table value (2.01) with degree of freedom 58, there is significance difference between the mean scores of post-test performance in control and experimental group.

Finding

Hence the Null Hypothesis is **rejected**.

From the above figure it may be clear that boys and girls mean scores are 30.22 and 36.94 respectively. It may be observed that Experimental Group show high mean than the Control Group students.

Hypothesis – 11

There is no significant difference between the mean scores of Control group students of pre-test and post-test performance in achieving certain competencies in physics among IX standard students.

Table 11

S. No	Test	N	Mean	Standard Deviation	t – value	Level of significance at 0.05 level
1	Pre - test	30	30.085	7.065	0.08	No significant
2	Post - test	30	30.22	6.905		

Interpretation

Since our obtained 't' - value (0.08) is less than the table value (2.01) with degree of freedom 58, there is no significance difference between the mean scores of pre-test and post-test performance in control group.

Finding

Hence the Null Hypothesis is **accepted**.

From the above figure it may be clear that boys and girls mean scores are 30.085 and 30.22 respectively. It may be observed that Post-test show high mean than the Pre-test students.

Hypothesis – 12

There is no significant difference between the mean scores of Experimental group students of pre-test and post-test performance in achieving certain competencies in physics among IX standard students.

Table 12

S. No	Test	N	Mean	Standard Deviation	t – value	Level of significance at 0.05 level
1	Pre - test	30	30.555	7.595	3.55	significant
2	Post – test	30	36.94	6.595		

Interpretation

Since our obtained 't' – value (3.55) is greater than the table value (2.01) with degree of freedom 58, there is significance difference between the mean scores of pre-test and post-test performances in experimental group.

Finding

Hence the Null Hypothesis is **rejected**.

From the above figure it may be clear that boys and girls mean scores are 30.555 and 36.94 respectively. It may be observed that Post-test show high mean than the pre-test students.

Conclusion

The researcher carried out the study of "Effectiveness of 3D Approach in Achieving Certain Competencies in Physics among IX Std Students". This study revealed that the effectiveness of students understanding physics is improved with the help of 3D approach concept. The pre test performance of the control group and experimental group level is minimum, when compared to the post test performance of control and experimental group. The experimental group having high level of performance in post test, when introducing the 3D approach in physics teaching. Both boys and girls performance better in experimental group of the post- test. The present research revealed that teacher should always teach certain competencies in physics concept by using novel method of 3D approach for easy understanding of physics.

Chapter V

Summary of Findings and Conclusion

Introduction

This chapter reveals origin of the research topic arises and introducing the problem of the present study. The investigator selected this topic and framed his work in a systematic manner.

Need and Significance of the Study

The present status of Physics is that most of the Physics students learn the subject, and forget the concept, facts, terms and principles when they go out. Unless some intervention is made, the student cannot comprehend the concept in the physics. Hence it is the duty of the physics teacher to make an instructional design that would support them in realizing and envisaged instructional objectives. So the investigator felt a need to select this topic to improve the easy understanding capacity of the students.

At present, the teacher in Indian schools take more time to complete the classroom instructions by the traditional method of teaching due to over loaded syllabi and lack of time in the classroom situation. Further the teachers are not able to concentrate on the development of all the cognitive skills. The investigator felt that this kind of study is needed particularly for secondary students to improve better understanding and application of their mind in enhancing their knowledge.

Statement of the Problem

Problem of the present research is to study the *"Effectiveness of 3D Approach in achieving certain competencies in physics Among IX Std Students"*.

Objectives of the Study

1. To find out whether there is any significant difference between the mean sources of boys and girls in pre-test of control group in achieving certain competencies in physics among IX standard students.
2. To find out whether there is any significant difference between the mean scores of boys and girls in pre-test of Experimental group in achieving certain competencies in physics among IX standard students.
3. To find out whether there is any significant difference between the mean scores of boys and girls in post-test of control group in achieving certain competencies in physics among IX standard students.
4. To find out whether there is any significant difference between the mean scores of boys and girls in post-test of Experimental group in achieving certain competencies in physics among IX standard students.
5. To find out whether there is any significant difference between the mean scores of boys in pre-test of Control and Experimental group in achieving certain competencies in physics among IX standard students.
6. To find out whether there is any significant difference between the mean scores of girls in pre-test of Control and Experimental group in achieving certain competencies in physics among IX standard students.

7. To find out whether there is any significant difference between the mean scores of Boys in post-test of Control and Experimental group in achieving certain competencies in physics among IX standard students.
8. To find out whether there is any significant difference between the mean scores of Girls in post-test of Control and Experimental group in achieving certain competencies in physics among IX standard students.
9. To find out whether there is any significant difference between the mean scores of Control and Experimental group students of pre-test performance in achieving certain competencies in physics among IX standard students.
10. To find out whether there is any significant difference between the mean scores of Control and Experimental group students in post-test performance in achieving certain competencies in physics among IX standard students.
11. To find out whether there is any significant difference between the mean scores of control group students of pre-test and post-test performance in achieving certain competencies in physics among IX standard students.
12. To find out whether there is any significant difference between the mean scores of Experimental group students of pre-test and post-test performance in achieving certain competencies in physics among IX standard students.

Summary of Findings:

1. There is no significant difference between the mean scores of boys and girls in pre-test performance in control group. **(Accepted)**
2. There is no significant difference between the mean scores of boys and girls in pre-test performance in experimental group. **(Accepted)**
3. There is no significant difference between the mean scores of boys and girls in post test performance in control group. **(Accepted)**

4. There is no significant difference between the mean scores of boys and girls in post-test performance in experimental group. **(Accepted)**
5. There is no significant difference between the mean scores of boys in control and experimental group of pre-test performance. **(Accepted)**
6. There is no significant difference between the mean scores of girls in control and experimental group of pre-test performance. **(Accepted)**
7. There is no significant difference between the mean scores of boys in control and experimental group in post-test performance. **(Accepted)**
8. There is significant difference between the mean scores of girls in control and experimental group in post-test performance. **(Rejected)**
9. There is no significant difference between the mean scores of control and experimental group students of pre-test performance. **(Accepted)**
10. There is significant difference between the mean scores of control and experimental group students in post-test performance. **(Rejected)**
11. There is no significant difference between the mean scores of control group students of pre-test and post-test performance. **(Accepted)**
12. There is significant difference between the mean scores of experimental group students of pre-test and post-test performance. **(Rejected)**

Research Implications

The findings of this experimental study show that, the 3 Dimensional approaches in Physics subject can be practiced in the classroom situation in order to attain better understanding the concepts of Physics by the students.

Suggestion for Further Research

1. It can be replicated with other science subjects like Physics, Mathematics, Botany and Zoology.
2. The present study was conducted among IX standard students only.
3. Therefore it is suggested that it may be conducted among the pupils if other classes also.
4. The Researcher conducted the Research in the urban area school. Hence it is suggested that this research also be implemented to rural area school for the development of the pupils.

Conclusion

The researcher carried out the study of "Effectiveness of 3D Approach in Achieving Certain Competencies in Physics among IX Std Students". This study revealed that the effectiveness of students understanding physics is improved with the help of 3D approach concept. The pre test performance of the control group and experimental group level is minimum, when compared to the post test performance of control and experimental group. The experimental group having high level of performance in post test, when introducing the 3D approach in physics teaching. Both boys and girls performance better in experimental group of the post- test. The present research revealed that teacher should always teach certain competencies in physics concept by using novel method of 3D approach for easy understanding of physics.

Bibiliography

1. Aggarwal (1990), "Statistical Methods, Concepts, Application and Computation", Sterling Publications, New Delhi.
2. Awasthy (1965), "Teaching Techniques in India" Allied Publishers Pvt. (Ltd), Bombay.
3. Dar (1965), "Science Teaching in Schools", Jallandhar – Sterling Publishers, Banglore.
4. Falk (1965), "Biology Teaching Methods", Johnwiley Publishers, London.

5. Herr, Norm and James Cunnigham (1999), "Hands – On Chemistry Activities with Real-Life Applications". John wiely/ Jossey-Bass, Publishers Northridge, California.
6. Jevons (1965), "The Teaching of Science", Allen and Unwin Ltd, Bombay.
7. Karmer (1975), "Teaching the Life Science", Macmilliam Publication, London.
8. Kiran Lata Pangwal and Shireesh Pal Singh (2011), "Emerging Trends in Education", A.P.H. Publishing Corporation, New Delhi.
9. Nair (1971), "Teaching Science in our Schools", S. Chand and Co. Pvt. Ltd., New Delhi.
10. Sharma (1992), "Modern Science Teaching", Dhanpat Rai & Sons Publishers, Delhi.
11. Sik. Gupta (1978), "Teaching Physical Sciences in Secondary Schools", Sterling Publishers Pvt. Ltd, New Delhi.
12. Vaidya, Narendera (1968), "Problem Solving in Science", S.Chand and Co. Pvt. Ltd., New Delhi.
13. Vaidya, Narendera (1970), "Some Aspects of Piaget's Work and Science Teaching", S.Chand and Co. Pvt. Ltd, New Delhi.
14. Schmalz, M.S. (2008). "IT/CS Workshop in Multimedia Courseware". Journal of Teaching Technical Concepts. 15. 23-30.
15. Johnstone, A.H. (1993). The development of Chemistry teaching. Journal of Chemical Education, 70(9), 701 ± 705.
16. Halimah (1999). "Multimedia Learning in Computer Science". Journal Pendidikan. 2. 1-5.
17. Gabel, D. (1998). The complexity of chemistry and implications for teaching. In B.J. Fraser & K.G. Tobin (Eds.), International handbook of science education (pp. 233 ± 248). Boston, MA: Kluwer Academic Publishers.
18. Krajcik, J.S. (1991). Developing students' understanding of chemical concepts. In S.M. Glynn, R.H. Yeany, & B.K. Britton (Eds.), The psychology of learning science: Indernational

perspective on the psychological foundations of technology-based learning environments (pp. 117 ± 145). Hillsdale, NJ: Erlbaum.

19. Kozma, R.B., Russell, J., Jones, T., Marx, N., & Davis, J. (1996). The use of multiple, linked representations to facilitate science understanding. In R.G.S. Vosniadou, E. Decorte, & H. Mandel (Eds.), International perspective on the psychological foundations of technology-based learning environments (pp. 41 ± 60). Hillsdale, NJ: Erlbaum..

20. Schmalz, M.S. (2008). "IT/CS Workshop in Multimedia Courseware". Journal of Teaching Technical Concepts. 15. 23-30.

21. Halimah (1999). "Multimedia Learning in Computer Science". Jurnal Pendidikan. 2. 1-5.

22. Johnstone, A.H. (1993). The development of chemistry teaching. Journal of Chemical Education, 70(9), 701 ± 705.

23. Griffths, A.K., & Preston, K.R. (1992). Grade-12 students' misconceptions relating to fundamental characteristics of atoms and molecules. Journal of Research in Science Teaching, 29(6), 611 ± 628.

24. Williamson, V.M., & Abraham, M.R. (1995). The effects of computer animation on the particulate mental models of college chemistry students. Journal of Research in Science Teaching, 32, 521 ± 534.

25. Hoffmann, R., & Laszlo, R. (1991). Representation in chemistry. Angewandte Chemie, 30, 1 ± 16.

26. Kozma, R.B., Chin, E., Russell, J., & Marx, N. (2000). The roles of representations and tools in the chemistry laboratory and their implications for chemistry instruction. Journal of the Learning Sciences, 9(2), 105 ± 143.

27. Gabel, D.L., Samuel, K.V., & Hunn, D. (1987). Understanding the particulate nature of matter. Journal of Chemical Education, 64, 695 ± 697.

28. Copolo, C.F., & Hounshell, P.B. (1995). Using three-dimensional models to teach molecular structures in high school chemistry. Journal of Science Education and Technology, 4(4), 295 ± 305.

29. Gabel, D., & Sherwood, R. (1980). The effect of student manipulation of molecular models on chemistry achievement according to Piagetian level. Journal of Research in Science Teaching, 17(1), 75 ± 81.

30. Barnea (2010), "Journal of Chemistry Education Research and Practice", Vol. 11, P-218.

31. Lyon (2011), "Journal of Natural Resources and Life Sciences Education", Vol. 40, P199.

32. Roberto (2011), "Journal of College Science Teaching", Vol 40, P85.

33. Rahayu (2011), "Journal of Research in Science and Technological Education", Vol. 29, P 169.

34. Briggs (2011), "Journal of Chemistry Education", Vol. 88, P-1034.

35. Carrio (2011), "Journal of Biological Education", Vol. 45, P-29.

36. Charles (2001), "Journal of Science Scope", Vol. 25, P-27.

37. Goodwin (2011), "Journal of School Science Review", Vol.92,P-49.

38. Leopold (2012), "Journal Learning and Instruction", Vol.7, P106.

39. Loverude (2011), "Journal of Physics Education Research", Vol 7, P106.

Chapter VI

Attitude of Creativity in Science Among Students

Introduction

Education is a basic right and more important a catalyst for economic growth and human development. It is a crucial tool for breaking the barrier of poverty. Specifically, primary education is the critical enabler required to improve the economic and social scenario in many pockets of the nation. We also need to ensure equal status for the girl children as citizens in their own right. For any country to progress, one half of its population cannot be denied the right to education. This denial is also a gross violation of many rights enshrined in the Indian Constitution, primary among them being the right to education and the right to equality. Global statistics reveal that 75% of the 130 million children who are out of school are girls. Illiterate girls grow up to be illiterate women. This results in lopsided development as it denies equal opportunities to equal citizens. Of the 960 million adults in the world who cannot read, two thirds are women. South Asia has the widest gender gaps compared to other countries of the world. There are many disparities between women and men across the world and they remain persistent in the areas of access to resources, opportunities and in matters of human rights. India is a signatory to many international commitments on women's and girls' development and has its own national commitments for development and education of girls. The first reference to equal opportunities for education of both girls and boys is made in India's

*National Policy on Education, 1968.*One of the principles of the development of education in the country listed in the 1968 policy was:

Equalisation of Educational Opportunity: "(c) The Education of girls should receive emphasis, not only grounds of social justice, but also because it accelerates social transformation".

The National Policy on Education, 1986 went beyond just specifying the need foremphasis on girls' education and laid down some specific strategies for education to achieve women's equality:

Foster the development of new values through.

1. Redesigned curricula, textbooks,
2. Training and orientation of teachers, decision-makers and administrators,
3. Active involvement of educational institutions
4. Removal of women's illiteracy and obstacles inhibiting their access to, and retention in school; elementary education to receive overriding priority through
5. Provision of special support services
6. Setting of time targets
7. Effective monitoring

The policies lack a clear gender perspective and do not touch upon many aspects that hinder education for girls, one of them being the sexual harassment of girls in schools.

Definition of Quality Education

Children have a right to an education, a quality education. Learners who are healthy, well-nourished and ready to participate and learn, and supported in learning by their families and communities; . Environments that are healthy, safe, protective and gender-sensitive, and provide adequate resources and facilities; Content that is reflected in relevant curricula and materials for the acquisition of basic skills, especially in the areas of literacy, numeracy and skills for life, and knowledge in such areas as gender, health, nutrition, HIV/AIDS prevention and peace. Processes through which trained teachers use child-centred teaching approaches in well-managed classrooms and schools and skilful assessment to facilitate learning and reduce disparities. Outcomes that encompass knowledge, skills and attitudes, and are linked to national goals for education and positive participation in society. This definition allows for an understanding of education as a complex system embedded in a political, cultural and economic context. (This paper examines research related to these dimensions). It is important to keep in mind education's systemic nature, however; these dimensions are interdependent, influencing each other in ways that are sometimes unforeseeable.

Secondary Education

Secondary education serves as a bridge between elementary and higher education and Prepares young person's between the age group of 14-18 for entry into higher education.

Function of Secondary Education

1. To prepare the young to live effectively and properly as adults in the society.
2. To develop the intellectual power of the young and transmit the knowledge and wisdom of the society to new generation.
3. To perpetuate the basic beliefs, value systems and socially approved modes behaviour .
4. To develop the powers and capabilities of the young so that may realise their potentialities and advance the life of the social group.

According to secondary education commission (1952-53). Development of the democratic citizenship, vocational efficiency development of personality, promoting leadership qualities and above all preservation and enrichment of our culture heritage should be the important aims of the secondary education in India.

Science

Science as defined above is sometimes called pure science to differentiate it from applied science, which is the application of research to human needs. Fields of science are commonly classified along two major lines:

1. Natural sciences, the study of the natural world, and
2. Social sciences, the systematic study of human behaviour and society.

Ypes of Science

Physical science

- Physics
- Chemistry

Earth science

- Ecology
- Oceanography
- Geology
- Meteorology

Life science

- Biology
- Zoology
- Human biology
- Botany

History of Science

Science as inquiry has a long history in science education. Here are a few milestones:

1. 1910: John Dewey writes about the importance of inquiry science.
2. 1927: Gerald Craig writes about the importance of teaching science through investigations.
3. 1947: Natural Sciences and Science Education (NSSE) Yearbook endorses science programs based on features that include problem-solving skills.
4. 1960s: Major revision of science education occurs through development of new science curricula that emphasize inquiry approaches (ESS [Elementary Science Study], SAPA [Science–A Process Approach], SCIS [Science Curriculum Improvement Study]).
5. 1970s: Science educators question effectiveness of "extreme" version of discovery science, i.e., minimal teacher intervention.
6. 1980s: Growing interest in the nature of science, including its implications for how authentic inquiry can be carried out in science classrooms.
7. 1990s: Domination of constructivist (see Glossary of Terms) learning theory, including emphasis on importance of children's existing ideas and how they affect what is learned during scientific inquiry.
8. 2000: Shift in emphasis in classroom scientific inquiry from a focus on "science processes" to a focus on evidence, explanation and current scientific knowledge.
9. (Note: A more detailed history of the inquiry approach can be found in Pine et al., 2006).

These milestones have had an ongoing impact on Alberta elementary science programs (Kamal, 2006).

Characteristics of Science

A good research question...

1. Answers something new! Replications, by themselves, are not good enough. The point of conducting research is to advanced knowledge—to test something in a unique way, to test the prediction of a theory, to explore new methodology, etc. It is

extremely important to show that a scientific finding can be replicated. Any valid scientific finding needs to be replicable...or in other words, reliable. The best kinds of research studies both replicate previous research while incorporating something new. That's not always possible in a single study; sometimes it takes two or three experiments to accomplish this. (That's why most journal articles will contain a number of research studies rather than a single study).

2. Is based on and builds upon previous research. A good research question tests the prediction of a theory. A research question that you generate off the top of your head can be useful, but almost always, research questions developed after an understanding of previous research and theory is much stronger and more relevant to science (and will be viewed more favorably by reviewers of your research). Is practical (e.g., Can you really do this study this semester? Do you have the equipment/ resources to sufficiently answer your question? Will you need a zillion subjects for the study?).

3. Is often simple. You don't have to answer the "big" questions of psychology – just add a little piece to existing research. *A good piece of advice when conducting research is "Keep it simple!" You don't want to be left with a pile of data that you don't know how to interpret. (You'd be surprised at how often that happens!).*[2]

4. Is based on primary (not secondary) sources. Primary source basically refers to the original source of research, usually from a publication. A secondary source, on the other hand, is a summary or description of the primary source. Newspapers, magazines, and topic books are secondary sources; journal articles are usually primary sources.

Main Features of Science

As diverse as sciences are, all scientific explanations have a lot in common. Psychological research, just like all other scientific research, adheres to these principles.

Scientific Explanations are Empirical

"Empirical" means "based on the senses." All scientific explanations must be based on empirical observations or experiments (or at the very least, be directly inferred when direct observation cannot be achieved).

Scientific Explanations are Tentative

This means that all findings are subject to change should there be enough evidence to necessitate a change. There is always a chance that the scientific theory is wrong, no matter how much supporting evidence there is for the theory. In other words, nothing is ever proven in science.

Scientific Explanations are Probabilistic

Nothing can be measured precisely; there is always a degree of uncertainty in one's measurement. This is especially true in psychology because humans are amazingly complex. In psychology, keep in mind that any finding is what's *likely* to be true but because of the impreciseness and variability in human observation, human behaviour, and measures we say there's only probability of a finding being true.

Scientific Explanations are Testable

There must exit an outcome that does not support the theory. An example of a non-testable theory is Freud's theory of personality. You can't test the id, the ego, or the superego. Thus, Freud's theory is not scientific. (The same applies to dream interpretation — certainly not scientific.)

Scientific Explanations are Parsimonious

If there are multiple theories that explain the data, the simplest one is usually correct. This is sometimes called the principle of simplicity. Here's a silly example that shows the principle: If I put on a blindfold and tell you how many fingers you're holding up, you can either explain this by a) telepathy (i.e., mind-reading), or b) that I cheated and saw your fingers. Which is the most parsimonious explanation? Clearly, the 'cheating' explanation is much simpler and requires the fewest assumptions.

Scientific Explanations Assume Cause & Effect

For every effect, there is a cause. If we assume no cause, the explanation is not scientific. In fact, much of psychological research is about finding the *causes* of human behaviour.

Scientific Explanations are General

Scientific findings must be applicable to other situations, to other people, to other scenarios, in other locations, at other times, etc. This is called "external validity." If the finding only happens once and does not apply to anyone or anything else, it's not scientific.

Introduction

Attitude

Education is the powerful tool which helps to modify the behaviour of the child according to the needs and expectancy of the society. Student's attitude is an integral part of learning and that it should, therefore become an essential component of second language learning pedagogy. Attitudes toward learning are believed to influence behaviour s such as selecting and reading books, speaking in a foreign language etc. Especially in Education, if the students have positive attitude towards any subject, they can achieve many things in that specific area. There is an interaction between language learning and the environmental components in which the students were grown up. Both negative and positive attitudes have a strong impact on the success of language learning.

"Attitude is determined by the individual's beliefs about outcomes or attributes of performing the behaviour (behaviour al beliefs), weighted by evaluations of those outcomes or attributes. Thus, a person who holds strong beliefs that positively valued outcomes will result from performing the behaviour will have a positive attitude toward the behaviour. Conversely, a person who holds strong beliefs that negatively valued outcomes will result from the behaviour will have a negative attitude." Attitude concept can be viewed from these three dimensions. Each one of these dimensions has different features to bring out language attitude results. Accordingly, the attitude concept has three components i.e., behaviour al, cognitive and affective. These three attitudinal aspects are based on the three theoretical approaches of behaviour ism, cognitivism and humanism respectively.

Typically, when we refer to a person's attitudes, we are trying to explain his or her behaviour . Attitudes are a complex combination of things we tend to call personality, beliefs, values, behaviour s, and motivations. As an example, we understand when someone says, "She has a positive attitude toward work" versus "She has a poor work attitude." When we speak of someone's attitude, we are referring to the person's emotions and behaviour s. A person's attitude toward preventive medicine encompasses his or her point of view about the topic (e.g., thought); how he or she feels about this topic (e.g., emotion), as well as the actions (e.g., behaviour s) he or she engages in as a result of attitude to preventing health problems. This is the tri-component model of attitudes. An attitude includes three components: an affect (a feeling), cognition (a thought or belief), and behaviour (an action).

Attitudes help us define how we see situations, as well as define how we behave toward the situation or object. As illustrated in the tricomponent model, attitudes include feelings, thoughts, and actions. Attitudes may simply be an enduring evaluation of a person or object (e.g., "I like John best of my coworkers"), or other emotional reactions to objects and to people (e.g., "I dislike bossy people" or "Jane makes me angry"). Attitudes also provide us with internal cognitions or beliefs and thoughts about people and objects (e.g., "Jane should work harder" or "Sam does not like working in this department"). Attitudes cause us to behave in a particular way toward an object or person (e.g., "I write clearly in patients' charts because it upsets me when I can't read someone else's handwriting").Although the feeling and belief components of attitudes are internal to a person, we can view a person's attitude from his or her resulting behaviour.

Definition of Attitude

Many psychologists have given different definitions for attitudes. According to Schneider (1988), 'Attitudes are evaluative reactions to persons, objects, and events. This includes your beliefs and positive and negative feelings about the attitude object.' He also added that attitude can guide our experiences and decide the effects of experience on our behaviours.

Besides that, Baron and Byrne (1987) also gave a similar definition of attitude which is, 'Attitudes can be defined as lasting, general evaluations of people (including oneself), objects, or issues. Attitude is lasting because it persists across time. A momentary feeling does not count as an attitude.' According to him attitudes are lasting since it remains across time.

Moreover, Vaughan & Hogg (1995) defined attitude as, 'A relatively enduring organization of beliefs, feelings and behavioural tendencies towards socially significant objects, groups, events or symbols or A general feeling or evaluation (positive/ negative) about some person, object or issue.' From this definition we could see that, attitudes are only relevant to socially significant objects.

In brief, it could be said that, attitude is a positive or negative evaluations or feelings that people have towards other people, objects, issues or events. Attitudes include the general way people feel towards socially significant objects and most attitudes are lasting.

For example, if you were once bitten by a cat and you dislike the feeling at that moment, that emotional response is regarded as just a feeling. However, if your experience of getting bitten by a cat made you hate all cats, then your hatred for cats is considered an attitude that you have towards cats.

Allport (1935) defined an attitude as a "mental or neural state of readiness, organised through experience, exerting a directive or dynamic influence on the individual's response to all objects and situations to which it is related. A simpler definition of attitude is a mindset or a tendency to act in a particular way due to both an individual's experience and temperament".

Creativity

The term creativity stands in need of precise distinctions among the referents it has acquired. Commonly used definitions of creativity vary in several ways. First of all, some definitions require socially valuable products if the act or person is to be called creative, while others see creativity itself as being intrinsically valuable, so that nothing of demonstrable social value need be produced; dreams thus may be creative, or unexpressed thoughts or simply the imaginative expressiveness or curiosity of a child. Definitions may vary also in terms of the level of accomplishment recognized as creative: difficulty of the problem seen or solved, e.g., or elegance or beauty of the product or the nature of the impact. A third kind of distinction is between creativity as achievement, creativity as ability, and creativity as disposition or attitude.

By way of illustration, let us take the two main categories of definition of a criterion of creativity actually used in large bodies of research: 1. creativity as socially recognized achievement in which there are novel products to which one can point as evidence, such as inventions, theories, buildings, published writings, paintings and sculptures and films; laws; institutions; medical and surgical treatments, and so on; and 2. creativity as an ability manifested by performance in critical trials, such as tests, contests, etc, in which one individual can be compared with another on a precisely defined scale.

The first category may lead to a definition of a field of activity and its products as intrinsically creative: all inventors, e.g., or all artists or all poets. This has led to a certain amount of research in which practitioners of a creative activity are compared with people in general, leading to a portrait of "the creative person" in terms of intellectual and personality differences between the criterion group and the generality. But these intrinsically creative products may differ among themselves in qualities such as originality, elegance, impact, and far-reachingness, Studies of individual differences as to creativity among members of such groups (architects, artists, mathematicians, and writers in the IPAR studies, for example) give a different picture of the components of creativity than do "field vs the generality" studies. A good example is measured intelligence. Creative architects do not score higher than comparison groups in architecture on standardized intelligence tests, but all architects studied scored an average of about two standard deviations higher than the general population (MacKinnon & Hall 1971). What does one then conclude about the relationship of creativity to intelligence? Many such examples could be given, not just in relationship to intelligence but to personality, interests, values, life history. The point is that results will appear confusing and contradictory unless the implications of the adopted definition of creativity and the assumptions of the methods are kept clearly in mind.

Creativity as an ability manifested by performance on tests is dogged by even more formidable difficulties. What kind of test is it? What abilities is it tapping? What effect do different methods of scoring it (and different, usually anonymous, scorers) have upon its correlates? How does timing affect the test? How do the instructions themselves affect performance in defining the implicit work schedule? The literature since 1970 reflects increasing sophistication about these difficulties as will be seen below.

Defining Creativity

Definitions of creativity are not straightforward, and many writers have contributed to the debate about what constitutes creativity, often hotly contesting different views. However, most theorists agree that the creative process involves a number of components, most commonly:

- originality (the ability to come up with ideas and products that are new and unusual)
- productivity (the ability to generate a variety of different ideas through divergent thinking)
- problem solving (application of knowledge and imagination to a given situation) the ability to produce an outcome of value and worth.

Where definitions of creativity differ most strikingly is the extent to which their proponents are attempting to identify creativity as a generic human characteristic, or to define what makes highly creative people special and different from others.

"All people are capable of creative achievement in some area of activity, provided that the conditions are right and they have acquired the relevant knowledge and skills".

Creativity in science

Creativity and intelligence are closely linked concepts, so much so that the existence of one is the measure of the other. Therefore, any attempt that brings clarity to one concept will be helpful to define the other. Lenat and Feigenbaum (1987) define intelligence in terms of "search", as the power to find a solution to a problem in animmense search space. Later, Feigenbaum defined intelligence in terms of "knowledge assembly rather than "search" (see, Engelmore & Morgan, 1988, vii). Accorclin to his definition, an intelligent system has the ability to assemble the necessary body of knowledge to conduct complex task. Scientific creativity can be investigated through five basic cognitive and computational concepts. These are

1. Motivation for scientific research.
2. Ability to correctly formulate research problems within a body of knowledge.
3. Ability to create a comprehensive search space for the solution of a scientific problem.
4. Ability to assemble (or induce) and implement of heuristics to reduce the search space.
5. Patience and stamina for the exhaustive search for solving the scientific problem within the constrained search space.

In view of these concepts, a creative scientist knows how-to correctly formulate research problems, can generate an extensive search space for a selected problem, can assemble or formulate the necessary methodological knowledge to reduce the search space into manageable dimensions, and can conduct exhaustive search in the reduced search space.

Modern scientific research is one of the most complex human activities, requiring the use of different types of general and specific knowledge. Knowledge necessary for modern scientific research can be divided into four types as a) Commonsense Knowledge, b) Technical Knowledge, c) Theoretical Knowledge, and d)Methodological Knowledge. Commonsense knowledge is simple, general and relatively unstructured knowledge about the world.

Statements such as 'Water extinguishes fire," "Fire burns paper" are examples of commonsense knowledge. Technical knowledge can be defamed as the knowledge about instruments, methods and processes. Knowledge about how to repair a TV set, how to control a chemical reactor, and how to fly an aeroplane can be considered as technical knowledge. Theoretical background is helpful, but not always essential, in acquiring thin kind of knowledge.

Technical knowledge can be descriptive as well as prescriptive. Theoretical knowledge is structured descriptive knowledge about the world, embodying classifications and numerous interrelated hypotheses. Typical examples of theoretical knowledge are the classical mechanics and electro-magnetism. Methodological knowledge, on the other hand, is exclusively prescriptive; it can be represented as condition action rules. Methodological knowledge includes knowledge about how to distinguish between scientifically interesting and interesting phenomena, how to choose between alternative goals, strategies and methods during scientific research, how to design experiments, how to propose new hypotheses, and how to generalise, test and evaluate them. It is mostly the extent of this type of knowledge that makes the difference between a research scientist and a non scientist. Unlike the inference rules in theoretical knowledge, many of the methodological rules rely on extra logical methods such as inductive generalizations, abduction, abstraction and analogy. Such rules are frequently used in formulating problem states, in constraining large search spaces, and in hypothesis formation during the activity of scientific research.

Need of the Study

1. To improve the students attitude of creativity in science.
2. To analyse variations in male and female students' attitude of creativity in science.
3. To analyse variations in government and government aided and self finance students' attitude of creativity in science.
4. To suggest possible strategies to improve the students' attitude of creativity in science.

Significant of the Study

1. Teachers, helps their students to improve their attitude and creativity.
2. Students should improve attitude and creativity by themselves.

3. Students should create new ideas in science.

Statement of the Problem

This is the title of the present study "A Study on the Attitude of Creativity in Science among Ix Standard Students in Pudukkottai Educational District."

Operational Definition Of Key Terms

Definition of Quality Education

Children have a right to an education, a quality education. Learners who are healthy, well-nourished and ready to participate and learn, and supported in learning by their families and communities; Environments that are healthy, safe, protective and gender-sensitive, and provide adequate resources and facilities; Content that is reflected in relevant curricula and materials for the acquisition of basic skills, especially in the areas of literacy, numeracy and skills for life, and knowledge in such areas as gender, health, nutrition, HIV/AIDS prevention and peace. Processes through which trained teachers use child-centred teaching approaches in well-managed classrooms and schools and skilful assessment to facilitate learning and reduce disparities. Outcomes that encompass knowledge, skills and attitudes, and are linked to national goals for education and positive participation in society. This definition allows for an understanding of education as a complex system embedded in a political, cultural and economic context. (This paper examines research related to these dimensions). It is important to keep in mind education's systemic nature, however; these dimensions are interdependent, influencing each other in ways that are sometimes unforeseeable.

Meaning of Attitude

"Attitude is determined by the individual's beliefs about outcomes or attributes of performing the behaviour (behaviour al beliefs), weighted by evaluations of those outcomes or attributes. Thus, a person who holds strong beliefs that positively valued outcomes will result from performing the behaviour will have a positive attitude toward the behaviour. Conversely, a person who holds strong beliefs that negatively valued outcomes will result from the behaviour will have a negative attitude." Attitude concept can be viewed from these three dimensions. Each one of these dimensions has different features to bring out language attitude results. Accordingly, the attitude concept has three components i.e., behaviour al, cognitive and affective. These three attitudinal aspects are based on the three theoretical approaches of behaviour ism, cognitivism and humanism respectively.

Creativity of Science

Creativity and intelligence are closely linked concepts, so much so that the existence of one is the measure of the other. Therefore, any attempt that brings clarity to one concept will be helpful to define the other. Lenat and Feigenbaum (1987) define intelligence in terms of "search", as the power to find a solution to a problem in an immense search space. Later, Feigenbaum defined intelligence in terms of "knowledge assembly rather than "search" (see, Engelmore & Morgan, 1988, vii). Accorclin to his definition, an intelligent system has the ability to assemble the neccessary body of knowledge to conduct a complex task. Scientific creativity can be investigated through five basic cognitive and computational concepts.

General Objectives

To find out the A Study on the Attitude of Creativity in Science among Ix Standard Students in Pudukkottai Educational Districts".

Objectives

1. To find out whether there is any significant difference between Male and Female students in their attitude of creativity in science of IX standard student's level.
2. To find out whether there is any significant difference between Rural and Urban students in their attitude of creativity in science of IX standard student's level.
3. To find out whether there is any significant difference between Government and Private school students in their attitude of creativity in science of IX standard student's level.

4. To find out whether there is any significant difference between Tamil medium and English medium students in their attitude of creativity in science of IX standard student's level.
5. To find out whether there is any significant difference between Boys school and Girls school students in their attitude of creativity in science of IX standard student's level.
6. To find out whether there is any significant difference between Government and Self employment parent students in their attitude of creativity in science of IX standard student's level.
7. To find out whether there is any significant difference between Literate and Illiterate parent's students in their attitude of creativity in science of IX standard student's level.

Hypotheses of the Study

1. There is no significant difference in the attitude of creativity in science of IX standard students on the basis of their gender (Male/ Female)
2. There is no significant difference in the attitude of creativity in science of IX standard students on the basis of their location of school. (Rural/Urban)
3. There is no significant difference in the attitude of creativity in science of IX standard students on the basis of their management of school. (Government/ Private)
4. There is no significant difference in the attitude of creativity in science of IX standard students on the basis of their medium of school. (Tamil/English)
5. There is no significant difference in the attitude of creativity in science of IX standard students on the basis of their type of school.(Boys/Girls)
6. There is no significant difference in the attitude of creativity in science of IX standard students on the basis of their parents occupation.(Government/Self Employee)
7. There is no significant difference in the attitude of creativity in science of IX standard students on the basis of their parent's educational qualification. (Literate/Illiterate)

Limitation of the Study

1. In this study questionnaire was administrated only for IX standard school students studying at Pudukkottai Educational District.
2. The sample was collected only from the government private school in Pudukkottai District.
3. The present information was collected only from 300 samples.

Population

The population is a set the totality of all objects or individuals. A population is by a group of individuals who have are studying in IX standard school students in Pudukkottai educational district.

Sample

A sample is a set of item of individuals selected from a larger aggregate or population. The sample selected for the present study consists of 300 IX standard school students from different school with the help of stratified random sampling technique.

Conclusion

This chapter deals with a detailed background of the quality education, objectives, attitude, creativity, creativity in science and hypotheses are discussed and valuable information about attitude of creativity in science. It also underlined and highlighted the improved of the student's ability. Moreover, this chapter helps the investigator to acquaint with related content of learning ability. Next chapter deals the review of related literature.

Chapter VII

Review of Related Literature

Introducation

This chapter reveals the previous related research studies in India and abroad. The main purpose of reviewing the literature understands the previous work done in the relevant field of study habit and academic achievement. Further the related literatures help the researcher to thoroughly analyse and scrutinise the methodological perspectives used in the previous studies may avoid unnecessary duplication of research in this chapter the investigator reviewed the related literatures and the area of study habit the available resources, the investigator collected some related studies and present in this chapter the previous studies are given below.

Importance of Review

Review of related literature allows the researcher to acquaint himself with current knowledge in the field or area in which he is going to conduct his research./ It also serves the following specific purposes.

1. The review of related literature enables the researches to define the limits of his field. It helps the researcher to delimit and define

his problem. The knowledge of related literature brings the researcher up – to – data on the work which others have done and to state the objectives clearly and concisely.

2. By reviewing the related literature the research can avoid in fruitful and unless problem areas. He can select those areas in which positive findings are likely to research and his endeavours would be likely to add to the knowledge in a meaningful way.
3. Through the review of related literature, the research can avoid an unintentional duplication of well established findings. There is no use to replicate a study when the stability and validity of its result have been clearly established.
4. The review of related literature gives the research understandings of the research methodology which refers to the way study is to be conducted. It helps the research to know about the books and instruments, which proved to be useful and promising the previous studies. The advantage of the related literature is also to provide insight into statistical methods through which validity of is to be established and
5. The final and important specific reason for reviewing the related literature is to know about the recommendations of previous research for further research which they have listed in their studies.

Value of the Review of Related Literature

It is a valuable guide to define the problem and recognize its significance. It helps in suggesting, promising data – gathering devices, appropriate study design and sources of data. It provides suggestions for possible modifications in the research to avoid unanticipated difficulties. It unfolds a backdrop of interpreting the results of the research study.

Oruces of Related Literature

The investigator identified several sources of related literature.

They included

1. Articles of Newspaper

2. Surveys of research in Education
3. Dissertation abstracts
4. Internet
5. Journals
6. E – Journals
7. E – Test books
8. Encyclopedia
9. Textbooks
10. Unpublished theses.

Research Studies Done in India and Abroad

Collins., (2000). The latter study was innovative in its use of focus groups to explore 16-year-old student's views and attitudes towards science in depth. Perhaps surprisingly, chemistry was found to be less appealing than physics.

Rua., (2000) using questionnaires with large samples. In the case of the American context, Jones et al. were forced to conclude, despite a large number of interventions undertaken in the 1980s and 1990s, 'that the future pipeline of scientists and engineers is likely to remain unchanged'.

Jones et al., (2000) would suggest that situation remains fundamentally unchanged. More importantly, Kahle argues that her data show conclusively that 'lack of experiences in science leads to a lack of understanding of science and contributes to negative attitudes to science'.

Gauld and Hukins., (2000). In essence, these are the features that might be said to characterize scientific thinking and are cognitive in nature. However, a clear distinction must be drawn between these attributes and the affective 'attitudes towards science', which are the feelings, beliefs and values held about an object that may be the enterprise of science, school science, the impact of science on society or scientists themselves.

Ajzen and Fishbein's., (2000) theory of reasoned action, which is concerned fundamentally with predicting behaviour. This theory focuses on the distinction between attitudes towards some 'object' and attitudes towards some specific action to be performed towards that 'object' (e.g. between attitudes towards science and attitudes towards doing school science). Ajzen and Fishbein argue that it is the latter kind of f attitude that best predicts behaviour. Thus,their theory represents a relationship between attitude, intention and behaviour.

Whitfield., (2000) argued that the rejection of science was accounted for by the perception that it was a difficult subject but his findings, based on data collected in the 1970s, now lack significance because of the considerable changes that have occurred in the science curriculum.

DeBoer, 2000 conducted a study With these conceptions of the nature of science, authentic science and scientific literacy comes the view that science education must involve much more than teaching children discrete facts that are narrowly aimed at increasing scores on standardized tests of science knowledge.

Munby., (2000) for the inconsistent results it produces and its lack of reliability. Moreover, a feature of this scale is that all the attitude objects are concerned with aspects of science in society and not attitude to science as a school subject. The result has been the development of a plethora of scales that give differing degrees of emphasis to a broader range of attitude objects.

Jones (2002) conducted a study on "The effects of video-based and activity-based instruction on high school students' knowledge, attitudes, and behaviour al intentions related to seat belt use. The purpose of the study was to determine the effect of video based science instruction and accompanying activity-based instruction on the knowledge, attitudes and behaviour al intentions of high school students' use of seat belt.

King., (2002), which suggests that one of the major factors in girls' antipathy towards science is their perception that they are better at other subjects. Preference ranking is simple to use and the results of such research are easily presented and interpreted. Its fundamental problem is that it is a relative scale.

Wellington., (2002) notes that there are “at least six types of activity” that take place in school science “that we would probably all class s practical work” teacher demonstrations: class practical’s, with all learners on similar tasks, working in small groups: a circus of ‘experiments with small groups engaged in different activities, rotating in a carousel: investigations, organized in one of the above two ways: and problem – solving activities.

Hurd (2002) observed that nothing much has changed despite the contexts of science and technology undergoing fundamental change. Science programs continue to feature an inquiry approach to teaching children science; frameworks of concepts (see Glossary of Terms), skills (see Glossary of Terms) and attitudes (see Glossary of Terms); and information about how children learn. These ideas have endured because they are good ideas that provide teachers with guidance about teaching practice.

Lubart et al., (2003) refined this model by including emotional factors. The confluence approaches recognise that cognitive and environmental factors contribute to the establishment and development of creativity.

Jebreel (2003) conducted a study to assess the effectiveness of Dimensions of Learning Model on Thinking Skills included in third Dimensions of Learning Model such as comparison, classification, induction, deduction, analyzing error, constructing support and analyzing perspectives with students in seven standards. The findings showed that Dimensions of Learning Model appeared generally encourage and develop Thinking Skills included in third Dimensions of Learning Model such as comparison, classification, induction, deduction, analyzing error, constructing support and analyzing perspectives.

Erduran and Simon (2004) observe, we live in a society in which scientific issues are increasingly dominating the cultural landscape. Recognition of the interdependency of science and technology and the inevitable role society plays in influencing and being influenced by science and technology, has led various researchers to speculate about what authentic learning experiences for children might look like, and why programs should feature opportunities for children to understand.

Al-Haroon (2003) carried out study by teaching biology through Dimensions of Learning Model. Participants included 70 tenth standard high school female students. A Achievement Test and Scale of Meta Cognition Skills were the tools of the study. Significance difference has been found in the mean scores of Achievement and Meta Cognition Skills of the Experimental Group. It was concluded that Dimensions of Learning Model was more effective than the conventional method.

Al-Baali (2003), through teaching of science using Dimensions of Learning Model, investigated Achievement and Science Processes Skills. Data were collected from 159 of eighth standard students. The sample was split into two groups Experimental Group was taught using Dimensions of Learning Model and Control Group was taught by conventional method. An Achievement Test and Science Processes Test were constructed by the Researcher. An Achievement Test and Science Processes Test were constructed for administering as pre-test and post-test. The results revealed students taught by Dimensions of Learning Model improved their Achievement and Science Processes Skills more than students taught by traditional approach; also it found a positive correlation between Achievement and Science Processes Skills.

Simpson., (2004) have all found that social support from peers and attitude towards enrolling for a course are strong determinants of student choice to pursue science courses voluntarily, which suggests that the theory has at least some partial validity. The main value of such a theory is its help in determining salient beliefs that can then be reinforced or downplayed to affect relevant behavioural decisions by students such as 'girls don't do science'.

Fleming. (2004), although this placed more emphasis on determining students' views of the nature of science. However, their items were determined from views expressed by students and, for this reason; their instrument is often seen as offering greater validity than others. It has been adapted most recently by Bennett (2001) to determine undergraduates' views of chemistry and develop profiles of students who held positive and negative views of the subject.

University of Louisiana at Monroe (2004) conducted a study entitled "the effect of an integrated, activity-based science curriculum on students' achievement, science process skills and attitude towards science" the study was intended to investigate the effect of the IASC (Integrated Activity-based Science Curriculum).

Dujari (2004) Conducted a Study aimed to determine the effect of tow components of the Dimensions of Learning Model on the Achievement of under prepared college science students, namely the Acquiring & Integrating Knowledge and Extending & Refining knowledge, the Study was applied to 61 students at Wilmington College in America, and an Achievement Test was used in this study, the results of this Study indicated that there was no significant difference between the Experimental and Control Groups, but the better improvement in score was observed within the Experimental Group. This clearly indicates that although there was no difference in instructional methods, students gained content knowledge when taught the strategy. The Study had limitations from small size and limited experimentation time.

Jerald (2005) carried out a study to examine the relationship between teachers' perception and implementation of inquiry instruction as well as their student' perception and performance on inquiry activities. A group of six science teacher and their students form grades seven to twelve were the subjects for this study. A mixed methodology was utilized.

Middleton, (2005) Research studies on STS have given rise to a closer inspection of the nature of technology and the goals of technology education. The strategies and settings that promote creative thinking in design and technology make the area suitable for addressing ethics and values and may be one of the major reasons for including design and technology programs in school curricula.

Comber, and Hargreaves., (2005), who found that there were significant gender differences among 11-year-old to 13-year-old pupils with girls favouring English and humanities, and boys favouring PE and science.

Saleh and Basheer (2005) conducted a study to assess using of Dimensions of Learning Model on Skills and Concepts associated with some educational experiences required for kindergarten child. The participants in this Study two classrooms of second KG. The results revealed that children taught by Dimensions of Learning Model acquire Skills more than students taught by traditional approach.

Weinburgh., (2005) covering the literature between 1970 and 1991. Both the latter two papers summarize numerous research studies to show that boys have a consistently more positive attitude to school science than girls, although this effect is stronger in physics than in biology. Interestingly, Weinburgh's work shows that this effect is highest for 'general science', and her finding raises the question of whether the introduction of 'balanced science' or integrated science courses during the past decade has had a similar effect in increasing the separation between boys' and girls' attitudes to science.

Hassaneen (2006) assessed the influence of Dimensions of Learning Model on Physical Concepts Acquisition, Complex Thinking and Attitude towards Physics. Compared to students in the Control Group who received conventional method, students in the Experimental Group taught using Dimensions of Learning Model. The result revealed that Dimensions of Learning Model was more effective than the conventional method in developing Physical Concepts Acquisition, Complex Thinking and Attitude towards Physics.

Wallace (2006) examined the effect of the Dimensions of Learning Model on the Epistemological Beliefs of students enrolled in general chemistry laboratory for post baccalaureate pre-medical students. The Experimental Group received twenty to thirty minute interactive instruction for each laboratory activity. This instruction for the Experimental Group was designed to include the five Dimensions of Learning. The Control Group received normal laboratory instruction which consisted of background information to complete the activities. Results indicated that there was not a significant difference between the two groups in the Epistemological Beliefs.

Buxton (2006) provides an overview of how the term "authentic science" is used in research literature. He reports that authentic science:

1. allows children to follow investigative pathways over time

2. includes natural problem-solving contexts with high degrees of complexity
3. requires the application of many cognitive processes
4. includes an accurate view of the nature of science
5. models what scientists do
6. addresses the culture of children
7. Involves applying scientific inquiry to public, social and community purposes.

Whitehead's., (2006) research has attempted to explore in more detail the influence of gender stereotyping on choice. She found that, although there were significant gender distinctions within pupils' perceptions of subjects, these were not significant influences on subject choice. Girls doing mainly 'feminine' subjects, who were the focus of her study, described themselves as high on the stereotypical masculine trait of competence and were highly intrinsically motivated. Boys in contrast, taking mainly 'masculine' subjects, were more likely to be extrinsically motivated for status, recognition and a highly paid job describing themselves as high on the traits of competence and aggression.

Campbell and Jane.,(2006). An example of this approach to pedagogy is the development of professional knowledge in the Creativity and Professional Development Project (C&PD) based in initial teacher education. Digital technologies, such as digital video for example, can provoke teachers' thinking about the media, the organisation, and the knowledge and skills required to support learners' creative activities.

Kesner (2008) assessed the affects of hands-on, inquiry-based instruction on student science achievement in a high-stakes testing environment. A quasi experimental design employing quantitative and qualitative methods was used. Results indicated a general improvement of students meeting mastery of fifth grade science state assessment when kits were implemented.

Al Saud (2009) conducted an experimental study comparing the effects of the Dimensions of Learning Model and the traditional method for teaching history in two secondary schools for girls. The main purpose of the Study was to compare the effectiveness of Dimensions of Learning Model and traditional method of teaching instructional unit on the Critical Thinking, Mental Features and Achievement in History. The participants in this study were 50 female students. The results indicated that the students in the Experimental Group performed significantly better than the students in Control Group in Critical Thinking, Mental Features and Achievement in History.

Saleh (2009) compared the Achievement levels in Science, Reasoning Thinking and Attitude towards Science of 42 male students (Experimental Group) who taught by Dimensions of Learning Model and 41 male students (Control Group) who taught through conventional method. The result revealed that there were significantly differences among students of the Experimental Group and the Control Group on Achievement in Science, Reasoning Thinking and Attitude towards Science in favour of students of the Experimental Group, besides; there were positive relationship between dependent variables of the study.

Barrows (2010) found the effects of teaching a science topic in the regents living environment course in a mini lesson instructional environment. The findings of the study reveal that the students had considerable difficulty with several areas relating to basic biology about the cell structure and functions and did not have an integrated conceptual understanding of the topic. The study revealed that mini lesson instruction appeared to impact student learning and understanding as to how to communicate and share ideas.

Powell (2010) found the effect of instructional methodology on high school students natural sciences standardized tests scores. The quasi experimental quantitative study comprised of two stages. First stage used a survey to identify teaching methods of a convenience sample of fifty seven teacher participants and determined level of inquiry used in instruction to place participants into instructional groups. Stage two used ANCOVA. Results demonstrated a statistically significant gain in test scores when taught using inquiry based instruction.

Although Simonton (2011) argues whilst knowledge does play a role it seems likely that blind variation is indeed at play. Gabora

(2005) argues that creativity evolves, but through a process of context driven actualization of potential and not via a Darwinian natural selection.

Study Conducted in India

Rajput et al (2000) carried out a survey of science laboratories in the western region. The objective of the survey was to study the role of laboratories in the basic education of science as perceived by science teachers. It intended to analyse the main objectives of laboratory work in the opinion of science teachers, the extent to which the objectives were realized, the area of the laboratory , the number of experimental tables in the laboratory, the total time allotted for laboratory work in each subject, the problem faced in conducting the laboratory classes, the procedure adopted for making purchases for the laboratory, the total grant available for the laboratory, the additional grant needed for the laboratory and the assistance in the conduct of laboratory work by trained laboratory attendants and helpers.

Cornelious (2000) investigated the factors affecting teacher competence of teacher trainees at the secondary level, revealed that intelligence, attitude towards teaching profession, and academic achievement of teacher trainees are the discriminating factors of the different groups of subjects.

Cornelius (2000) in a study on teacher competency of the B.Ed trainees found that intelligence, attitude towards teaching profession and academic achievement are the discriminating factors of different group of teachers.

Pugh Ava and Others (2000) conducted a study, an Investigation of Pre-service Teachers' Attitude toward Theory and Practical Application in Teacher preparation. To determine program effectiveness, students were surveyed at the end of the spring and fall semesters for 6 years, examining their attitudes towards theory and practical application in teacher education. The study noted whether they felt competent about subject matter, audiovisuals, classroom management and routine, and communication. Results found their attitudes more positive in the fall on all four measures.

Ruscoe, Gordon and Others (2000) conducted a study the Qualitative and quantitative perspectives on Teacher Attitudes. Since 1988, teacher analysis suggests that simultaneous involvement with more than one type of restructuring has a positive effect on teacher attitudes. In subsequent interviews with teachers and administrators. While showing appreciation for shared decision making, teachers more often accounted for their positive attitudes by describing a supportive administrative style.

Gitlin (2000) conducted in a study, examined teacher's attitudes about professional voice involved discussion among group of colleagues about professional issues, addressing three areas of concern about dialogue: teacher interest, administrative support from the teacher's perspective and constraints. They suggested the importance of personal narratives to encourage teacher voice and teacher interest.

Chandrasekhar (2000) conducted a study "In an in-depth analysis of India's economic reform package Patnaik and considered the crisis of 1991 purely 'speculative in nature' caused by speculative outflows from Indian economy that continued the pressure on balance of payments despite reduction in trade deficit. A very vital, daring and worrisome feature of India's economic reform according to them was that, there was no urgent need of bringing about structural changes in 1991 since the condition could have come under control by low conditionality of IMF loans. It was the 'liberalisation lobby' that consisted of Fund, Bank, government elements and Indian business class that made use of this unprecedented economic crisis by introducing 'liberalisation'.

Muddu (2000) conducted a study entitled 'A study of prevalent status of instructional procedures in biology in high schools'. The objectives of the study were to evaluate the facilities provided to teachers, such as laboratories, audio visual aids, to find out the type of instruction adopted in teaching biology in accordance with the concepts envisaged in the syllabi, and to find out the extent to which the instructional procedures met the demands of biology syllabi in the process of reorganizing the scheme of secondary education.

Swaranamma (2001) conducted a study entitled 'An enquiry into the teaching of biology in the upper primary schools of Kerala'. The major objectives of the study were to identify topics to be deleted from the biology syllabus of standards VI and VII from the point of view of pupils, to identify activities which are found rather difficult by pupils of standards VI and VII, to identify the techniques of teaching adopted by the teachers teaching biology at the upper primary classes in the Trivandrum district, to identify the objectives aimed at by the teachers of biology of the upper primary stage and to find out the level of attainment of pupils of standard VII in biology.

Kumar (2001) carried out an experimental study of the relative effectiveness of three methods of instruction exposition method, programmed learning method and multimedia method in science education. The main objectives of the study were to find out the relative effectiveness of the three methods of instruction, to study the relative retention in learning through the three methods.

Thaker (2001) Effectiveness of Mastery Learning Programme with reference to Science Teaching. The major objectives were to construct a 'Mastery Learning Programme' for the Science subject and to test the influence of Mastery Learning Programme with reference to 'General class teaching' on students' Science Learning.

Vijay Kumari (2002) studied the effect of different methods of teaching Science on the achievement, basic science process skills and scientific attitude of pupils with The objectives of study were to study the effect of methods, levels of pre-acts and their interaction on achievement of knowledge, understanding and application objectives separately by taking intelligence as covariate, to compare variation in interaction patterns due to change in prior achievement levels of pupils with respect to Teacher Demonstration Method (TDM), Guided Discovery (GD) and Cooperative Learning Method (GDLM & CLM) of teaching science, to explain the relationship between significant differences in achievement, improvement of scientific attitude and Basic Science Process Skills (BSPS) in terms of differences in teaching process.

Ravindranath (2002) developed a multimedia instructional strategy for teaching science (biology) at class VIII. The main objectives of the study were to develop a duly validated multimedia instructional strategy for teaching the course in biology at standard VIII, to study the relationship between students achievement and intelligence, to study the feasibility of the strategy in terms of cost and time and to develop alternative instructional components for teaching few concept and their relative effectiveness

Sharma (2002) carried out a study entitled growth and development of science education in Bihar. The objectives of the study was to analyse the aims, curriculum, textbooks and techniques, materials and equipment, teacher training programmes, supervision and inspection and agencies of the improvement of science education in Bihar. Data were collected from ten primary schools, ten middle schools, ten secondary schools and the State Council for Educational Research and Training. Five science teacher educators of secondary education colleges and ten science teacher educators of primary teacher education colleges were interviewed with the help of a specially prepared interview schedule.

Barman (2003) conducted study entitled the origin and development of modern science in pre-independence India. The main aim of the research was to study the origin and development of modern science in pre- independence period. The historical survey method was adopted. Some of the major conclusion were modern science grew in India as part of British occupation in the country. It was primarily an extension of British science and purported to serve the needs of colonial power.

Aziz (2004) conducted a study of science education programmes in the secondary schools of Bangladesh. The major objectives of the inquiry were to study the science education programmes mainly in terms of physical facilities, budget allocation, science teachers, procedure of teaching, evaluation, to study science education practices in some selected schools with better than usual results and varied physical facilities.

Bajracharya (2006) conducted a study of science education in the secondary schools of Nepal with a view to evolving a functional model for improving the science education. The objectives of the study were to study the existing conditions of secondary science education in Nepal, to identify the problems of the existing secondary science education in Nepal, and to evolve a functional model for improving secondary science education in Nepal.

Shaikh (2007) conducted a study of teaching competency of secondary school science teachers of Dhaka city. Major objectives of the study were, to identify the competencies of science teachers in teaching of science, to identify the competent science teachers with the help of the rating scale constructed by the researcher, to study the competent science teachers in relation to the different attributes such as inherent capacity environmental facilities home and school and academic background.

Vaidya (2007) reported a total of sixty one studies during the period covered by fifth. The area where the research was concentrated were Environmental Studies (nine), Science Curriculum Syllabus and textbook (seven), learning science and models of teaching (fifteen), teaching strategies (four), outcomes of science education (scientific temper, attitude, skills and interests) (eight), correlates of achievements in science (seven), educational technology (three).

Umashree (2009) conducted a study entitled science curriculum and its transaction: an exploratory study in secondary schools of Vadodara. The objectives of study were: to study the intentions of science curriculum at the secondary level under operation in schools at Vadodara, to study the curriculum transaction in science in the classroom situations in schools at Vadodara, to gather the teachers' opinion about the different aspects of science curriculum through classroom observation, questionnaire and interviews, to evaluate the congruency between the intended and transacted curriculum.

Al-Ahmadi (2008) in her study aimed to examine the effect of Brainstorming on Creative thinking and Written Expression in Arabic Language. The participants in this Study were 40 female students in ninth standard. The Creative Thinking Test and Written Expression Test were constructed by the Researcher. The results revealed that Brainstorming was more effective than the conventional method in developing Creative Thinking and Written Expression Skills.

Al-Itabi (2009) conducted an experimental study to determine the Ability of six elementary standard females on Deductive Thinking and Creative Thinking and Problem Solving and their relation to Achievement in Science. Data were collected from 853 of sixth standard female students. The Deductive Thinking and Creative Thinking and Problem Solving Tests were constructed by the

Investigator. The result revealed that the general Ability on Deductive and Creative Thinking and Problem Solving exceed the minimum limit of the accepted performance (75%) of the total mark measure on the level of the three branched measures, also there is not a statistically significant correlation between the students' abilities orders in Deductive and Creative Thinking and Problem Solving in Science and their Achievement orders in Science and there is not a statistically significant effect for the students' abilities orders in Deductive and Creative Thinking and Problem Solving in science on their Achievement orders level in Science.

Amin (2011) developed and implemented an activity based science teaching programme for pre service student teachers. The researcher studied effectiveness of the developed programmes in terms of content knowledge of science and technology, experimental ability, understanding about nature of science, teaching qualities enhanced as science teachers, understanding about science teaching. The sample consisted of 40 student teachers.

Conclusion

This chapter review of related literature discussed about the importance of the related studies. More which also discussed about the studies done in India and abroad connected with the present study. The third chapter will present the research methodology of the present study.

Chapter VIII

Methodology

Introduction

The chapter of Research Methodology deals with plan and procedure that are adopted for present study. This chapter reveals objectives, Hypotheses, construction and validation of Research tool, sampling procedure, Data collection, Data analysis and Delimitation of study. The Researcher explains systematic procedure used in the study is given below.

Statement of the Problem

This is the title of the present study "A Study on the Attitude of Creativity in Science among Ix Standard Students in Pudukkottai Educational District."

Objectives Of The Study

General Objectives

To find out the "A Study on the Attitude of Creativity in Science among Ix Standard Students in Pudukkottai Educational Districts".

Specific Objectives

1. To find out whether there is any significant difference between Male and Female students in their attitude of creativity in science of IX standard students level.
2. To find out whether there is any significant difference between Rural and Urban students in their attitude of creativity in science of IX standard students level.
3. To find out whether there is any significant difference between Government and Private school students in their attitude of creativity in science of IX standard students level.
4. To find out whether there is any significant difference between Tamil medium and English medium school students in their attitude of creativity in science of IX standard students level.
5. To find out whether there is any significant difference between boys school and girls school students in their attitude of creativity in science of IX standard students level.
6. To find out whether there is any significant difference between government and self employment parent students in their attitude of creativity in science of IX standard students level.
7. To find out whether there is any significant difference between Literate and Illiterate parents students in their attitude of creativity in science of IX standard students level.

Hypotheses of the Study

1. There is no significant difference in the attitude of creativity in science of IX standard students on the basis of their gender.(Male/ Female)
2. There is no significant difference in the attitude of creativity in science of IX standard students on the basis of their location of school.(Rural/Urban)
3. There is no significant difference in the attitude of creativity in science of IX standard students on the basis of their management of school.(Government/Private)

4. There is no significant difference in the attitude of creativity in science of IX standard students on the basis of their medium of school.(Tamil/English)
5. There is no significant difference in the attitude of creativity in science of IX standard students on the basis of their type of school.(Boys/Girls)
6. There is no significant difference in the attitude of creativity in science of IX standard students on the basis of their parents occupation.(Government/ Self employment)
7. There is no significant difference in the attitude of creativity in science of IX standard students on the basis of their parents educational qualification.(Literate/Illiterate)

Limitation of the Study

1. In this study questionnaire was administrated only for IX standard school students studying at Pudukkottai Educational District.
2. The sample was collected only from the government and Privates school in Pudukkottai District.
3. The present information was collected only from 300 samples.

Population

The population is a set the totality of all objects or individuals. A population is by a group of individuals who have are studying in the IX standard school students in pudukkottai educational districts.

Sample

A sample is a set of item of individuals selected from a larger aggregate or population.

The sample selected for the present study consists of 300 IX standard school students from different school with the help of stratified random sampling technique.

Research Method

The investigator used normative survey method to collect date from IX standard students. In the study the investigator collected the data from various school located Pudukkottai district.

Research Tool

The investigator used questionnaire to collect data to attitude of creativity in science in IX standard students.

Construction of Research Tool

Before constructing the research tool the investigator visited a few schools located in Rural and Urban areas and collected opinion from high school level students.

Since the investigator himself faced some problems when he was studying at high school level this experience and student's suggestions mostly helped the researcher to frame the present research tool.

Description of the Research Tool

A questionnaire on attitude of creativity in science in IX standard students has 30 items. All the items of questionnaire of focused on varieties of ideas regarding attitude of creativity in science. The researcher adopted two point scaling procedure for measuring the level of attitude of creativity in science.

Namely, "Known" carries One Marks, "Unknown" carries Zero mark in positive statement. These marks are indicating the level of attitude of creativity in science among IX standard school students level.

The scale is

(1) Known (k)

(2) Unknown (UK)

Scale Items	Scoring Procedure	
	Positive Questions Marks	Negative Questions Marks
Known(K)	1	0
Unknown (UK)	0	1

Pilot Study

The Researcher conduct a pilot study nearby school of government boy's high school in Pudukkottai.

Before administering the research tool, the researcher give some instruction regarding how can answer all questions, then allowed all the students to rise the difficulties related to some questions and difficult items were discussed and clarified to students for better understanding. After getting response for all the items the researcher give frequencies to each and every item and these frequencies were tabulated used to find out reliability. In order to find out the usability of the proposed study, the researcher felt that the pilot study is an essential study.

Reliability

The reliability of the research tool was established by using "Split half method". The top and bottom items of the questionnaire were taken and frequencies were given to those items based on the "Known" response. This total frequency of (top and bottom) considers finding out the correlation and then the researcher used the "Spearman Brown prophecy" formula of split half method to find out reliability.

FORMULA: - $r = 2r / 1+r$

$= 2(0.732) / 1+ 0.732$

$r= 0.84$

Validity

The investigator established content and face validity of the research tool. The items of the questionnaire were given to experts in the field of education to see their opinion in relation to its objective and worthiness of items. Further the experts view the each and every items of the questionnaire and provide of some suggestions to modify some of the questions. Based on the opinions some of the questions are eliminated and modified. The above process brought a sufficient content and face validity to research questioner of this study.

Sampling Technique

The sample procedure is used to collect the data is satisfied random sampling. The researcher collected sample only from high school level students, the school located in Pudukkottai Educational District. The total samples taken for the present study is 300 Number of students.

Data Collections

The researcher himself visited high school students located in Pudukkottai area by getting permission from the Head Master of various schools. Before administering the research tool the researcher explain the aim and purpose of the study and then administered a research tool for IX standard school level students. Then the researcher asked all the students to response for each and every item that are given in the questionnaire the response were recorded and the demographic particulars were collected from students. Then the researcher gave frequencies for all items and this frequency was entering in the Master table for data analysis. The researcher used statistical techniques, such as percentage analysis and test of significant to analysis data for this study.

Data Analysis

The investigator used statistical techniques such as mean, standard deviation and "t" test to find out whether there is any significant difference between the different biographical variables of the attitude of creativity in science among IX standards school students.

The Arithmatic Mean

The mean of the distribution is commonly understood as the arithmetic average. The term grade point average, familiar to student is a mean value. It is computed by dividing the sum of all the scores by the number of scores. It is probably most useful of all statistical measures for in addition to the information that it provides, it is the base from which many other important measures are computed, $\acute{x} = \frac{\sum x}{N}$.

The Standard Deviation (S.d)

Standard Deviation is most widely used measure of dispersion of a series and is commonly denoted by the symbol 'σ'(sigma). S.D is defined as the square root of the average of the squares of deviation for the values of individual items in a series are obtained from the arithmetic average.

Standard Deviation (S.D), $\sigma = \sqrt{\left(\frac{\Sigma f d^2}{n}\right) - \left(\frac{\Sigma f d}{n}\right)^2} \times C.I$

'T' (**t –Test**)

'T' test is based on t-distribution and is a sample mean (or) judging the significance of difference between the means of the sample in case of small samples when population variance is not known. In case of two samples paired t - test is used for judging the significance of the mean of difference between the two related samples. The relevant test statistic is calculated from the sample data then compared with portable value based on t - distribution at a specified level of significance for concerning degrees of freedom for accepting (or) rejecting the null hypothesis. This test applies only in case of small samples when population variance is not known.

Where, M_1 = Highest Mean value, M_2 = Lowest Mean value.

S_1 = SD for highest Mean value, S_2 = SD for Lowest Mean value.

N_1 = Highest mean value of case, N_2 = Lowest mean value of case.

Limitation of the Study

1. In this study questionnaire was administrated only for IX standard school students studying at Pudukkottai Educational District.
2. The sample was collected only from the government schools, and private school in Pudukkottai district.
3. The present information was collected only from 300 samples.

Table 1

School – Wise Distribution of the Sample

SI. No	Name of the school	School locality	Boys	Girls	Total
1.	Sri Bragathambal Hr.Sec.School	Pudukkottai	—	50	50
2.	Ranee's Girls Hr Sec. School.	Pudukkottai	50	—	50

SI. No	Name of the school	School locality	Boys	Girls	Total
3.	Government Hr. Sec. School.	Vennavelkudi	20	30	50
4.	St Joseph Hr. Sec. School	Venkatakulam	30	20	50
5.	Mount Zion Matric.Hr.Sec.School	Pudukkottai	23	27	50
6.	Government Hr. Sec. School	Arimalam	27	23	50
	Total		150	150	300

It is inferred from above table that of them different number of students were taken in the schools.

Table 2

Sex – Wise Distribution of the Sample

Sex	Number	Percentage
Boys	150	50%
Girls	150	50%
Total	300	100%

It is inferred from the above table that 50% of them were boys and 50% of them were girls.

Table 3

Place – Wise Distribution of the Sample

Place of the School	Number	Percentage
Rural	140	46.7%
Urban	160	53.3%
Total	300	100%

It is inferred from the above table that 46.7% of them were Rural and 53.3% of them were Urban.

Table 4

Management Wise Distribution of the Sample

Type of school	Number	Percentage
Government	160	53.3%
Self – Finance	140	46.7%
Total	300	100%

It is inferred from above table that of them were taken Government 53.3% and Self finance 46.7% of them students.

Conclusion

This chapter explained about the methodology employed for the present study. Preparation research tool, construction of research too, pilot study reliability and validity, sampling technique, data collection and data analysis also presented in the chapter. The next chapter will be about the analysis and interpretation of the collected data.

Chapter IX

Analysis Data

Introduction

The chapter highlights the result of the research. The result are presented in systematic manner after all the hypotheses of the study is tested and verified applying suitable statistical such as "t" test.

One of the important parts of any investigation is analysis and interpretation of data. The data collected in any field of activity becomes meaningful and useful only when they are subjected to statistical analysis and inference.

Analysis of data means studying the organized material in order to discover inherent facts. The data are studied from as many angels as positive to explore the new facts. Once the research data have been collected, data analysis should be made. Then the research can proceed to the stage of interpreting the result. The process of interpret on is essentially needed to stage what the result show. The research data become meaningful only after they are being analyses and interpreted.

Meaning

The analysis and interpretation of data involves the objective material in the possession of the research and his subjective reactions and desire to drive from the data, the inherent meaning in their reactions to the problem.

The Mean and Standard Deviation of Creativity In Science Scores of the Entire Sample and its Sub Sample

Sample	N	Mean	SD	Significant
Male	150	13.67	6.69	1.71
Female	150	15.00	6.83	
Rural	140	15.71	7.04	3.35
Urban	160	13.13	6.36	
Government	160	13.13	6.81	3.35
Private	140	15.71	6.58	
Tamil Medium	150	16.33	6.71	5.33
English medium	150	12.33	6.30	
Boys School	200	14.00	6.24	0.89
Girls School	100	15.00	7.75	
Government Employee	126	16.11	7.15	3.87
Self Employee	174	13.05	6.21	
Literate parents	119	14.16	6.43	0.37
Illiterate parents	181	14.45	7.02	

Null Hypotheses – 1

There is no significant difference in the attitude of creativity in science of IX standard students on the basis of their gender (Male/ Female)

Table 1

Difference Between Male and Female Students in their Attitude of Creativity in Science Among IX Standard Students Level.

S.No	Gentral	No.s	Mean	SD	"t" Value	Level of Significant (0.05)
1	Male	150	13.67	6.69		
2	Female	150	15.00	6.83	1.71	Not Significant

(For df = 298 at 5% Level of significance the table value of 't' is 1.96)

Since the calculated "t" – Value of 1.71is less than the table–value (1.96) at 5% level, there is no significant difference between the mean scores of attitude of creativity in science among Male and Female at IX standard school students. Hence the null hypothesis is accepted.

Finding:

Female student's attitude of creativity in science is same as well as male student's attitude of creativity in science among IX standard students level.

Null Hypotheses – 2

There is no significant difference in the attitude of creativity in science of IX standard students on the basis of their location of school. (Rural/Urban)

Table 2

Difference Between Rural and Urban Students in their Attitude of Creativity in Science Among IX Standard Students Level.

S.no	Location of the School	Nos	Mean	SD	"t" Value	Level of significant(0.05)
1	Rural	140	15.71	7.04		Significant
2	Urban	160	13.13	6.36	3.35	

(For df = 298 at 5% Level of significance the table value of 't' is 1.96)

Since the calculated "t" – Value of 3.35 is higher than the table "t" – value (1.96) at 5% level, there is significant difference in the attitude of creativity in science of IX standard students on the basis of their location of the school. Hence the null hypothesis is rejected.

Finding:

Urban student's attitude of creativity in science is not same as rural student's attitude of creativity in science among IX standard students level.

Null Hypotheses – 3

There is no significant difference in the attitude of creativity in science of IX standard students on the basis of their management of school. (Government/ Private)

Table 3

Difference Between Governmetnt and Private School Students In their Attitude of Creativity in Science Among IX Standard Students Level

S.no	Location of the School	Nos	Mean	SD	"t" Value	Level of significant(0.05)
1	Government	160	13.13	6.81		
2	Private	140	15.71	6.58	3.35	Significant

(For df = 298 at 5% Level of significance the table value of 't' is 1.96)

Since the calculated "t" – Value of 3.35is higher than the table "t" – value (1.96) at 5% level, there is significant difference in the attitude of creativity in science of IX standard students on the basis of the management of the school students. Hence the null hypothesis is rejected.

Finding:

Government student's attitude of creativity in science is not same as Private student's attitude of creativity in science among IX standard students level.

Null Hypotheses – 4

There is no significant difference in the attitude of creativity in science of IX standard students on the basis of their medium of school. (Tamil/English)

Table 4

Difference Between Tamil and English School Students in their Attitude of Creativity in Science Among IX Standard Students Level

S.no	Type of School	Nos	Mean	Sd	"t" Value	Level of significant(0.05)
1	Tamil	150	16.33	6.71		
2	English	150	12.33	6.30	5.33	Significant

(For df = 298 at 5% Level of significance the table value of 't' is 1.96)

Since the calculated "t" – Value of 5.33 is higher than the table "t" – value (1.96) at 5% level, there is significant difference in the attitude of creativity in science of IX standard students on the basis of medium of school students. Hence the null hypothesis is rejected.

Finding:

English Medium student's attitude of creativity in science is not same as Tamil medium student's attitude of creativity in science among IX standard students level.

Null Hypotheses – 5

There is no significant difference in the attitude of creativity in science of IX standard students on the basis of their type of school.(Boys/Girls)

Table 5

Difference Between Boys School and Girls School Students in Their Attitude of Creativity in Science Among IX Standard Students Level

S.no	Type of the School	Nos	Mean	SD	"t" Value	Level of significant(0.05)
1	Boys school	200	14.00	6.24		
2	Girls school	100	15.00	7.75	0.89	Not significant

(For df = 298 at 5% Level of significance the table value of 't' is 1.96)

Since the calculated "t" – Value of 0.89 is less than the table "t" – value (1.96) at 5% level, there no is significant difference in the attitude of creativity in science of IX standard students. On the basis of their type of the school. Hence the null hypothesis is accepted.

Finding:

Boys school student's attitude of creativity in science is same as well as Girls school student's attitude of creativity in science among IX standard students level.

Null Hypotheses - 6

There is no significant difference in the attitude of creativity in science of IX standard students on the basis of their parents occupation (Government/Self Employee).

Table 6

Difference Between Government Employee and Self Employee Parents Students in their Attitude of Creativity in Science Among IX Standard Students Level

S.no	Parents Occupation	Nos	Mean	SD	"t" Value	Level of significant(0.05)
1	Government Employee	126	16.11	7.15	3.87	Significant
2	Self - Employee	174	13.05	6.21		

(For df = 298 at 5% Level of significance the table value of 't' is 1.96)

Since the calculated "t" - Value of 3.87 is higher than the table "t" - value (1.96) at 5% level, there is significant difference in the attitude of creativity in science of IX standard students on the basis of their occupation of school. Hence the null hypothesis is rejected.

Finding:

Self Employee parents student's attitude of creativity in science is not same as Govt. Employee parent student's attitude of creativity in science among IX standard students level.

Null Hypotheses - 7

There is no significant difference in the attitude of creativity in science of IX standard students on the basis of their parents educational qualification. (Literate/Illiterate)

Table 7

Difference Between Literate and Illiterate Parents Students in Their Attitude of Creativity in Science Among IX Standard Students Level.

S.no	Parents Qualification	Nos	Mean	SD	"t" Value	Level of significant(0.05)
1	Literate	119	14.16	6.43		
2	Illiterate	181	14.45	7.02	0.37	Not Significant

(For df = 298 at 5% Level of significance the table value of 't' is 1.96)

Since the calculated “t” – Value of 0.37 is less than the table “t” – value (1.96) at 5% level, there no is significant in the attitude of creativity in science of IX standard students on the basis of the parent education qualification of school. Hence the null hypothesis is accepted.

Finding:

Illiterate parents student’s attitude of creativity in science is same as well as Literate parents student’s attitude of creativity in science among IX standard students level.

Conclusion

Thus the score were subjected to statistical treatment to find out the validation on attitude of creativity in science among IX standard students. These collected data calculated, analysed and interpreted. The next chapter deals with the summary of the findings and conclusion.

Chapter X

Summary and Conclusion

Introduction

"Attitude is determined by the individual's beliefs about outcomes or attributes of performing the behaviour (behavioural beliefs), weighted by evaluations of those outcomes or attributes. Thus, a person who holds strong beliefs that positively valued outcomes will result from performing the behaviour will have a positive attitude toward the behaviour. Conversely, a person who holds strong beliefs that negatively valued outcomes will result from the behaviour will have a negative attitude." Attitude concept can be viewed from these three dimensions. Each one of these dimensions has different features to bring out language attitude results. Accordingly, the attitude concept has three components i.e., behaviour al, cognitive and affective. These three attitudinal aspects are based on the three theoretical approaches of behaviour ism, cognitive and humanism respectively.

Creativity and intelligence are closely linked concepts, so much so that the existence of one is the measure of the other. Therefore, any attempt that brings clarity to one concept will be helpful to define the other. Lenat and Feigenbaum (1987) define intelligence in terms of "search", as the power to find a solution to a problem in an immense search space. Later, Feigenbaum defined intelligence in terms of "knowledge assembly rather than "search" (see, Engel more & Morgan, 1988, vii). Accorclin to his definition, an intelligent system has the ability to assemble the necessary body of knowledge to conduct a complex task. Scientific creativity can be investigated through five basic cognitive and computational concepts. These are

1. Motivation for scientific research.
2. Ability to correctly formulate research problems within a body of knowledge.
3. Ability to create a comprehensive search space for the solution of a scientific problem.
4. Ability to assemble (or induce) and implement a of heuristics to reduce the search space.
5. Patience and stamina for the exhaustive search for solving the scientific problem within the constrained search space.

In view of these concepts, a creative scientist knows how to correctly formulate research problems, can generate an extensive search space for a selected problem, can assemble or formulate the necessary methodological knowledge to reduce the search space into manageable dimensions, and can conduct exhaustive search in the reduced search space.

NEED AND SIGNIFICANCE OF THE STUDY

1. To improve the students attitude of creativity of science.
2. To analyse variations in male and female students' attitude of creativity in science.
3. To analyse variations in rural and urban students' attitude of creativity in science.
4. To analyse variations in government and government aided and self finance students' attitude of creativity in science.
5. To suggest possible strategies to improve the students' attitude of creativity in science.

SIGNIFICANT OF THE STUDY

1. Teachers help our students to improve their attitude and creativity.
2. Students improve them self attitude and creativity.
3. Students are create new ideas in science.

STATEMENT OF THE PROBLEM

This is the title of the present study "A study on the attitude of creativity in science among IX standard students in pudukkottai educational district."

GENERAL OBJECTIVES

To find out the "A Study on the Attitude of Creativity in Science among Ix Standard Students in Pudukkottai Educational Districts".

SPECIFIC OBJECTIVES

1. To find out whether there is any significant difference between male and female students in their attitude of creativity in science of IX standard students level.
2. To find out whether there is any significant difference between Rural and urban students in their attitude of creativity in science of IX standard students level.
3. To find out whether there is any significant difference between government and private school students in their attitude of creativity in science of IX standard students level.
4. To find out whether there is any significant difference between Tamil and English medium students in their attitude of creativity in science of IX standard students level.
5. To find out whether there is any significant difference between Boys school and Girls school students in their attitude of creativity in science of IX standard students level.
6. To find out whether there is any significant difference between government and self employment parent students in their attitude of creativity in science of IX standard students level.

7. To find out whether there is any significant difference between Literate and Illiterate parents students in their attitude of creativity in science of IX standard students level.

HYPOTHESES OF THE STUDY

1. There is no significant difference in the attitude of attitude of creativity in science of IX standard students on the basis of their gender (Male/Female)
2. There is no significant difference in the attitude of creativity in science of IX standard students on the basis of their location of school.(Rural/Urban)
3. There is no significant difference in the attitude of creativity in science of IX standard students on the basis of their management of school.(Government/Private)
4. There is no significant difference in the attitude of creativity in science of IX standard students on the basis of their medium of school.(Tamil/English)
5. There is no significant difference in the attitude of creativity in science of IX standard students on the basis of their type of school.(Boys/Girls)
6. There is no significant difference in the attitude of creativity in science of IX standard students on the basis of their parents occupation.(Government/Self Employee)
7. There is no significant difference in the attitude of creativity in science of IX standard students on the basis of their parents educational qualification.(Literate/Illiterate)

POPULATION

The population is a set the totality of all objects or individuals. A population is by a group of individuals who have are studying in the IX standard school students in pudukkottai educational districts.

SAMPLE

A sample is a set of item of individuals selected from a larger aggregate or population.

The sample selected for the present study consists of 300 IX standard school students from different school with the help of stratified random sampling technique.

RESEARCH METHOD

The investigator used normative survey method to collect date from IX standard students. In the study the investigator collected the data from various school located Pudukkottai district.

RESEARCH TOOL

The investigator used questionnaire to collect data to attitude of creativity in science in IX standard students.

CONSTRUCTION OF RESEARCH TOOL

Before constructing the research tool the investigator visited a few school located in Rural and Urban areas and collected opinion from high school level students.

Since the investigator himself faced some problems when he was studying at high school level this experience and student's suggestions mostly helped the researcher to frame the present research tool.

DESCRIPTION OF THE RESEARCH TOOL

A questionnaire on attitude of creativity in science in IX standard students has 30 items. All the items of questionnaire of focused on varieties of ideas regarding attitude of creativity in science. The researcher adopted two point scaling procedure for measuring the level of attitude of creativity in science.

Namely, "Known" carries One Marks, "Unknown" carries Zero mark in positive statement. These marks are indicating the level of attitude of creativity in science among IX standard school students level. The scale is,

(1) Known (k)

(2) Unknown (UK)

Scale Items	Scoring Procedure	
	Positive Questions Marks	Negative Questions Marks
Known(K)	1	0
Unknown (UK)	0	1

PILOT STUDY

The Researcher conduct a pilot study nearby school of government boy's high school in Pudukkottai.

Before administering the research tool, the researcher give some instruction regarding how can answer all questions, then allowed all the students to rise the difficulties related to some questions and difficult items were discussed and clarified to students for better understanding. After getting response for all the items the researcher give frequencies to each and every item and these frequencies were tabulated used to find out reliability. In order to find out the usability of the proposed study, the researcher felt that the pilot study is an essential study.

RELIABILITY

The reliability of the research tool was established by using "Split half method". The top and bottom items of the questionnaire were taken and frequencies were given to those items based on the "Known" response. This total frequency of (top and bottom) considers finding out the correlation and then the researcher used the "Spearman Brown prophecy" formula of split half method to find out reliability.

VALIDITY

The investigator established content and face validity of the research tool. The items of the questionnaire were given to experts in the field of education to see their opinion in relation to its objective and worthiness of items. Further the experts view the each and every items of the questionnaire and provide of some suggestions to modify some of the questions. Based on the opinions some of the questions are eliminated and modified. The above process brought a sufficient content and face validity to research questioner of this study.

SAMPLING TECHNIQUE

The sample procedure is used to collect the data is stratified random sampling. The researcher collected sample only from high school level students, the school located in Pudukkottai Educational District. The total samples taken for the present study is 300 Number of students.

DATA COLLECTIONS

The researcher himself visited high school students located in Pudukkottai area by getting permission from the Head Master of various schools. Before administering the research tool the researcher explain the aim and purpose of the study and then administered a research tool for IX standard school level students. Then the researcher asked all the students to response for each and every item that are given in the questionnaire the response were recorded and the demographic particulars were collected from students. Then the researcher gave frequencies for all items and this frequency was entering in the Master table for data analysis. The researcher used statistical techniques, such as percentage analysis and test of significant to analysis data for this study.

DATA ANALYSIS

The investigator used statistical techniques such as mean, standard deviation and “t” test to find out whether there is any significant difference between the different biographical variables of the attitude of creativity in science among IX standards school students.

THE ARITHMATIC MEAN

The mean of the distribution is commonly understood as the arithmetic average. The term grade point average, familiar to student is a mean value.

It is computed by dividing the sum of all the scores by the number of scores. It is probably most useful of all statistical measures for in addition to the information that it provides, it is the base from which many other important measures are computed.

THE STANDARD DEVIATION (S.D)

Standard Deviation is most widely used measure of dispersion of a series and is commonly denoted by the symbol (sigma). S.D is defined as the square root of the average of the squares of deviation for the values of individual items in a series are obtained from the arithmetic average.

Standard Deviation (S.D), $\sigma = \sqrt{\left(\frac{\Sigma f d^2}{n}\right) - \left(\frac{\Sigma f d}{n}\right)^2} \times C.I$

'T' **(t –Test)**

'T' test is based on t-distribution and is a sample mean (or) judging the significance of difference between the means of the sample in case of small samples when population variance is not known. In case of two samples paired t - test is used for judging the significance of the mean of difference between the two related samples. The relevant test statistic is calculated from the sample data then compared with portable value based on t - distribution at a specified level of significance for concerning degrees of freedom for accepting (or) rejecting the null hypothesis. This test applies only in case of small samples when population variance is not known.

$$t = \frac{M_1 - M_2}{\sqrt{\frac{S_1^2}{N_1} + \frac{S_2^2}{N_2}}}$$

Where, = Highest Mean value, M_2= Lowest Mean value.

S_1=SD for highest Mean value, S_1 = SD for Lowest Mean value.

N_1= Highest mean value of case, N_2= Lowest mean value of case.

LIMITATION OF THE STUDY

1. In this study questionnaire was administrated only for IX standard school students studying at Pudukkottai Educational District.
2. The sample was collected only from the government schools, and private school in Pudukkottai istrict.
3. The present information was collected only from 300 samples.

MAJOR FINDINGS

1. Female student's attitude of creativity in science is same as well as male student's attitude of creativity in science among IX standard students level.
2. Urban student's attitude of creativity in science is not same as rural student's attitude of creativity in science among IX standard students level.
3. The Government school students are found to be higher than Private school students in their attitude of creativity in science among IX standard students level.
4. The English Medium school students are found to be higher than Tamil medium school students in their attitude of creativity in science among IX standard students level.
5. The Boys school students are found to be higher than Girls school students in their attitude of creativity in science among IX standard students level.
6. The Self employee parents students are found to be higher than Government Employee parents students in their attitude of creativity in science among IX standard students level.
7. The Illiterate Parents students are found to be higher than literate Parents students in their attitude of creativity in science among IX standard students level.

SUGGESTIONS FOR FUTHER RESEARCH

The following research topics are suggested for further research in this area.

1. Every institution should take care and motivate the studetns on attitude and creativity.
2. The same study may be conducted and developed students attitude and creativity.
3. Some variables may also be taken for further study.
4. The investigation may be extended to higher secondary level for find out attitude and creativity.

5. The investigation area may be extended to some more districts, state and national level.
6. Furthermore this study can be extended at research and developed level (M.Phil and Ph.D) to find out the efficacy.

RECOMMENDATIONS OF THE STUDY

1. Research study may be conducted on development of attitude and creativity to all level students.
2. Research study may be conducted on development of attitude and creativity to higher secon dary level.
3. Research study may be conducted to villeage students.
4. Research study may be conduct to Tamilnadu science research centres.

CONCLUSION

In the recent research that the students attitude and creativity of science IX standard school students level. Further the research also reveals that the student belong to Female category be higher level than the counterpart. Finally the research study concluded that the students belong to Government school students is found to be higher level of attitude of creativity in science of ix standard students level while compare to Private school students. English medium school students is found to be higher level of attitude of creativity in science of ix standard students level while compare to Tamil medium school students.

References

1. Giancarlo, C.A., &Facione, P (2001), A look across four years of the disposition toward Critical thinking among undergraduate students Journal of General Education.
2. Duchscher, J.E.B (2003). Critical Thinking: Perceptions of newly graduated female baccalaureate nurses, journal of Nursing Education.
3. Bower, L. (2005). Everyday learning about imagination. Early Childhood Australia Inc.: Goanna Print, Canberra.

4. Laius, A., Rannikmäe, M. (2005). The Influence of STL Teaching on Students' Creative Thinking. ESERA Conference Contributions of Research to Enhancing Students' Interest in Learning Science.
5. Kind, P. M., &Kind, V. (2007).Creativity in science education: Perspectives and challenges for developing school science. Studies in Science Education.
6. Matud, M. P., Rodriguez, C. ve Grande, J. (2007). Gender differences in creative thinking. Personality and Individual Differences.
7. HOGÖRÜR, V., BILASA, P. (2009). „The problem of creative education in information society". ÎnProcedia – Social and Behaviour al Sciences: World Conference on Educational Sciences – New Trends and Issues in Educational Sciences.
8. MAKEL, M. C. (2009). „Help Us Creativity Researchers, You're Our Only Hope". În Psychology of Aesthetics, Creativity and the Arts.
9. CHIEN, Chu-ying, HUI, Anna N.N. (2010). „Creativity in early childhood education: Teachers' perceptions in three Chinese societies". In Thinking Skills and Creativity.
10. TOJANOVA, Biljana. (2010). „Development of creativity as a basic task of the modern educational system". In Procedia – Social and Behaviour al Sciences: Innovation and Creativity in Education.
11. Zampetakis, l. a., bouranta, nancy, moustakis, v. s. (2010). „On the relationship between individual creativity and time management". In Thinking Skills and Creativity.
12. Ghassib, H. B. (2010). Where does creativity fit into a productivity industrial model of knowledge production. Gifted and Talented International.

Difficulties Encounted in Understanding

Chapter XI

Introduction and Conceptual Frame Work

Introduction

In English the term "Education" has been derived from two Latin words Educare (Educere) and Educatum. "Educare" means to train or mould. It again means to bring up or to lead out or to draw out, propulsion from inward to outward. The term "Educatum" denotes the act of teaching. It throws light on the principles and practice of teaching. The term Educare or Educere mainly indicates development of the latent faculties of the child. But child does not know these possibilities. It is the educator or the teacher who can know these and take appropriate methods to develop those powers.

In Hindi, the term "Siksha" has come from the Sanskrit word "Shash". "Shash" means to discipline, to control, to order, to direct, to rule etc. Education in the traditional sense means controlling or disciplining the behaviour of an individual. In Sanskrit "Shiksha" is a particular branch of the Sutra literature, which has six branches – Shiksh, Chhanda, Byakarana, Nirukta, Jyotisha and Kalpa. The Sutra literature was designed to learn the Vedas. Sikṣha denotes rules of pronunciation.

There is another term in Sanskrit, which throws light on the nature of education. It is "Vidya" which means knowledge. The term "Vidya" has originated from "Bid" meaning knowledge. If we mention certain definitions of education of great educators of the East and the West, we may have a clear picture of the nature and meaning of the term education.

1. "Education is the manifestation of perfection already in man. Like fire in a piece of flint, knowledge exists in the mind. Suggestion is the friction; which brings it out"- Swami Vivekananda
2. "Education according to Indian tradition is not merely a means of earning a living; nor is it only a nursery of thought or a school for citizenship. It is initiation into the life of spirit and training of human souls in the pursuit of truth and the practice of virtue"- Radhakrishnan

SPECIAL FEATURES OF EDUCATION

1. Education is both unilateral as well as bi-polar in nature.
2. It is a continuous process.
3. It is knowledge or experience.
4. It is development of particular aspects of human personality or a harmonious integrated growth.
5. It is conducive for the good of the individual or the welfare of the society.
6. It is a liberal discipline or a vocational course.
7. It is stabilizer of social order, conservator of culture, an instrument of change and construction.

NEED OF AIMS OF EDUCATION

Education is a purposeful activity. By education we intend to bring certain desirable changes in the students. Education is a conscious effort and, as such, it has definite aims and objectives. In the light of these aims the curriculum is determined and the academic achievements of the student are measured. Education without aim is like a boat without its rudder. Aims give direction to activity. Absence of an aim in education makes it a blind alley. Every stage of human development had some aim of life. The aims of life determine aims of education. The aims of education have changed from age to age and thus it is dynamic because the aims of life are dynamic.

SECONDARY EDUCATION COMMISSION

For reconstruction of Secondary Education, Secondary Education Commission was set up (1952-53) under the chairmanship of Dr. Lakshmanswami Mudaliar, a noted educationist and ex-Vice Chancellor of the Madras University. The Commission has made important recommendations for the reconstruction and development of secondary education in the country. The Commission formulated the following aims of Secondary Education after considering the dominant needs of India. These are, mainly, four:

DEVELOPING DEMOCRATIC CITIZENSHIP

The adoption of the goals of democracy and socialism necessitate the development of habits, attitude and qualities of character, which will enable its citizens to bear worthily the responsibilities of democratic citizenship. Among these qualities, which are to be fostered through curricular and co-curricular activities in secondary schools, are:

1. The capacity for clear thinking (clearness in speech and writing);
2. The scientific attitude of mind;
3. Receptivity to new ideas;
4. Respect for the dignity and worth of every individual;
5. The ability to live harmoniously with one another
6. A sense of true patriotism; and
7. A sense of world citizenship.

VOCATIONAL EFFICIENCY

One of the urgent problems of the country was to improve productive efficiency and to increase the national wealth and thereby to raise the standard of living. In this respect the commission recommended fostering dignity of manual labour and promotion of work and technical skill for the advancement of industry and technology.

DEVELOPMENT PERSONALITY OR CHARACTER

An important aim of democratic education is the all-round development of every individual's personality. This requires that education should take into account his entire needs- psychological, social, emotional, and practical and cater to all of them. It should provide in him the sources of creative energy so that he may be able to appreciate his cultural heritage, to cultivate rich interests, which he can pursue in his leisure, and contribute in later life to the development of this heritage. Hence, education should be so organized that subjects like life, art, craft, music, dancing and the development of creative hobbies should find place of honour in the curriculum.

EDUCATION FOR LEADERSHIP

Since the youth of today assume leadership in different walks of life tomorrow, special function of the secondary education is to train persons who will be able to assume the responsibility of leadership in social, political, industrial and cultural fields. To achieve success in this work, the qualities of justice, courage, discipline, tolerance, wisdom, sacrifice, initiative, understanding of social issues, civic as well as vocational efficiency should be developed in the young men and women of our country.

PROCESS OF EDUCATION

The supporters of the theory of education by accretion hold that knowledge is essential means of prompting human welfare. With the invention of the conventional symbols of language, it was easy to record, pressure and to transmit human experiences systematically.

The theory is really narrow and unsound. It neglects the essential elements in the theory of knowledge .It regards knowledge as information of facts and statements to be condensed into compact and logical forms and memorized by the pupils.

This theory is quite un-psychological as it neglects the child who is to be educated, his innate equipments for bearing, his inherited potentialities, propensities, attitudes and abilities, the psychological processes and products of learning.

EDUCATION AS FORMATION OF MIND

Education as formation tries to form the mind by a proper presentation of arterials. It is formation of mind by setting up certain association or connection of content by means of a subject matter.

EDUCATION AS PREPARATION

Education as preparation is a process of preparation or getting ready for the responsibilities and privileges of adult life- preparation for "complete living", this theory is the outcome of modern scientific tendency in education and has for its exponents men like Herbert Spencer, T. H. Huxley and others.

EDUCATION AS MENTAL DISCIPLINE

The theory of mental discipline is a traditional concept of education. It was in vogue in the Western countries for many centuries. It is still highly popular even today in our country. According to this theory, the process of learning is more important than the thing learned. This theory is based upon the traditional "Faculty Theory" of psychology according to which the mind is divided into a good number of separate faculties such as memory, attention, reasoning, imagination, perception, thinking judgment etc. Johan Locke was the classic representative of this theory. The outer world presents the material or content of knowledge, through passively received sensations. After the simple stuff of experience is furnished by the senses, one's ideas, judgments, etc. are formed through the perfection of intellect.

EDUCATION AS GROWTH AND DEVELOPMENT

It is a modern concept of education. Change is the law of nature. Man undergoes changes and transformations from cradle to grave.

These changes may be of different types such as physical, mental, moral and emotional. Two factors, training and environment condition every change. The original nature of man can be changed either by training on by his reaction to the environment. Whenever there is change there is growth. Through change, a living organism can take entirely a new shape and this again gives him powers to grow. Thus, Growing is education and getting education is growing.

EDUCATION AS DIRECTION

Educate a child means directing the child in the proper direction. The young earners have innate powers, attitudes, interests and instincts. It is the essential function of education to direct those inborn instincts and powers properly in socially acceptable and desirable channels. The native impulses of the child may not conform to the socially accepted norms and behaviour patterns. So the child has to be directed, controlled or guided. It is the duty of the teacher to see that the active tendencies of children are not dispersed aimlessly. These are to be directed at various phases of life for their proper satisfaction.

EDUCATION AS ADJUSTMENT AND SELF-ACTIVITY

Adjustment is essential to an individual for self-development. Education gives an individual the power of adjustment in an efficient manner. Through education, the child learns to adjust with the environment. That is why it is said education is adjustment and adjustment is education. In the process of continuous growth man has to adjust in multifarious and diverse life situations and environment. This is called adjustment and it requires self-activity. So education is nothing but adjustment through self-activity.

EDUCATION AS SOCIAL CHANGE AND PROGRESS

A society is a well-organized human community. A conglomeration of people may not create a society. There must be active co-operation and intimate interaction among the members of the community. A society is not constant or static. It is rather dynamic and subject to change. A society is composed of individuals and when the ideas of individuals change the society is bound to change. According to Maciver social change is a process, which influences and change human life in different directions. Change is the law of human life and society. The function of education is to maintain this progressive trend.

EDUCATION AS PROCESS SOCIALIZATION

Education is a process both in the narrower as well as in the wider sense. Ancient people used to collect facts and information about nature for survival. This is nothing but education. In the wider sense, education is acquisition of experience throughout life. Experience brings changes in human life and behaviour. It is the primary function of formal education to accelerate and facilitate social progress.

QUALITY EDUCATION INCLUDES:

"Learners who are healthy, well-nourished and ready to participate and learn, and supported in learning by their families and communities; Environments that are healthy, safe, protective and gender-sensitive, and provide adequate resources and facilities;„ Content that is reflected in relevant curricula and materials for the acquisition of basic skills, especially in the areas of literacy, numeracy and skills for life, and knowledge in such areas as gender, health, nutrition, HIV/AIDS prevention and peace;

1. "Processes through which trained teachers use child-centred teaching approaches in well-managed classrooms and schools and skilful assessment to facilitate learning and reduce disparities;
2. " Outcomes that encompass knowledge, skills and attitudes, and are linked to national goals for education and positive participation in society

QUALITY LEARNERS

School systems work with the children who come into them. The quality of children's lives before beginning formal education greatly influences the kind of learners they can be. Many elements go into making a quality learner, including health, early childhood experiences and home support.

GOOD HEALTH AND NUTRITION

Physically and psychosocially healthy children learn well. Healthy development in early childhood, especially during the first three years of life, plays an important role in providing the basis for a healthy life and a successful formal school experience (McCain & Mustard, 1999). Adequate nutrition is critical for normal brain development in the early years, and early detection and intervention for disabilities can give children the best chances for healthy development. Prevention of infection, disease and injury prior to school enrolment are also critical to the early development of a quality learner.

EARLY CHILDHOOD PSYCHOSOCIAL DEVELOPMENT EXPERIENCES

Positive early experiences and interactions are also vital to preparing a quality learner. A large study in 12 Latin American countries found that attendance at day care coupled with higher levels of parental involvement that includes parents reading to young children is associated with higher test scores and lower rates of grade repetition in primary school (Willms, 2000).

REGULAR ATTENDANCE FOR LEARNING

When they reach school age, research demonstrates that to achieve academically, children must attend school consistently. A child's exposure to curriculum - his or her 'opportunity to learn'- significantly influences achievement, and exposure to curriculum comes from being in school (Fuller et al., 1999). A study of village-based schools in Malawi found that students with higher rates of attendance had greater learning gains and lower rates of repetition, a finding consistent with many other studies (Miske, Dowd et al., 1998).

FAMILY SUPPORT FOR LEARNING

Parents may not always have the tools and background to support their children's cognitive and psychosocial development throughout their school years. Parents' level of education, for example, has a multifaceted impact on children's ability to learn in school. In one study, children whose parents had primary school education or less were more than three times as likely to have low test scores or grade repetition than children whose parents had at least some secondary schooling (Willms, 2000).

HIGH SCHOOL EDUCATION

Secondary education serves as a bridge between elementary and higher education and Prepares young person's between the age group of 14-18 for entry into higher education.

IMPORTANCE OF HIGH SCHOOL EDUCATION

Secondary education is an improvement stage in the educational leader. It has well defined structure of its own. The overall development of the individual and the balanced development of a region are determined in the higher secondary education.

A number of types of regional disparities may exit performance of the system. If so, it is imperative to explore, the ways men by which the regional education can be overcome and also to find out factor which facilitate or inhibit the performance of secondary school systems. Such discussions will provide light for future polities in establishment of secondary schools. They will enable the planner to reduce and obviate the sick and the chronically sick schools as well as strengthen the number of good schools.

FUNCTION OF HIGH SCHOOL EDUCATION

1. To prepare the young to live effectively and properly as adults in the society.
2. To develop the intellectual power of the young and transmit the knowledge and wisdom of the society to new generation.
3. To perpetuate the basic beliefs, value systems and socially approved modes behaviour.
4. To develop the powers and capabilities of the young so that may realise their potentialities and advance the life of the social group.

According to secondary education commission (1952-53). Development of the democratic citizenship, vocational efficiency development of personality, promoting leadership qualities and above all preservation and enrichment of our culture heritage should be the important aims of the secondary education in India.

CONCEPTUAL FRAME WORK

GEOGRAPHY

Geography claims a substantial segment of the national academic space. If one goes by the numerical strength of the geographical community in terms of students admitted to various geography programmes in different universities and colleges and the strength of the faculty, Indian geography has certainly made impressive gains during the past eight decades. More geographers now attend summits, workshops, seminars symposia and conferences in geography both at national and international level. Yet, Indian Geography does not feature prominently in the international arena. This is despite attempts to include every possible change in the development of the subject into the geography curriculum. Geographers in India have been alive to every new tool and technique that has appeared on its door step. Yet, the geographical enterprise has failed to reap dividends nationally or internationally. Teaching and research in Geography is channelized through a large number of geography departments spread all over the country.

The period under review has witnessed establishment of many new departments of geography particularly in the North-Eastern region of India. But the inherent dichotomy in nature of geography continues to affect its position in the highly structured university system that treats the subject either as a natural science or as a social science. The placement of geography in the university system continues to baffle generations of students. Geography continues to be placed under the faculty of sciences in many universities enabling them to procure funds and projects from funding agencies as well as to establish laboratories. On the other hand departments which are placed under arts/social sciences continue to be eternally starved of funds for their minimal needs. This has created not only inequality between departments of geography, but also affects the quality of teaching and research.

Private universities which have come up in large numbers in recent years have largely ignored geography as a serious area of teaching and research. Even some of the traditional departments of geography which have made significant contribution in geography teaching and research have (or are in the process of) begun to cultivate new techniques such as geo-informatics on the wake of advances made in GIS and Remote Sensing technology. A number of geography departments now proudly display on their websites courses on GIS, Remote Sensing and Geo-informatics. There is nothing wrong in this trend except that an impression has gathered about a new image of geography as cultivation of these techniques. Many researchers now find it prestigious to add suffix using GIS techniques- to the title of their research papers. Geography teaching and research is transforming in many departments to aggressively accommodate itself to this new trend. Yet there are many geography departments in universities and colleges which lack even computers to do word processing. Such is the state of affairs in geography that occupies a substantial segment of the national academic space.

DEFINITION OF GEOGRAPHY

Cluster of definitions that "I think of as geographers' geography has a status that sets it apart from the others. It reflects the way experts and practitioners in geography think of their field. Because geographers' definitions of geography are the product of academic study and discussion, they cluster around a set of conventional definitions, including geography as the study of place and space and geography as the study of spatial patterns and processes at the earth's surface. Geographers also commonly describe geography as encompassing human geography, physical geography, and human-environment interaction".

GEOGRAPHY CONTINENTS

1. Asia
2. Europe
3. North America
4. South America
5. Africa
6. Australia
7. Antartica

CLIMATOLOGY, SOIL GEOGRAPHY AND BIO-GEOGRAPHY

As these fields of geography thrive on links with disciplines like meteorology, soil science and life sciences, the range of non-geographers' contributions to the study of climate, soil and bio resources is considerable compared to that of the geographers. Although Climatology traditionally occupies an important position in Physical Geography considering the renewed interest world over on the topic of climate change, study of climate, finds little proportionate weight age in the hands of Indian geographers. Apart from a few purely pedagogical studies, contributions from geographers in the area of soil geography leave much to be desired. Biogeography continues to be less emphasized despite its growing importance in the field of environmental studies.

TYPES OF GEOGRAPHY

AGRICULTURAL GEOGRAPHY

Agriculture continues to be the backbone of Indian economy and rightly remains a major thrust area in geography. Agricultural geographers in India have diversified their interests and have ventured into significant areas of analysis such as land capability classification, agro-ecological concerns, crop diversification and diffusion, problems of food security and vulnerability, dairy farming apart from social and institutional framework of agriculture.

INDUSTRIAL GEOGRAPHY

In spite of tremendous potential in this field of research, particularly in the post liberalization phase, not much work appears to have been made. Very few papers have been published in this branch of geography in leading journals of India. As industry along with agriculture is the backbone of the nation's economy, the geographers can neglect this field of inquiry only at their own peril. This is particularly true in the context of a vibrant trend of research in this field during the eighties and nineties.

POPULATION GEOGRAPHY

Population related issues remained central to geographical discourse during the period under review. Issues that have caught geographers' attention include population distribution; density and growth; population composition; fertility and reproductive health; mortality and morbidity, migration and human development. Migration, both internal and international, appears to be one of the major focuses of researches. Besides; migration from across the international borders, which has led to conflicts and political unrest in the frontier states has attracted attention from population geographers. Concern for a better quality of life, reduction of poverty, gender equity and equality has led to several studies in Human Development, management of human resources and sustainable development. However, continued dependence on census based data has been a limiting factor. There is an urgent need to go beyond census based data to an understanding of poverty, inter-ethnic differentials in population and characteristics of displaced.

POPULATIONS

Population Change and Migration Regarded as a special area of interest within population geography, studies undertaken in this area are a mix of both general and contemporary-specific population issues relating to population growth/change and migration. There is little change in the focus of research during the period under review. It is necessary that studies pertaining to the impact of rapid population growth, migration, population pressure, ageing and globalization etc. need to be taken up with urgency for their important role in population change.

SETTLEMENT GEOGRAPHY

This is a traditionally important area of research that has attracted good number of researches. Moving away from the conventional analysis of size, form and location of settlements, Indian geographers have made important contribution to studies on functional aspects and vocational characteristics of human activities as well as patio functional organization of economic landscape. Issue pertaining to the impacts emanating from hyper-urbanization and diversified urban systems are recommended as important areas for future research.

URBANIZATION

Urban geography is one of the most dynamic sub-disciplines of geography. It has been moving forward in its philosophical perspectives and thematic contents. However, the urban process as is viewed by geographers has been perceived more as a demographic phenomenon drawing largely on data available from successive census operations. Nevertheless, Indian urban geography has been unfolding several new dimensions including environmental issues of the built environment and sustainability of the present urban systems. More intensive research is recommended for studies on ecological implications of urban fringe, the natural and human induced hazards and disasters in the urban context and alternative models of indigenous city which is energy efficient, eco-friendly and sustainable.

REGIONAL DEVELOPMENT AND PLANNING

Economic reforms initiated in India in the nineties and its regional impacts-both apparent and likely-have dominated researches in this field of study. The review however reflects a vast range of interests and research areas covered by geographers in relation to issues of regional development. The studies indicate that the shackles of a centralised planning perspective has largely become unrecognisable and on the other hand, a more local based concern, grass-root based issues but not entirely discounting the broader canvass, have come to stay in the subject as it has been evolving in India over a decade or so.

HISTORICAL GEOGRAPHY

Historical geography has never been a priority area in Indian geography, though its importance can hardly be overemphasized. Most of the studies cited in the review do not come from geographers, nor can they strictly be considered as historical-geographical researches. Nevertheless, acceptance and emergence of new notions, ways, perspectives, subaltern views, oral history, biographical resources, heritage ecology, etc. are some of the recent concerns enriching the field of historical geography of India. All such studies can provide essential raw material for a meaningful historical-geographical interpretation.

SOCIAL GEOGRAPHY

Though this specialism is characterized by a more than desirable dose of eclecticism, the sub-discipline has received adequate attention by a number of geographers during the period under review. The most important feature of the growth of the sub-discipline has been an accent on theory impinging more on epistemological issues at the cost of empirical research. More contributions have come in the form of chapters in edited volumes rather than articles in leading journals. This cannot be taken as a healthy development. The immediate cause for a shift in interest in socio-geographical research appears to be the post-modern discourse that has caught the attention of Indian geographers following their western counterparts. A few geographers have however continued with studies of caste and morphology of rural settlements, spatial aspects of language and shifts in language and ethnic conflicts and the like.

CULTURAL GEOGRAPHY

The post-modern discourse has certainly given a new meaning to studies in cultural geography and cultural geography in India has become a shadow of its western incarnation. But, this branch has mostly been used as a way and approach narrating or analyzing landscape and culture, putting aside the theoretical construction and critique of the philosophical ideas as popular in the West. More western scholars than Indian have evinced interest in cultural forms, mostly of its mythical dimension. The geographical implication of cultural pluralism has hardly received any attention. While ancient Indian traditions have been overemphasized, few talk about contemporary cultural development including globalization of culture and its impact.

GENDER ISSUES IN GEOGRAPHY

Integrating gender issues into geographical research has been a formidable exercise. In spite of serious efforts made by a few enthusiastic geographers in India, gender in geography has not achieved the heights it deserves. This is despite instances of inclusion gender studies in the syllabi offered by a few universities. Most works in the sub-field continue to be descriptive rather than analytical. The engagement of space with gender and vice versa remains largely glossed over by geographers. The larger research input into these themes has come not from geographers but sociologists or economists. Most geographers equate site with space and sex with gender. Conspicuous by their paucity are studies which engage directly with the themes of gendered experience of space, gendered spaces and spatiality's of gender. Limitations in the current level of research notwithstanding, gender issues in geography holds an important social position in understanding larger issues of female subordination and deprivation.

GEOGRAPHY OF HEALTH

As a branch, Geography of Health has made significant strides in the period under review. It has progressed from studies in ecological associations of diseases and attempts at disease mapping, to investigations into a wider perspective of health and health care with a focus on human welfare. Cultural and the structural approaches to address the problems of health and place are dimensions that distinguishes this field of enquire from its past. However, many, if not all studies stop at a cartographic representation of diseases showing inter-state or inter-district variation in the prevalence pattern and hardly move beyond the level of description.

SOCIAL WELLBEING AND TRANSFORMATION

Studies pertaining to health dominate in this field while issues concerning housing and social pathology remain neglected. Most studies continue to rely on cartographic representation of facts without placing the issues in a proper theoretical context. Recent impacts of globalization, liberalization and economic restructuring which are bound to have immense effects on the process of social transformation and social well-being find rare mention by Indian geographers.

POLITICAL GEOGRAPHY

Political geography in India has been a neglected field of inquiry in the past, and continues to be marginalized even at present. This is in spite of tremendous potential of the sub discipline in contributing to varied political problems directly linked to geographical backgrounds and territorial identification as well as external space-relations. Unfortunately barring a few notable exceptions, much of the interest is centred on electoral geography. The field needs to shed its conventional mould and concentrate on issues of urgent national importance such as political implications of social and cultural pluralism and related issues of conflict as well as integration, problems of nation building, federalism and above all the political geography of underdevelopment.

ADMINISTRATIVE GEOGRAPHY

There has been world over, a significant increase in the expression of concern for the neglect of policy-relevant research in human geography. Only a few geographers in India have evinced interest in this vitally important area in which geographers should contribute significantly with their skills of understanding the 'natural' and 'human' in synthesis rather than in isolation.

REMOTE SENSING AND GEOGRAPHICAL INFORMATION SYSTEM

During the last decade urgency has been shown by geographers for an increased application of remote sensing techniques and GIS not only as part of the curriculum but also in the researchers conducted mostly confined, though not restricted to physical geography. Such techniques are crucially dependent on computer as a tool. Only a few elitist centres have been able to introduce such courses and are increasingly using these techniques in their researches.

CLIMATE AND WATER RESOURCES

India is situated in the Northern hemisphere and the tropic of cancer divides the country into roughly two equal parts. The southern part enjoys a low temperature range while the North is cold in winters and warm for greater part of the year exhibiting much greater range in its temperature. Though generally described as a tropical country, India experiences varied climatic conditions in different regions. The north is more affected by a continental climate while the south has more maritime influence (Arabian Sea, Bay of Bengal and Indian Ocean). Much of the rain is a gift of the monsoon and is primarily orographic. The annual rainfall of 116 cms is only marginally higher than the global mean of 99 cms. Spatial distribution of rainfall in India is characterized by great unevenness. While Mawsynram, located in the southern face of Meghalaya plateau receives the highest annual rainfall in world, India also has one of the driest regions of world i.e. Jaisalmer located in the western part of the country. Generally rainfall decreases from east to west.

India has 4 per cent of the freshwater reserve of the world. The annually 'replenishable' groundwater has been estimated at 432 billion cubic meters (BCM). The Ganga basin has the highest potential followed by the Godavari and the Brahmaputra. The Indo-Gangetic alluvial plain with an area of around 25,000 km is one of the largest groundwater reservoirs in the world. Of the total groundwater of India, only 30 per cent has been harnessed. Overuse of groundwater in almost all the states of India has led to ground water depletion in large parts of the country. In certain areas, like Punjab, the level of groundwater exploitation is over 98 per cent. India is rich in terms of surface water wealth. It has some of the largest rives of world e.g. the Brahmaputra (2900 Kms), the Indus (2810kms) and the Ganga (2525 Kms). Besides, there are many other large river basins, with basin area of more than 20,000 km.

Some of its lakes are internationally known e.g. Chilka, Wular, Sambhar etc. Rainfall is the main source of surface water in India. It receives about 4000 BCM of water from precipitation. Of this, monsoon rainfall accounts for about 3000 BCM. The total utilizable water is about 690 BCM in the country.

India is one of the most disaster prone areas of world. Nearly 57 per cent of the country's land is prone to earthquakes included in the seismic zones III-IV. About 8 per cent of the land is vulnerable to cyclones of varying intensity. About 68 per cent of the net sown area and 5 per cent of the total land are vulnerable to droughts and floods (40 million ha). India alone accounts for 20 per cent of the deaths caused by floods in the world.

Forests, Biodiversity and Land Use Great variation in climatic conditions has given appearance to variety of forest types including tropical and sub-tropical forests in the Western Ghats and eastern Himalaya, temperate and alpine forests in central and western Himalaya and desert forests in the arid and semi-arid regions of the country. According to Forests Survey of India (2003), about 6, 78,333 km, constituting 20.64 per cent of its geographical area is under forest cover in the country. Very dense forest (VDF) however accounts for only 1.56 per cent while the moderately dense forest (MDF) and open forest account for 10.32 per cent and 8.76 per cent respectively. The total forest and tree cover of the country is estimated to account for 23.68 per cent of the country's land.

India contains a great wealth of biodiversity in its forests, wetlands and marine areas. The country has 7 per cent of the mammals, 12.6 per cent birds, 6.2 per cent reptiles, 4.4 per cent amphibians, 11.7 per cent fishes and 6 per cent flowing plants of the world. Among plants, endemism is estimated as 33 per cent. India contains 172 species (2.9 per cent of world's total) of animals considered globally threatened species. The Western Ghats and eastern Himalaya are biodiversity hotspots. The faunal species of India is estimated to be about 81,000, representing about 6.4 per cent world's fauna. Besides other invertebrates, there are about 2546 fish species, 204 amphibians, 428 reptiles, 1228 birds and 372 mammals. About 4,900 species of flowering plants are endemic to the Indian subcontinent. Among the endemic species, 2532 species are found in the Himalaya and adjoining areas, followed by1782 species in Peninsular India. About 1500 endemic flowering species are facing varying degree of threats of extinction. The number of plant species in India is estimated to be over 45,000 representing about 7 per cent of world's flora. India is home to 14 biosphere reserves, of which 3 are in the world network of biosphere reserve viz. Sundarban, Gulf of Mannar, and Nilgiri.

Agriculture is the backbone of Indian economy. Agriculture and allied sectors like forestry, logging and fishing accounted for about 16 per cent of GDP and employed about 60 per cent of India's population. About 43 per cent of total geographical area of the country is used for the agricultural practices. Despite a steady decline of its share in the GDP, agriculture remains largest economic sector and plays a significant role in the overall socio-economic development of India. Indian agriculture is dependent on monsoon and is called "Gamble of Monsoon". Among the non-food crops, oilseeds, fiber crops, several plantation crops and forage crops are important. Rice and wheat are the principal food crops grown over the large tract (about 70 per cent of agricultural land) of the country.

CULTURE, ETHICS AND UNITY IN DIVERSITY

A grand synthesis of cultures, religions and languages of the people belonging to different castes and communities has upheld its unity and cohesiveness. It is this synthesis which made India a unique mosaic of cultures. People belonging to several faiths-Hinduism, Jainism, Buddhism, Islam, Sikhism and Christianity have coexisted for centuries in a shared space. Diversity in India is not merely confined to racial, religious and linguistic distinctions but also permeates deep into patterns of living, life styles, land tenure systems, occupational pursuits, inheritance and succession law, together with local practices, rites and rituals related to social norms and values. The Indian cultural tradition is unique. The notions of dharma (normative order), karma (personal moral commitment) and jati (caste) as the hierarchical principle of social stratification are basic to Indian society. Twenty three Indian languages are listed in our constitution and more than 544 dialects are spoken in the country. Pali language was prominent in ancient India. Sanskrit enjoyed the status of carrying Hindu Sanskritic culture throughout the country. These were followed by the modern Indo-Aryan languages. The institutional basis of social order and socio-economic interaction among communities like Jajmani system remained unchanged to a large extent.

A plural and multi-ethnic society like India would have an overlapping of ethnic, caste and class groupings. There are more than 285 ethnic tribal communities in India accounting for over 8 per cent of her population. The tribes themselves are not a homogenous group, but display remarkable heterogeneity in their racial, linguistic, religious composition as also in their modes of living and levels of development as well as in the level of socio-cultural integration. In spite of this great diversity, India continues to swear by its commitment to secularism and practices democratic form of governance. The federal principle of governance has provided a sense of identity to most people.

GEOGRAPHY OF HEALTH

Geography of Health as a branch of study has been making significant strides in the universities in India where the subject is being taught. Over the years, it has progressed from studies in ecological associations of diseases and attempts at disease mapping, to investigations into a wider perspective of health and health care. Researches in India have been laying greater stress on changing environmental factors and its impact on health as a system and on health care. The focus of most research has been human welfare and various attempts have been made to adopt the cultural and the structural approaches to address the problems of health and place. Some of the publications that have been reviewed here may be divided into different categories based on the central theme of these studies.

DISEASE ECOLOGY

It is interesting to note that disease ecology studies have shifted from the traditional communicable diseases to the more modern diseases such as SARS, Bird flu and HIV/AIDS. Hazra (2004) has highlighted the factors that contributed to the occurrence of SARS in China and has traced the diffusion of the disease from China to other parts of the world. She also examines the social and economic implications of the disease. In yet another study, Hazra has looked at the global threat of Bird 'flu (under publication).

Since India has the largest number of HIV/AIDS cases in the world, the disease continues to attract the attention of Indian geographers. Choubey (2007a & b) has highlighted the distribution pattern of the disease in India and has shown to what extent it is associated with sex workers in Greater Mumbai. Hazra (2007b) too, identifies the environmental factors that are causatively associated with the occurrence of the disease.

NUTRITION AND HEALTH

The period under review has witnessed a surge of interest in studies establishing the relation between nutrition and health. Choubey (2004a) has studied the nutritional status among different tribal communities of Madhya Pradesh and has quantified the extent of deficiency of the required nutrients within the community. A significant contribution in this area has been the publication of a book (Ashraf, 2006) which stresses the link between environmental factors, agricultural practices, nutrition levels, health and disease.

MATERNAL AND CHILD HEALTH

Maternal and child health has been another emerging area of concern of a number of geographers in the recent years. The need, availability and utilization of Maternal and Child Health (MCH) care services have been the main focus of these studies. Banerjee and Das (2006) have analyzed how the use of MCH services has played a significant role in reducing infant mortality rates in different states of India with special reference to West Bengal. Choubey (2005) and Dubey (2005) have carried out investigations into the reproductive and child health care status in different parts of the state of Madhya Pradesh.

WOMEN'S HEALTH

The environment, including physical, biological and socio-cultural conditions, plays a dominant role in determining the health status of women. This has been highlighted by De (2005). Malnutrition, anaemia, low birth weight of children, vulnerability to infectious diseases due to under-nutrition, increasing incidences of tuberculosis, bronchial asthma, lung and breast cancer due to exposure to air pollution, skin diseases due to contact with polluted water and soil, urinary tract infection due to poor sanitary conditions, and stresses and strains of the physical and social environment leaving their imprint on the mental health are some of the problems faced by women that have been highlighted in this paper.

HEALTH CARE PLANNING

Location of health care facilities has been a significant area of study by medical geographers. Availability of modern tools and quantitative techniques have further facilitated such studies and enabled geographers to contribute towards the planning of health care services. Ahmad and Shamim (2004) have used quantitative techniques to reveal the gap between distribution of settlements and settlements having health facilities. Rubeena and Kumaran (under publication) have assessed the possibilities of employing geo-informatics in promoting the use of Local Health Traditions and thereby provide affordable health care options within the reach of the common man. Using a participatory approach, in another study, Rubeena and Kumaran (under publication) have looked into the problems faced by local health practitioners in Kerala. They have tried to examine the viability of complementing the modern system of medicine with Local Health Traditions.

Choubey (2004) has pointed out the paucity of allopathic health care facilities in tribal areas of Madhya Pradesh and the factors that inhibit provision of health care in such areas (Choubey, 2006).

HEALTH AND SOCIAL WELL-BEING

A number of papers have been published within the last four years concerning the close link between health and social well-being. Mukhopadhyay (2007) seeks clarification of the concept of well-being from an interdisciplinary perspective and demonstrates its relevance with respect to the changing mode of the discipline of geography. De (2004) establishes the link between health and social well-being and identifies the role of geographers, vis-à-vis other scientists, in the domain of health. Aliar (2007) has broken new ground by dealing with issues pertaining to the rights of the community and traditional medicine for Local Health Traditions as an intellectual property.

PERCEPTION OF GEOGRAPHY

Unfortunately, the popular perception of geography is very different. I find the understanding of geography that I encounter on a daily basis to fit the stereotype that geographers refer to as "place-name and location" geography frighteningly often. Most people I encounter, regardless of their level of educational attainment, view geography as a body of discrete knowledge about the world that includes names and locations of countries, cities, bodies of water, and major geological features and facts about those places.

Most people I talk to consider map reading and way finding to be the only skills that geography teaches, and if they are aware that one can study geography at an advanced level or practice geography professionally, they believe the focus of that geography is mapmaking.

From the perspective of geography education, the popular perception of geography is as pernicious as it is widespread. People are increasingly aware that factual knowledge is of limited value in the Internet age, so it is difficult to have a productive conversation about the value of geography education with someone who believes geography is about factual understanding and thinks its usefulness for careers is limited to the obscure profession of cartography. Unfortunately, it can be very difficult to change this perception of geography, especially in a single conversation, when the individual has had no personal exposure to systematic geographic reasoning or problem solving.

SCHOOL GEOGRAPHY

The third cluster of definitions I encounter is what I call "school geography." This is what is taught in schools under the label of geography. School geography is typically a little broader than the popular perception of geography but dramatically narrower than geographers' geography.

In the United States, the overwhelming distinction between school geography and geographers' geography is that school geography focuses almost exclusively on human geography. To the extent that physical geography is taught as geography in the United States, it is taught as background and context for human geography. This is not to say that physical geography is not taught in American schools. Some physical geography is taught, but it is taught under the labels of earth science, environmental science, and geo-science rather than geography. Anything that is taught with the label geography is taught as part of the social studies curriculum and focuses on the geography of people.

The second characteristic of school geography is that it focuses primarily on factual knowledge. It would not be fair to modern curriculum designers, textbook authors, or teachers to say that geography education today focuses exclusively on facts, but it is fair to say that school geography is so dominated by the teaching of facts that it has not done anything to change the popular perception of geography as being about knowledge of discrete facts.

Geographers and geography educators have worked hard to change the definition of school geography through the development and dissemination of standards that reflect the subset of geographers' geography they believe K–12 students should learn. However, the impact of these efforts on the geography that is taught in schools is still limited. Like the popular definition of geography, the school definition of geography is a problem for conversations about geography education. It leaves out the critical component of physical geography and makes it difficult to talk about the study of human-environment interaction. Likewise, the focus on factual knowledge makes it hard to make the case of the importance of geography education in our modern world.

NEED OF THE STUDY

1. To solve the students difficulties in geographical map.
2. To analyse variations in male and female students' difficulties encounted in understanding geographical map.
3. To analyse variations in government and government aided and self finance students' difficulties encounted in understanding geographical map.
4. To suggest possible strategies to improve the students' difficulties encounted in understanding geographical map.

SIGNIFICANT OF THE STUDY

1. Teachers, helps their students to solve their difficulties.
2. Students should improve their memory in geographical map.
3. Students should create new ideas in geographical map.

STATEMENT OF THE PROBLEM

This is the tiltle of the present study "*Difficulties Encounted in Understanding Geographical Maps among High School Students.*"

OPERATIONAL DEFINITION OF KEY TERMS

GEOGRAPHY

Geography claims a substantial segment of the national academic space. If one goes by the numerical strength of the geographical community in terms of students admitted to various geography programmes in different universities and colleges and the strength of the faculty, Indian geography has certainly made impressive gains during the past eight decades. More geographers now attend summits, workshops, seminars symposia and conferences in geography both at national and international level. Yet, Indian Geography does not feature prominently in the international arena. This is despite attempts to include every possible change in the development of the subject into the geography curriculum. Geographers in India have been alive to every new tool and technique that has appeared on its door step.

Difficulties

Biofilms are bacterial colonies enveloped in a matrix of extracellular polymeric secretions. Confocal scanning laser microscopy has been used in conjunction with different image analysis techniques to investigate the structure of bio-films. A major goal is to reconstitute the three- dimensional structure of bio-films, and computer or estimate the bio-volumes. Our previous research focused on the utilization of remote sensing techniques and Geographical information systems for quantitative analyses of co focal images. The present study investigates potential problems in microbial imaging, and use two approaches, the program COMSTAT and a Geographical information systems- based method, to reconstitute three- dimensional structures and estimate bio-volumes. Volumes of thirty fluorescent polymeric microspheres with a known diameter were estimated and used as a approaches were used to estimate the bio-volume of a section through a pseudomonas aeruginosa biofilm. Difficulties were encountered indicate that the Geographical due to the optical properties of the micro beads. Our results indicate that the geographical information systems approach produced results consistent with the existing COMSTAT approach, and close to theoretical values, despite many problems inherent to each phase of this process. Also, the image classification process encountered several limitations. It is suggested that the unique constraints of the microscopic world may generated additional problems, especially related to image classification

Encounted

1. If any difficulty arises in giving effect to the provisions of this Act, the central Government may, by order published in the official Gazette, make such provisions not inconsistent with the

provisions of this Act as may appear to be necessary for removing the difficulty: Provided that no order shall be made under this section after the expiry of five years from the commencement of this Act.

2. Every order made under section shall, as soon as may be after it is made, be laid before each House of parliament.

Understanding

Specifically focuses on Civil Services Examination Over 3300 entries pertaining to: oceans, mountains, peaks, plateaus, peninsulas, trenches, rivers, deltas, estuaries, lakes, glaciers, waterfalls, river- projects dames, biosphere reserves, national parks, bird sanctuaries, sea- beaches, tourist resorts, cities, seaports, industrial and mining centres, national highways and trans-continental railways. Precise informative write- up on each entry.

High School geographical map

What's new in this edition?

1. Restructured, Updated and covered in two parts
2. Part I Covers the main geographical entries of the world
3. Part II covers the main geographical entries of the world
4. 300 new and contemporary entries included in this revised edition
5. Entries arranged topic- wise in alphabetical order.

Understanding geographical map

Understanding Geographical Map Entries: Map based questions is an important feature of the civil Services Main Examination for aspirants with Geography as an optional subject. The revised, updated edition of this popular book written by an eminent academician equips aspirants with the precise knowledge and the skill to plot geographical entries correctly. It also equips with the resources to write a precise and informative note on each entry. The book should of interest to the ordinary reader and also be of valuable help to teachers of geography who would like to keep themselves updated on the subject.

HIGH SCHOOL EDUCATION

High school education serves as a bridge between elementary and higher education and Prepares young person's between the age group of 14-18 for entry into higher education.

OBJECTIVES OF THE STUDY

GENERAL OBJECTIVES

To find out the *Difficulties Encounted in Understanding Geographical Maps Among High School Students."*

OBJECTIVES THE STUDY

1. To find out whether there is any significant difference between the mean score of male and female students in respect of a study on basis of difficulties encounted in understanding geographical map among high school students.
2. To find out whether there is any significant difference between the mean score of rural and urban school students in respect of a study on basis of difficulties encounted in understanding geographical map among high school students.
3. To find out whether there is any significant difference between the mean score of government and private school students in respect of a study on basis of difficulties encounted in understanding geographical map among high school students.
4. To find out whether there is any significant difference between the mean score of government boy's school and government aided girls school in respect of a study on basis of difficulties encounted in understanding geographical map among high school students.
5. To find out whether there is any significant difference between the mean score of government boy's school and co – education private school students in respect of a study on basis of difficulties encounted in understanding geographical map among high school students.
6. To find out whether there is any significant difference between the mean score of government aided Girls School and Co-

Education Private school students in respect of a study on basis of difficulties encounted in understanding geographical map among high school students.

7. To find out whether there is any significant difference between the mean score of government employee and self employee parents students in respect of a study on basis of difficulties encounted in understanding geographical map among high school students.

HYPOTHESES OF THE STUDY

1. There is no significant difference in the difficulties encounted in geographical map among high school students on the basis of their gender.
2. There is no significant difference in the difficulties encounted in geographical map among high school students on the basis of their location of school.
3. There is no significant difference in the difficulties encounted in geographical map among high school students on the basis of their type of school.
4. There is no significant difference in the difficulties encounted in geographical map among high school students on the basis of their management of school.
5. There is no significant difference in the difficulties encounted in geographical map among high school students on the basis of their type of school.
6. There is no significant difference in the difficulties encounted in geographical map among high school students on the basis of their type of school.
7. There is no significant difference in the difficulties encounted in geographical map among high school students on the basis of their employment of school.

LIMITATION OF THE STUDY

1. In this study questionnaire was administrated only for high school students studying at Pudukkottai District.

2. The sample was collected only from the government and private school in Pudukkottai District.

3. The present information was collected only from 300 samples.

POPOULATION AND SAMPLE

POPULATION

The population is a set the totality of all objects or individuals. A population is by a group of individuals who have are studying in high school students in Pudukkottai educational district.

SAMPLE

A sample is a set of item of individuals selected from a larger aggregate or population. The sample selected for the present study consists of 300 high school students from different school with the help of stratified random sampling technique.

CONCLUSION

This chapter is deals with a detailed background of the education, special features of education geography meaning, definition and types of geography and hypotheses are discussed and valuable information about difficulties encounted in understanding geographical map it also underlined and highlighted the improved of the students ability. Moreover, this chapter helps the investigator to acquaint with related content of difficulties. Next chapter deals the review of related literature.

Chapter - II

Review of Related Literature

INTRODUCATION

This chapter reveals the previous related research studies in India and abroad. The main purpose of reviewing the literature understands the previous work done in the relevant field of study habit and academic achievement. Further the related literatures help the researcher to thoroughly analyse and scrutinise the methodological perspectives used in the previous studies may avoid unnecessary duplication of research in this chapter the investigator reviewed the related literatures and the area of study habit the available resources, the investigator collected some related studies and present in this chapter the previous studies are given below.

IMPORTANCE OF REVIEW

Review of literature is a very important aspect of any research. A literature review is a description of the literature relevant to a particular field or topic. Every piece of ongoing research needs to be connected with the work which has been done already. The review of literature is needed to attain an overall relevance and purpose. It tells the reader about aspects that have already established or concluded by other researchers. It is a link between the research proposed and the studies already done. A careful review of the research journals, books, dissertations, theses and other sources of information on the problem to be investigated is one of the important steps in the planning of any research study. It is also important to highlight differences in opinions, contradictory evidence and the different explanations given for their conclusions.

A literature review is a body of text that aims to review the critical points of current knowledge including substantive findings as well as theoretical and methodological contributions to a particular topic. Literature reviews are secondary sources and as such, do not report any new or original experimental work.

A literature review usually precedes a research proposal and results section. Its ultimate goal is to bring the reader up to date with current literature on a topic and forms the basis for another goal, such as future research that may be needed in the area a familiarity with the literature in any problem area helps the students to discover what is already known, what others have attempted to find out. Afolabi (1992) states that a good literature review requires knowledge of the use of indexes and abstracts, the ability to conduct exhaustive bibliographic searches, ability to organise the collected data meaningfully, describe, critique and relate each source to the subject of the inquiry, and present the organised review logically, and last, but by no means least, to correctly cite all sources mentioned.

VALUE OF THE REVIEW OF RELATED LITERATURE

It is a valuable guide to define the problem and recognize its significance. It helps in suggesting, promising data – gathering devices, appropriate study design and sources of data. It provides suggestions for possible modifications in the research to avoid unanticipated difficulties. It unfolds a backdrop of interpreting the results of the research study.

SOUCES OF RELATED LITERATURE

The investigator identified several sources of related literature.

They included

1. Articles of Newspaper
2. Surveys of research in Education
3. Dissertation abstracts
4. Internet
5. Journals
6. E – Journals
7. E – Test books
8. Encyclopaedia
9. Textbooks
10. Unpublished theses.

RESEARCH STUDIES DONE IN INDIA AND ABROAD

FOREIGN STUDY

Pang (2001) conducted a study found that Junior College students who had experienced dynamic and interactive visualisations through a Geographical Information System had 'positive educational effect, especially in terms of creative and visual thinking'.

ESRI, (2003). Conducted a study the cycle of Geographic Inquiry is a simple and useful 5-step framework for teachers to use when planning to implement GIS in the classroom:

1. Ask geographic questions
2. Acquire geographic resources
3. Explore geographic data
4. Analyse geographic information
5. Act upon geographic knowledge

Evans (2003) showed that students with learning disabilities were satisfied with the accommodations they received in their university-related geography courses. It was reported that students with learning disabilities performed better in a class that is reserved for them than students enrolled in open sections.

Stamp, (2005). This concept and plan of World Land Use Survey was brought forward by Volkenberg. He proposed the World Land use at the International Geographical Congress at Lisbon in April 1949. It was proposed that land use may be undertaken on a uniform scale of 1:1000000 and each map sheet be accompanied by an explanation text. In 1953 under the chairmanship of Van Volkenberg at the International Geographical Congress proposed to carry out land use survey in many parts of the world.

Brosseau (2004), where the stance is purposely critical, arguing that in literary geography the text itself should function more as a target of research.

Owen (2005) conducted on the comparison of mathematical problem-solving errors between third-grade students with learning disabilities and peers without disabilities indicated that students with learning disabilities made more errors in the translation of word problems than in computation.

Maite & Mete (2006) revealed that one third of all the mistakes in division of fractions were due to the student's negligence to invert the divisor before the process of multiplication; one fourth of all mistakes in the division of fractions were due to the student's lack of comprehension of the process involved.

Hartmann (2007) showed that students with low geography achievement had more computational errors but fewer translation errors when compared to students with geography learning disabilities who had conceptual difficulties in the areas of analyzing, reasoning and abstract thinking.

Michaelson (2007) suggested that for many children, geography is an inherently difficult subject to learn. Between 5 and 8 percent of children between the ages of 6 and 14 have a particular type of cognitive deficiency that limits their aptitude to acquire knowledge and understanding of fundamental ideas in numeracy?

Snow (2008) identified several individual risk factors for learning disabled- family history of reading difficulties, poor pre literacy skills either because of inherent cognitive limitation or home environment, poor literacy, related cognitive linguistic processing especially phonological awareness, confrontational naming, sentences/ story recall and general language ability, a diagnosis of specific language impairment, hearing impairment and a primary medical diagnosis in which reading problems tend to occur as a secondary symptom. Among the group factors listed as risk factors for LD by Snow et al are poor schools, low income/ poor neighbourhoods, limited proficiency in medium of instruction and dialectal differences in language.

Belmarez (2008) on doing a research on the relationship between co-teaching and the geography achievement of groups of students with and without learning disabilities found that: (1) students with learning disabilities do not achieve greater academic gains by receiving Mathematics instruction in a co-taught classroom rather than in a resource classroom; (2) students with learning disabilities in the co-taught classroom attained significantly higher standardized test scores; (3) with the exception of the case significantly higher standardized test scores, the co-taught classroom in this study was not conducive to greater geography achievement for students with learning disabilities and (4) no significant difference existed in Mathematics achievement for co taught, experimental groups of students without learning disabilities when compared to that of the control groups who received geography instruction in the general classrooms.

Inglis and Swain (2012) explored the views of men with learning difficulties living in a secure environment. The findings suggest that the men are very positive about their lives reporting that they have many attributes and talents and views that having a learning difficulty as an advantage at times.

Bane et al. (2012) explored the perspectives of people with learning disabilities on relationships and supports in the Republic of Ireland. A national research network consisting of 21 researchers with learning disabilities, 12 supporters and 7 university researchers conducted the study. Findings suggested that people with learning disabilities have a diversity of experiences and views on relationships and support needed to keep them. People with learning disabilities taking part in the focus groups identified that they need more support from friends, family, and services staff to develop new relationships and keep their existing ones.

Schieve (2012) found that children in all developmental disabled groups also had significantly higher estimates for health care use, impact, and unmet needs than children without disability. This study provides empirical evidence that children with disability require increased pediatric and specialist services, both for their core functional deficits and concurrent medical conditions.

INDIAN STUDY

Kumar (2003) on studying the effectiveness of certain instructional strategies to overcome learning disabilities in historical map among secondary level school children, it was found that there was significant difference in the post-test performance of learners than pre-test by using various instructional strategies.

Rao and Hossain,(2003). The different land utilization studies have been carried out in United State of America and European countries. Developed nations like United State of American and USSR have completed extensive soil surveys and mapped out all types of soil. In U.S.A. State Planning Board has maked the culmination of land utilization surveys conceived on the broadest possible basis. The United Kingdom and Denmark applied industrial and agricultural economic base and brought out the land utilization survey on the top of the list of countries in the world.

Shankaran (2003) dissects the tradition and development of literary geography from a more critical perspective. Other overviews instead dissect the course of research from certain theoretical perspectives, such as the overview offered.

Kavitha subramanian (2004) claimed that students with learning disability have rather differential learning characteristics from low achievers so that they can be clearly differentiated. Understanding learner characteristics of learning disabled children also can be helpful in that the implications from the literature are conducive to develop intervention programme for low achievers in geography class.

Apsira (2007), an edited collection, attempts to be, as its title suggests, "a meeting of the disciplines." In taking a look at the development of the geographic study of literature, several fresh articles include good overviews of the development in the field.

Pocock 2008 takes a decent chronological look at how literature has been used in the course of geographic studies. Some overviews include a specific critical argument, as with the excellent coverage.

Shamir and Baruch (2012) found that geography learning difficulties can originate at an early age. The findings revealed that following the e-book intervention, children in the experimental e-book group improved both their vocabulary and early Mathematics skills as compared to the control group who engaged in their regular pre-school activities.

Compton (2012) examined the cognitive and academic profiles associated with Learning disability (LD) in reading comprehension, word reading, applied problems and calculations. Results supported the hypothesis that unexpected under achievement is associated with LD.

Balakumaran (2012) have shown that children with historical Map difficulties (MD) have weaknesses in multiple areas of Map. The study builds on this recent finding and aims at a more profound understanding of the difficulties that children with MD experience with telling time. This finding is in line with Geary's theory of subtypes in MD, which argues that children with MD have problems and understanding with map procedures and semantic memory retrieval.

CONCLUSION

The chapter review of related literature discussed about the importance of the related studies. More which also discussed about the studies done in India and abroad connected with the present study. The third chapter will present the research methodology of the present study.

Chapter III

Methodology

INTRODUCTION

The chapter of Research Methodology deals with plan and procedure that are adopted for present study. This chapter reveals objectives, Hypotheses, construction and validation of Research tool, sampling procedure, Data collection, Data analysis and Delimitation of study. The Researcher explains systematic procedure used in the study is given below.

NEED AND SIGNIFICANCE OF THE STUDY

NEED OF THE STUDY

1. To solve the students difficulties in geographical map.
2. To analyse variations in male and female students' difficulties encountered in understanding geographical map.
3. To analyse variations in government and government aided and self finance students' difficulties encountered in understanding geographical map.
4. To suggest possible strategies to improve the students' difficulties encountered in understanding geographical map.

SIGNIFICANT OF THE STUDY

1. Teachers, helps their students to solve their difficulties.
2. Students should improve their memory in geographical map.
3. Students should create new ideas in geographical map.

STATEMENT OF THE PROBLEM

This is the title of the present study *"Difficulties Encounted in Understanding Geographical Maps among High School Students."*

OPERATIONAL DEFINITION OF KEY TERMS

GEOGRAPHY

Geography claims a substantial segment of the national academic space. If one goes by the numerical strength of the geographical community in terms of students admitted to various geography programmers' in different universities and colleges and the strength of the faculty, Indian geography has certainly made impressive gains during the past eight decades. More geographers now attend summits, workshops, seminars symposia and conferences in geography both at national and international level. Yet, Indian Geography does not feature prominently in the international arena. This is despite attempts to include every possible change in the development of the subject into the geography curriculum. Geographers in India have been alive to every new tool and technique that has appeared on its door step.

OBJECTIVES OF THE STUDY

1. To find out whether there is any significant difference between the mean score of male and female students in respect of a study on basis of difficulties encounted in understanding geographical map among high school students.
2. To find out whether there is any significant difference between the mean score of rural and urban school students in respect of a study on basis of difficulties encounted in understanding geographical map among high school students.

3. To find out whether there is any significant difference between the mean score of government and private school students in respect of a study on basis of difficulties encounted in understanding geographical map among high school students.
4. To findout whether there is any significant difference between the mean score of government boys school and government aided girls school in respect of a study on basis of difficulties encounted in understanding geographical map among high school students.
5. To find out whether there is any significant difference between the mean score of government boys school and co-education private school students in respect of a study on basis of difficulties encounted in understanding geographical map among high school students.
6. To find out whether there is any significant difference between the mean score of government aided girls School and Co-Education Private school students in respect of a study on basis of difficulties encounted in understanding geographical map among high school students.
7. To find out whether there is any significant difference between the mean score of government employee and self employee parents students in respect of a study on basis of difficulties encounted in understanding geographical map among high school students.

HYPOTHESES OF THE STUDY

1. There is no significant difference in the difficulties encounted in geographical map among high school students on the basis of their gender residence type of school.
2. There is no significant difference in the difficulties encounted in geographical map among high school students on the basis of their location of school.
3. There is no significant difference in the difficulties encounted in geographical map among high school students on the basis of their management of school.

4. There is no significant difference in the difficulties encountered in geographical map among high school students on the basis of their type of school.
5. There is no significant difference in the difficulties encountered in geographical map among high school students on the basis of their type of school.
6. There is no significant difference in the difficulties encountered in geographical map among high school students on the basis of their type of school.
7. There is no significant difference in the difficulties encountered in geographical map among high school students on the basis of their medium of school.

POPULATION

The population is a set the totality of all objects or individuals. A population is by a group of individuals who have are studying in the high school students.

SAMPLE

A sample is a set of item of individuals selected from a larger aggregate or population. The sample selected for the present study consists of 300 high school students from different school with the help of stratified random sampling technique.

RESEARCH METHOD

The investigator used normative survey method to collect data from high school students. In the study the investigator collected the data from various school located Pudukkottai district.

RESEARCH TOOL

The investigator used questionnaire to collect data to difficulties encountered in understanding geographical map among high school students.

CONSTRUCTION OF RESEARCH TOOL

Before constructing the research tool the investigator visited a few schools located in Rural and Urban areas and collected opinion from high school students level.

Since the investigator himself faced some problems when he was studying at high school level this experience and student's suggestions mostly helped the researcher to frame the present research tool.

DESCRIPTION OF THE RESEARCH TOOL

A questionnaire on difficulties encounted in understanding geographical map among high school students has 30 items. All the items of questionnaire of focused on varieties of ideas regarding attitude towards economics. All the items should specific YES/NO Namely, "YES" carries One Marks, "NO" carries Zero mark in positive statement.. This frequency revealed the level of on difficulties encounted in understanding geographical map among high school students.The scale is,

(1) Yes (Y)
(2) No (N)

Scale Items	Scoring Procedure Positive Questions Marks
YES (Y)	1
NO (N)	0

PILOT STUDY

The Researcher conduct a pilot study nearby school of government girl's High School in Pudukkottai.

Before administering the research tool, the researcher give some instruction regarding how can answer all questions, then allowed all the students to rise the difficulties related to some questions and difficult items were discussed and clarified to students for better understanding. After getting response for all the items the researcher give frequencies to each and every item and these frequencies were tabulated used to find out reliability. In order to find out the usability of the proposed study, the researcher felt that the pilot study is an essential study.

RELIABILITY

The reliability of the research tool was established by using "Split half method". The top and bottom items of the questionnaire were taken and frequencies were given to those items based on the "Known" response. This total frequency of (top and bottom) considers finding out the correlation and then the researcher used the "Spearman Brown prophecy" formula of split half method to find out reliability.

VALIDITY

The investigator established content and face validity of the research tool. The items of the questionnaire were given to experts in the field of education to see their opinion in relation to its objective and worthiness of items. Further the experts view the each and every items of the questionnaire and provide of some suggestions to modify some of the questions. Based on the opinions some of the questions are eliminated and modified. The above process brought a sufficient content and face validity to research questioner of this study.

SAMPLING TECHNIQUE

The sample procedure is used to collect the data is stratified random sampling. The researcher collected sample only from high school level students, the school located in Pudukkottai District. The total samples taken for the present study is 200 Numbers.

DATA COLLECTIONS

The researcher himself visited high school students located in Pudukkottai area by getting permission from the Head Master of various schools. Before administering the research tool the researcher explain the aim and purpose of the study and then administered a research tool for High School level students. Then the researcher asked all the students to response for each and every item that are given in the questionnaire the response were recorded and the demographic particulars were collected from students. Then the researcher gave frequencies for all items and this frequency was entering in the Master table for data analysis. The researcher used statistical techniques, such as percentage analysis and test of significant to analysis data for this study.

DATA ANALYSIS

The investigator used statistical techniques such as mean, standard deviation and "t" test to find out whether there is any significant difference between the different biographical variables of the difficulties encountered in understanding geographical map among high school students.

THE ARITHMATIC MEAN

The mean of the distribution is commonly understood as the arithmetic average. The term grade point average, familiar to student is a mean value.

It is computed by dividing the sum of all the scores by the number of scores. It is probably most useful of all statistical measures for in addition to the information that it provides, it is the base from which many other important measures are computed.

THE STANDARD DEVIATION (S.D)

Standard Deviation is most widely used measure of dispersion of a series and is commonly denoted by the symbol (sigma). S.D is defined as the square root of the average of the squares of deviation for the values of individual items in a series are obtained from the arithmetic average.

Standard Deviation (S.D), $\sqrt{\frac{fd^2}{n} \quad (\frac{fd^2}{n}})\text{xC.I}$

'T' (t –Test)

'T' test is based on t-distribution and is a sample mean (or) judging the significance of difference between the means of the sample in case of small samples when population variance is not known. In case of two samples paired t - test is used for judging the significance of the mean of difference between the two related samples. The relevant test statistic is calculated from the sample data then compared with portable value based on t - distribution at a specified level of significance for concerning degrees of freedom for accepting (or) rejecting the null hypothesis.

Where, M_1 = Highest Mean value, M_2=Lowest Mean value.

S_1 = SD for highest Mean value, S_2= SD for Lowest Mean value.

N_1 = Highest mean value of case, N_2 =Lowest mean value of case.

LIMITATION OF THE STUDY

1. In this study questionnaire was administrated only for high school students studying at Pudukkottai Educational District.
2. The sample was collected only from the Government and private school in Pudukkottai District.
3. The present information was collected only from 300 samples.

TABLE 1

SCHOOL – WISE DISTRIBUTION OF THE SAMPLE

SI. NO	Name of the school	School locality	Students
1.	Sri Bragathambal Govt. Higher secondary school	Pudukkottai	50
2.	Ranee's Govt.Girls High secondary school.	Pudukkottai	50
3.	Government Boys High secondary school	Thirumayam	60
4.	Sacred Heart Girls Higher secondary school	Pudukkottai	50
5.	P.S.K Matric.Higher Secondary School.	Narthamalai	50
6.	ADR Matric Hr.Sec.School	Kaikkuruchi	40
	Total		300

It is inferred from above table that of them different number of students were taken in the schools.

TABLE 2

SEX – WISE DISTRIBUTION OF THE SAMPLE

Sex	Number	Percentage
Male	150	%
Female	150	50%
Total	300	100%

It is inferred from the above table that 50% of them were male and 50% of them were female.

TABLE 3

PLACE – WISE DISTRIBUTION OF THE SAMPLE

Place	Number	Percentage
Rural	150	50%
Urban	150	50%
Total	300	100%

It is inferred from the above table that 50% of them were rural students and 50% of them were urban students.

TABLE 4

MANAGEMENT - WISE DISTRIBUTION OF THE SAMPLE

Management	Number	Percentage
Government	160	53.33
Private	140	46.67
Total	300	100%

It is inferred from the above table that 80% of them were government and 70% of them were private school students.

TABLE 5

MEDIUM - WISE DISTRIBUTION OF THE SAMPLE

Management	Number	Percentage
Tamil medium	180	60%
Engliah medium	120	40%
Total	300	100%

It is inferred from the above table that 60% of them were government and 40% of them were private school students.

CONCLUSION

This chapter explained about the methodology employed for the present study. Preparation research tool, construction of research tool, pilot study reliability and validity, sampling technique, data collection, data analysis also presented in the chapter. The next chapter will be about the analysis and interpretation of the collected data.

Chapter - IV

Analysis of Data

INTRODUCTION

This chapter deals with data analysis of data, the data were recorded in the master sheet in form of frequencies and this frequency were converted into percentage which indicate the level of difficulties encounted in understanding geography map among high school students. The investigated also identified the level of difficulties encounted in understanding geography map among high school students who belongs to different groups of demographic variable such as sex, location of school, type of school. Further the 't' test was applied by the investigator to find out the difficulties encounted in understanding geography map among high school students differentiate and base of different biographical variables.

MEANING

The analysis and interpretation of data involves the objective material in the possession of the research and his subjective reactions and desire to drive from the data, the inherent meaning in their reactions to the problem.

NEEDS FOR ANALYSIS

In the present study, we have obtained a series of paired data which are to be analysis because these are correlated. The nature and extent of relation is essential to make decisions, formulate policies and estimate future. The study of relation makes decision making more effective and useful. The provide valuable information which analyst can employ to support a judgment concerning the existence of a cause effect relationship between the variable selected for analysis.

STATISTICAL TECHNIQUES APPLIED IN DATA ANALYSIS

The following statistical techniques were applied to analyses and interpret the collected data.

HYPOTHESES: 1

There is no of significant difference between the mean score of difficulties encountered in understanding geographical map of Male and Female students at high school level students.

TABLE 1

S.No	GENDER	Nos.	MEAN	SD	"t" VALUE	at 0.05 level
1.	Male	150	18.47	6.82		
2.	Female	150	18.53	6.76	0.08	Not Significant

Interpretation:

Since the calculated "t" – Value of 0.08 is lesser than the table "t" – value (1.96) at 0.05% level, there is significant difference between the mean scores of difficulties encountered in understanding geographical map of **Mal**e and **Female** high school students. **Hence the research hypothesis is accepted**.

FINDING:

Male and female student's difficulties encountered in understanding geographical map among high school students level are to be same.

HYPOTHESES: 2

There is no significant difference between the mean score of difficulties encounted in understanding geographical map of Rural and Urban students among high school level students.

TABLE 2

S.No	Locality	Nos.	MEAN	SD	"t" VALUE	at 0.05 level
1.	Rural	160	19.52	6.71		
2.	Urban	140	17.48	6.95	2.72	Significant

Interpretation:

Since the calculated "t" – Value of 2.72 is greater than the table "t" – value (1.96) at 0.05 % level, there is no significant difference between the mean scores of difficulties encounted in understanding geographical map of **Rural** and **Urban** at high school level students. **Hence the research hypothesis is rejected.**

FINDING:

Rural student's difficulties are higher than urban student's difficulties encounted in understanding geographical map among high school level.

HYPOTHESES: 3

There is no significant difference between the mean score of difficulties encounted in understanding geographical map of Government and Private school students among high school level students.

TABLE 3

S.No	Type of School	Nos.	MEAN	SD	"t" VALUE	at 0.05 level
1.	Government	150	18.23	6.23		
2.	Private	150	18.87	7.14	0.84	Not Significant

Interpretation

Since the calculated "t" – Value of 0.84 is lesser than the table "t" – value (1.96) at 0.05% level, there is significant difference between the mean scores of difficulties encounted in understanding geographical map of **Government** and **Private** school level students. **Hence the research hypothesis is accepted**.

FINDING:

Government and private school student's difficulties encounted in understanding geographical map among high school students level are to be same.

HYPOTHESES: 4

There is no significant difference between the mean score of difficulties encounted in understanding geographical map of Boys school and Girls school students at high school level.

TABLE 4

S.No	Type of School	Nos.	MEAN	SD	"t" VALUE	at 0.05 level
1.	Boys school	100	17.43	6.33		
2.	Girls school	100	18.52	6.81	1.17	Not Significant

Interpretation:

Since the calculated "t" – Value of 1.17 is lesser than the table "t" – value (1.96) at 0.05% level, there is significant difference between the mean scores of difficulties encounted in understanding geographical map of Boys school and Girls school students. Hence the research hypothesis is accepted.

FINDING:

Girls school student's difficulties awareness is higher than Boys school student's difficulties encounted in understanding geographical map of high school students level.

HYPOTHESES: 5

There is no significant difference between the mean score of difficulties encounted in understanding geographical map of Boys school and Co - education school students among high school level students.

TABLE 5

S.No	Type of School	Nos.	MEAN	SD	"t" VALUE	at 0.05 level
1.	Boys school	100	17.43	6.33		
2.	Co– education	100	19.75	7.22	2.42	Significant

Interpretation:

Since the calculated "t" – Value of 2.42 is greater than the table "t" – value (1.96) at 0.05% level, there is no significant difference between the mean scores of difficulties encountered in understanding geographical map of **Boys school** and **Co – education of high school** level students. **Hence the research hypothesis is rejected.**

FINDING:

Co – education school student's difficulties is higher than Boys school student's difficulties encountered in understanding geographical map of high school students level.

HYPOTHESES: 6

There is no significant difference between the mean score of difficulties encountered in understanding geographical map of Girls school and Co-education school students among high school level students.

TABLE 6

S.No	Type of School	Nos.	MEAN	SD	"t" VALUE	at 0.05 level
1.	Girls school	100	18.52	6.81		
2.	Co- education	100	19.75	7.22	1.26	Not Significant

Interpretation:

Since the calculated "t" – Value of 1.26 is lesser than the table "t" – value (1.96) at 0.05% level, there is significant difference between the mean scores of difficulties encountered in understanding geographical map of **English medium** and **Tamil medium** among high school level students. **Hence the research hypothesis is accepted.**

FINDING

Girls school students attitude is same as well as **Co-education school students** in difficulties encountered in understanding geographical map among high school students level.

HYPOTHESES: 7

There is no significant difference between the mean score of difficulties encountered in understanding geographical map of Govt. Employee and Self employee parents students among high school level students.

TABLE 7

S.No	Parents occupation	Nos.	MEAN	SD	"t" VALUE	at 0.05 level
1.	Govt.Employee	170	19.17	6.79		
2.	Self Employee	130	17.43	6.36	2.29	Significant

Interpretation:

Since the calculated "t" – Value of 2.29 is greater than the table "t" – value (1.96) at 0.05% level, there is significant difference between the mean scores of in difficulties encountered in understanding geographical map among high school students level of **Government Employee** and **Self Employee school students. Hence the research hypothesis is rejected.**

FINDING:

Govt. Employee parents difficulties is same as well as Self employee parents **student's** difficulties encountered in understanding geographical map among high school students level.

CONCLUSION

Thus the score were subjected to statistical treatment to find out the difficulties encountered in understanding geographical map among high school students. These collected data calculated, analysed and interpreted. The next chapter deals with the summary of the findings and conclusion.

Chapter - V

Summary and Conclusion

INTRODUCTION

Geography claims a substantial segment of the national academic space. If one goes by the numerical strength of the geographical community in terms of students admitted to various geography programmes in different universities and colleges and the strength of the faculty, Indian geography has certainly made impressive gains during the past eight decades. More geographers now attend summits, workshops, seminars symposia and conferences in geography both at national and international level. Yet, Indian Geography does not feature prominently in the international arena. This is despite attempts to include every possible change in the development of the subject into the geography curriculum. Geographers in India have been alive to every new tool and technique that has appeared on its door step. Yet, the geographical enterprise has failed to reap dividends nationally or internationally. Teaching and research in Geography is channelized through a large number of geography departments spread all over the country.

The period under review has witnessed establishment of many new departments of geography particularly in the North-Eastern region of India. But the inherent dichotomy in nature of geography continues to affect its position in the highly structured university system that treats the subject either as a natural science or as a social science. The placement of geography in the university system continues to baffle generations of students. Geography continues to be placed under the faculty of sciences in many universities enabling them to procure funds and projects from funding agencies as well as to establish laboratories. On the other hand departments which are placed under arts/social sciences continue to be eternally starved of funds for their minimal needs. This has created not only inequality between departments of geography, but also affects the quality of teaching and research.

NEED OF THE STUDY

1. To solve the students difficulties in geographical map.
2. To analyse variations in male and female students' difficulties encounted in understanding geographical map.
3. To analyse variations in government and government aided and self finance students' difficulties encounted in understanding geographical map.
4. To suggest possible strategies to improve the students' difficulties encounted in understanding geographical map.

SIGNIFICANT OF THE STUDY

1. Teachers, helps their students to solve their difficulties.
2. Students should improve their memory in geographical map.
3. Students should create new ideas in geographical map.

STATEMENT OF THE PROBLEM

This is the title of the present study *"Difficulties Encounted in Understanding Geographical Maps among High School Students."*

OPERATIONAL DEFINITION OF KEY TERMS

GEOGRAPHY

Geography claims a substantial segment of the national academic space. If one goes by the numerical strength of the geographical community in terms of students admitted to various geography programmes in different universities and colleges and the strength of the faculty, Indian geography has certainly made impressive gains during the past eight decades. More geographers now attend summits, workshops, seminars symposia and conferences in geography both at national and international level. Yet, Indian Geography does not feature prominently in the international arena. This is despite attempts to include every possible change in the development of the subject into the geography curriculum. Geographers in India have been alive to every new tool and technique that has appeared on its door step.

Difficulties

Bio films are bacterial colonies enveloped in a matrix of extracellular polymeric secretions. Confocal scanning laser microscopy has been used in conjunction with different image analysis techniques to investigate the structure of bio films. A major goal is to reconstitute the three- dimensional structure of bio films, and computer or estimate the bio volumes. Our previous research focused on the utilization of remote sensing techniques and Geographical information systems for quantitative analyses of confocal images. The present study investigates potential problems in microbial imaging, and use two approaches, the program COMSTAT and a Geographical information systems- based method, to reconstitute three- dimensional structures and estimate bio volumes. Volumes of thirty fluorescent polymeric microspheres with a known diameter were estimated and used as a approaches were used to estimate the bio volume of a section through a pseudomonas aeruginosa bio film. Difficulties were encountered indicate that the Geographical due to the optical properties of the micro beads. Our results indicate that the geographical information systems approach produced results consistent with the existing COMSTAT approach, and close to theoretical values, despite many problems inherent to each phase of this process. Also, the image classification process encountered several limitations. It is suggested that the unique constraints of the microscopic world may generated additional problems, especially related to image classification.

Encounted

1. If any difficulty arises in giving effect to the provisions of this Act, the central Government may, by order published in the official Gazette, make such provisions not inconsistent with the provisions of this Act as may appear to be necessary for removing the difficulty: Provided that no order shall be made under this section after the expiry of five years from the commencement of this Act.
2. Every order made under section shall, as soon as may be after it is made, be laid before each House of parliament.

Understanding

Specifically focuses on Civil Services Examination over 3300 entries pertaining to: oceans, mountains, peaks, plateaus, peninsulas, trenches, rivers, deltas, estuaries, lakes, glaciers, waterfalls, river- projects dames, biosphere reserves, national parks, bird sanctuaries, sea- beaches, tourist resorts, cities, seaports, industrial and mining centres, national highways and trans-continental railways. Precise informative write- up on each entry

High School geographical map

What's new in this edition?

1. Restructured, Updated and covered in two parts
2. Part I Covers the main geographical entries of the world
3. Part II covers the main geographical entries of the world
4. 300 new and contemporary entries included in this revised edition
5. Entries arranged topic- wise in alphabetical order.

Understanding geographical map

Understanding Geographical Map Entries: Map based questions is an important feature of the civil Services Main Examination for aspirants with Geography as an optional subject. The revised, updated edition of this popular book written by an eminent academician equips aspirants with the precise knowledge and the skill to plot geographical entries correctly. It also equips with the resources to write a precise and informative note on each entry. The book should of interest to the ordinary reader and also be of valuable help to teachers of geography who would like to keep themselves updated on the subject.

STATEMENT OF THE PROBLEMS

To find out the "*Difficulties Encounted in Understanding Geographical Maps among High School Students.*"

OBJECTIVES THE STUDY

1. To find out whether there is any significant difference between the mean score of male and female students in respect of a study on basis of difficulties encounted in understanding geographical map among high school students.
2. To find out whether there is any significant difference between the mean score of rural and urban school students in respect of a study on basis of difficulties encounted in understanding geographical map among high school students.
3. To find out whether there is any significant difference between the mean score of government and private school students in respect of a study on basis of difficulties encounted in understanding geographical map among high school students.
4. To find out whether there is any significant difference between the mean score of government boys school and government aided girls school in respect of a study on basis of difficulties encounted in understanding geographical map among high school students.
5. To find out whether there is any significant difference between the mean score of government boys school and co – education private school students in respect of a study on basis of difficulties encounted in understanding geographical map among high school students.
6. To find out whether there is any significant difference between the mean score of government aided girls School and Co-Education Private school students in respect of a study on basis of difficulties encounted in understanding geographical map among high school students.

7. To find out whether there is any significant difference between the mean score of government employee and self employee parents students in respect of a study on basis of difficulties encounted in understanding geographical map among high school students.

HYPOTHESES OF THE STUDY

1. There is no significant difference in the difficulties encounted in geographical map among high school students on the basis of their gender residence type of school.
2. There is no significant difference in the difficulties encounted in geographical map among high school students on the basis of their location of school.
3. There is no significant difference in the difficulties encounted in geographical map among high school students on the basis of their management of school.
4. There is no significant difference in the difficulties encounted in geographical map among high school students on the basis of their type of school.
5. There is no significant difference in the difficulties encounted in geographical map among high school students on the basis of their type of school.
6. There is no significant difference in the difficulties encounted in geographical map among high school students on the basis of their type of school.
7. There is no significant difference in the difficulties encounted in geographical map among high school students on the basis of their medium of school.

POPULATION

The population is a set the totality of all objects or individuals. A population is by a group of individuals who have are studying in high school students in Pudukkottai educational district.

SAMPLE

A sample is a set of item of individuals selected from a larger aggregate or population. The sample selected for the present study consists of 300 high school students from different school with the help of stratified random sampling technique.

RESEARCH METHOD

The investigator used normative survey method to collect data from high school students. In the study the investigator collected the data from various school located Pudukkottai district.

RESEARCH TOOL

The investigator used questionnaire to collect data to difficulties encounted in understanding geographical map among high school students.

CONSTRUCTION OF RESEARCH TOOL

Before constructing the research tool the investigator visited a few school located in Rural and Urban areas and collected opinion from high school students level.

Since the investigator himself faced some problems when he was studying at higher secondary school level this experience and student's suggestions mostly helped the researcher to frame the present research tool.

DESCRIPTION OF THE RESEARCH TOOL

A questionnaire on difficulties encounted in understanding geographical map among high school students has 30 items. All the items of questionnaire of focused on varieties of ideas regarding attitude towards economics. All the items should specific YES/NO Namely, "YES" carries One Marks, "NO" carries Zero mark in positive statement.. This frequency revealed the level of on difficulties encounted in understanding geographical map among high school students.

PILOT STUDY

The Researcher conduct a pilot study nearby school of government girl' s high secondary school in Pudukkottai.

Before administering the research tool, the researcher give some instruction regarding how can answer all questions, then allowed all the students to rise the difficulties related to some questions and difficult items were discussed and clarified to students for better understanding. After getting response for all the items the researcher give frequencies to each and every item and these frequencies were tabulated used to find out reliability. In order to find out the usability of the proposed study, the researcher felt that the pilot study is an essential study.

RELIABILITY

The reliability of the research tool was established by using "Split half method". The top and bottom items of the questionnaire were taken and frequencies were given to those items based on the "Known" response. This total frequency of (top and bottom) considers finding out the correlation and then the researcher used the "Spearman Brown prophecy" formula of split half method to find out reliability.

VALIDITY

The investigator established content and face validity of the research tool. The items of the questionnaire were given to experts in the field of education to see their opinion in relation to its objective and worthiness of items. Further the experts view the each and every items of the questionnaire and provide of some suggestions to modify some of the questions. Based on the opinions some of the questions are eliminated and modified. The above process brought a sufficient content and face validity to research questioner of this study.

SAMPLING TECHNIQUE

The sample procedure is used to collect the data is stratified random sampling. The researcher collected sample only from high school level students, the school located in Pudukkottai District. The total samples taken for the present study is 300 Numbers.

DATA COLLECTIONS

The researcher himself visited high school students located in Pudukkottai area by getting permission from the Head Master of various schools. Before administering the research tool the researcher explain the aim and purpose of the study and then administered a research tool for high school level students. Then the researcher asked all the students to response for each and every item that are given in the questionnaire the response were recorded and the demographic particulars were collected from students. Then the researcher gave frequencies for all items and this frequency was enter in the Master table for data analysis. The researcher used statistical techniques, such as percentage analysis and test of significant to analysis data for this study.

DATA ANALYSIS

The investigator used statistical techniques such as mean, standard deviation and "t" test to find out whether there is any significant difference between the different biographical variables of the difficulties encountered in understanding geographical map among high school students.

THE ARITHMATIC MEAN

The mean of the distribution is commonly understood as the arithmetic average. The term grade point average, familiar to student is a mean value.

It is computed by dividing the sum of all the scores by the number of scores. It is probably most useful of all statistical measures for in addition to the information that it provides, it is the base from which many other important measures are computed.

THE STANDARD DEVIATION (S.D)

Standard Deviation is most widely used measure of dispersion of a series and is commonly denoted by the symbol 'σ'(sigma). S.D is defined as the square root of the average of the squares of deviation for the values of individual items in a series are obtained from the arithmetic average.

'T' (t –Test)

'T' test is based on t-distribution and is a sample mean (or) judging the significance of difference between the means of the sample in case of small samples when population variance is not known. In case of two samples paired t - test is used for judging the significance of the mean of difference between the two related samples. The relevant test statistic is calculated from the sample data then compared with portable value based on t - distribution at a specified level of significance for concerning degrees of freedom for accepting (or) rejecting the null hypothesis. This test applies only in case of small samples when population variance is not known.

LIMITATION OF THE STUDY

1. In this study questionnaire was administrated only for high school students studying at Pudukkottai District.
2. The sample was collected only from the government and private school in Pudukkottai District.
3. The present information was collected only from 300 samples.

MAJOR FINDINGS

1. **Male and female** student's difficulties encounted in understanding geographical map among high school students level are to be same.
2. **Rural school student's** difficulties are higher than urban student's difficulties encounted in understanding geographical map of high school student's level.
3. **Government and private school** student's difficulties encounted in understanding geographical map among high school students level are to be same.
4. **Girls school student's** difficulties is higher than **Boys school student's** difficulties encounted in understanding geographical map of high school students level.
5. **Co – education school student's** difficulties is higher than **Boys school student's** difficulties encounted in understanding geographical map of high school students level.
6. **Girls school student's** difficulties is higher than **Co – education school student's** difficulties encounted in understanding geographical map of high school students level.
7. **Government Employee** difficulties are higher than **Self Employee Parents Students** difficulties encounted in understanding geographical map of high school students level.

CONCLUSION

In the recent research that the students difficulties encounted in understanding geographical map among high school level. Further the research also reveals that the student belong to Male category be higher level than the counterpart. Finally the research study concluded that the students difficulties belong to Government Aided school students is found to be higher level of difficulties encounted in understanding geographical map while compare to Government school students and private school students.

BIBILIOGRAPHY

1. Baker, T. R. (no date). The History and Application of GIS in K-12 Education. Retrieved 27 March 2006 from http://www.gisdevelopment.net/Education/papers/edpa0003.htm
2. Baker, T. R. (2005). Internet-Based GIS Mapping in Support of K-12 Education. The Professional Geographer, 57(1) 2005, 44-50. Blackwell Publishing, Oxford, U.K.
3. Baker, T. R. & Bednarz, S. W. (2003). Lesson Learned from Reviewing Research in GIS Education. Journal of Geography, 102: 231-233. National Council for Geographic Education.
4. Baker, T. R. & White, S. H. (2003). The Effects of GIS on Students' Attitudes, Self-efficacy, and Achievement in Middle School Science Classrooms. Journal of Geography, 102, 243-254.
5. Brown, J. S., Collins, A. & Duguid, P. (1989). Situated Cognition and the Culture of Learning. Educational Researcher, 18(1), 32-42.
6. Burrough, P.A & McDonnell, R.A. (1998), Principles of Geographical Information Systems: Oxford University Press.
7. Davis, B. (1996). GIS: A Visual Approach. Onward Press, Thomson Learning, Canada.
8. Environmental Systems Research Institute. (1995). Exploring Common Ground: The Educational Promise of GIS. Environmental Systems Research Institute Inc.
9. Environmental Systems Research Institute. (2003). Geographic Inquiry: Thinking Geographically.

Problems Faced in Solving Equations

Chapter - I

INTRODUCTION

In olden days, Education was teacher centered, now the trend is changing towards Pupil or child centeredness, here arises the wide scope of teaching aids as a supportive measure, the national policy on Education (1986) observes that Education must serve as a powerful instrument of social, economic and cultural transformation necessary for the realization of the national goals.

Higher Education provides people with an opportunity to reflect on the critical social, economic, cultural, and spiritual issues facing humanity. It contributes to national, Development through dissemination of specialized Knowledge and skills. It is therefore a crucial factor for survival, Being at the apex of the Educational pyramid, it has also a key role in producing teachers for the Education system.

In the context of the unprecedented explosion of Knowledge, higher Education has to become dynamic as before, constantly entering uncharted areas. In view of mixed experiences with the system of affiliation, autonomous colleges will be helped to develop in large numbers until the affiliating system is replaced by a freer and creative association of universities with colleges, similarly, the creation of autonomous departments within universities on a selective basis will be encouraged. Autonomy and freedom will be accompanied by accountability. Courses and programmers will be redesigned to meet the demands of specialization better. Special emphasis will be laid on linguistic competence. There will be increasing flexibility in the combination of courses.

State Level planning and coordination of higher Education will be done through Councils of Higher Education. The UGC and these Councils will develop coordinative methods to keep a watch on standards.

Provision will be made for minimum facilities and admission will be regulated according to capacity major effort will be directed towards the transformation of teaching methods. Audio-visual aids and electronic equipment will be introduced; development of science and technology curricula and material, research, and teacher orientation will receive attention. This will require preparation of teachers at the beginning of the service as well as continuing Education thereafter. Teacher Performance will be systematically assessed. All posts will be filled on the basis of merit.

Research in the universities will be provided enhanced support and steps will be taken to ensure its high quality. Suitable mechanisms will be set up by the UGC for coordinating research in the universities, particularly in thrust areas of science and technology, with research undertaken by other agencies, an effort will be made to encourage the setting up of national research facilities within the university system, with proper forms of autonomous management.

Research in Ideology, the humanities and social sciences will receive adequate support. To fulfil the need for the synthesis of Knowledge, inter-disciplinary research will be encouraged Efforts will be made to delve into India's ancient fund of Knowledge and to relate it to contemporary reality.

In the interest of greater coordination and consistency in policy, sharing of facilities and developing interdisciplinary research, a national body covering higher Education in general, agricultural, medical, technical, legal and other professional fields will be set up.

The implementation of the National policy on Education 1986 was evaluated by two committees, namely the Ramamurti Committee (1990) and the Janardhaana Committee (1992). As a result of the recommendations of these two committees, slight modifications were made in the NPE in 1992. Education refers to the process by which society, through its different institutions deliberately transmits its cultural heritage to the young.

As a selector of instructional strategies an effective teacher will.

1. Plan to influence directly the learning process by varying his behaviour.

1. Arrange a variety of media including books, Lecture notes, home work, visual aids, Programs, discussion and Laboratory experience.

EDUCATION

Meaning

Education of man does not begin at school it begins of birth. It ends not when he graduates from the university but at his death. Hence Education is a lifelong process. Any modification brought about in the behaviour of an individual as a result of his interaction with the environmental constituted learning.

Education is an activity which goes on the society. It attempts to develop the personality of an individual and then prepares him for membership in a society. Man without Education would still be living just like an animal. It is Education which transforms man from a more 'tow legged animal' into a human.

The realization of the interlinked twin objectives of individual growth and social progress implies a well planned and efficiently operated system of Education. The primary meaning of 'Education' appears to be 'bringing up' 'leading up' or 'making manifest' and explicit the potentialities talent in a child.

The word Education is derived from the Lain word "Educate" which means to train to put in the instruction. It also means to draw out to lead forth.

WHAT IS SCIENCE?

The word Science Comes from a Latin word "Sciatica" Which means 'to know'. Science is nothing but the Knowledge gained through the systematic observations and experiments, Scientific methods include the Systematic observations, reasoning, modelling and theoretical prediction.

Science is mankind's rational attempts to organize and explain the perceived things and events of the world. The greatly changing conditions of life and world events are demanding a new perspective of teaching science.

CHEMISTRY

Chemistry is one of the most important branches of science; it enables learners to understand what happened around them. Because chemistry topics are generally related to or based on the structure of matter, chemistry proves a difficult subject for many students. Chemistry curricula commonly incorporate many abstract concepts, which are central to further learning in both chemistry and other sciences. The branch of science concerned with the substances of which matter is composed, the investigation of their properties and reactions, and the use of such reactions to form new substances.

Chemistry is often regarded as a difficult subject, an observation that sometimes repeals learners from continuing with studies in chemistry. With the establishment of new syllabuses in chemistry for secondary schools in different countries in the last decayed. One of the essential characteristics of chemistry is the constant interplay between the macroscopic and microscopic levels of thought, and it is thesis aspect of chemistry (and physics) learning that represents a significant challenge to novices.

The imperative character of education for individual growth and social development is now accepted by everyone. Man is highly enterprising being. He is always on the lookout for inventing new innovations in all walks of life. Human like has improved tremendously as a result of the growth in science and technology. Education is a social institution that has also been influenced by technological development. The impact of changes is described as modernization.

Educational technology has great potential for improving the teaching-learning process Educational technology is the development, application and evaluation of systems, techniques and also aids in the field of human learning. One of the important contributions of educational technology is individualized instruction, which enables in to make use of self-instructional programmes.

The teacher-cantered and group cantered approaches are inadequate nice they hardly make any provision for individual difference of the learner, the premise is that strictly speaking no two students in the class are alike and that there are many permutations and combinations of individuals different us.

MEANING

A chemical equation is the symbolic representation of a chemical reaction wherein the reactant entities are given on the left-hand side and the product entities of the right-hand side. The coefficients next to the symbols and formulae of entities are the absolute values of the stanchion metric numbers.

DEFINITION

A chemical equation is shorthand written description of what happens in a chemical reaction. It includes the reactants, products, direction(s) of the reaction, and may also include charge and states of matter. All Chemical Reactions Can Be Placed Into One Of Six Categories. Here They Are, In No Particular Order

COMBUSTION

A combustion reaction is when oxygen combines with another compound to form water and carbon dioxide. These reactions are exothermic, meaning they produce heat. An example of this kind of reaction is the burning of naphthalene:

C10H8 + 12 O2

All Chemical Reactions Can Be Placed Into One Of Six Categories. Here They Are, In No Particular Order

COMBUSTION

A combustion reaction is when oxygen combines with another compound to from water and carbon dioxide. These reactions are exothermic, meaning they produce heat. An example of this kind of reaction is the burning of naphthalene:

$$C_{10}H_8 + 12\ O_2 \longrightarrow 10\ CO_2 + 4\ H_2O$$

SYNTHESIS

A synthesis reaction is when two or more simple compounds combine to form a more complicated one. These reactions come in the general form of:

$$A + B \longrightarrow AB$$

One example of a synthesis reaction is the combination of iron and sulfur to form iron (II) sulfide:

$$8\ Fe + S_8 \longrightarrow 8\ FeS$$

DECOMPOSITION

A decomposition reaction is the opposite of a synthesis reaction - a complex molecule breaks down to make simpler ones. These reactions come in the general From:

$$AB \longrightarrow A + B$$

One example of a decomposition reaction is the electrolysis of Water to make oxygen and hydrogen gas:

$$2\ H_2O \longrightarrow 2\ H_2 + O_2$$

SINGLE DISPLACEMENT

This is when one element trades places with another element in a compound These reactions come in the general form of:

$$A+BC \longrightarrow AC+B$$

One example of a single displacement reaction is when magnesium replaces hydrogen in water to make magnesium hydroxide and hydrogen gas:

$$Mg + 2\ H_2O \longrightarrow Mg\ (OH)_2\ H_2$$

DOUBLE DISPLACEMENT

This is when the anions and cations of two different molecules switch places, forming g two entirely different compounds. These reactions are in the general form:

$$AB + CD \longrightarrow AD + CB$$

One example of a double displacement reaction is the reaction of lead (II) nitrate with potassium iodide to form lead (II) iodide and potassium nitrate:

$$Pb(NO_3)2 + 2\ KI \longrightarrow PbI_2 + 2\ KNO_3$$

ACID-BASE

This is a special kind of double displacement reaction that takes place when an avid and base react with each other. The H^+ion in the acid reacts with the OH' ion in the base, causing the formation of water. Generally, the product of this reaction is some ionic salt and water:

$$HA + BOH \longrightarrow H_2O + BA$$

One example of an acid-base reaction is the reaction of hydrotropic acid (HBr) with sodium hydroxide:

$$HBr + NaOH \longrightarrow NaBr + H_2O$$

GENERAL CHEMISTRY/REACTION MECHANISMS

Chemists often write chemical equations for reactions as a single step, which only shows the net result of a reaction. However, most chemical reactions occur in a series of steps called elementary reactions. All of these elementary reactions must add up to equal the overall balanced equation. "The complete sequence of these elementary steps is called a reaction mechanism." The reaction mechanism is the sep-by-step process by which reactants actually become products. It is the "how" o 1" the reaction, whereas the overall balanced equation only shows the "what" of the reaction.

RATE-DETERMINING STEPS

Sometimes, intermediate substances are created in the process that disappears in the end. Take the following example of a homogeneous reaction (where products and reactants are all in the same phase):

$$CO + NO_2 \text{ —> } CO_2 + NO$$

There are actually two reactions occurring at different speeds.

- o $2NO_2$ —> NO_3 + NO (slow)
- o NO_3 + CO —>NO_2 + CO_2 (fast)

1. Since the first step is the slowest, and the entire reaction must wait for it, it is known as the rate-determining step. The overall reaction rate depends almost entirely on the rate of the *slowest step. The other steps are fast enough that their rate is insignificant, as they are always waiting for the slower step to complete.
2. Why is the first step slower? Collision theory explains whether for not particles react when they collide. The particles must collide with a minimum energy and a proper orientation if a reaction is to occur. The minimum energy needed for a reaction to occur is its activation energy. The particles must be moving fast enough for their collision to satisfy the activation energy. Without the necessary energy, the particles will bounce off each other with no reaction. A good example of activation energy is butane lighter, which needs a spark before the fluid burns. The spark
3. Provides enough energy to the particles to make their collisions effective. Reactions with high activation energy will be slower than those with low activation energy. With high activation energy, less particles are likely to generate the needed energy when they collide. Reactions that break bonds, especially double or triple covalent bonds, will have higher activation energy.

The particles must also collide with the proper orientation. For example, the faction in the animation above shows an ammonium ion reacting with a NCO‘ ion. For the reaction to occur, the ammonium ion must collide with the nitrogen of ne NCO: If the ions don’t collide in the right place while facing in the right reaction, the reaction cannot occur.

Reactions that have very specific requirements for the orientation of the colliding particles will be much slower. Reactions that can occur without a specific orientation will happen faster.

Determining the Validity of an Elementary Step Model

In order for a proposed elementary step equation to be valid it must fulfill these requirements.

1. The rate equation of the slow step much matches the rate equation of the overall reaction.'
2. The reactants and products of all the elementary steps added together must equal the one of the actual equation.
3. The rate law for the elementary step must be able to be written without the concentration of the intermediates, because the intermediates are too small to be accurately measured. For example, if given this equation and asked to prove the rate mechanism

Equation $2O_3 \longrightarrow 3O_2$ + NO

Proposed Mechanism

O3 —>O2 + O(fast)

O3O —>2O2(slow)

rate = $k [O_3]^2 [O_2]$

We know that when the reaction occurs backwards, the k changes from k to k {-l}. So, we substitute in the backwards rate for O3, and plug it into the slow sup. Then, take the rate equation of the slow step. We find that it is the same as the rate law for the overall equation and meets the three 'criteria above, so this proposed mechanism is valid.

HERE IS A LIST OF ITEMS, WE HAVE TALKED ABOUT IN THIS PIECE

CLOCK

At the primary stage, imparting the concept of time becomes crucial, and equally so for a visually impaired student. It cannot be taught without a concrete presentation. A good idea is to devise a clock-face made of a thermocol placed on cardboard. Special care should be taken while designing the clock to make it graspable and comprehensible. Buttons can be used to demarcate the hours, while we hands can be shown through the use of matchsticks.

GEOMETRY-KIT

This is a kit adapted for use by visually impaired students. It consists of a thick rubber sheet, with a box containing a tactile scale, tactile angle-constructers, tactile compass and a tactile divider. A thick sheet of paper is placed on the rubber sheet draw the desired shapes and figures. Not only this, the graphs used in economics statistics can also be easily drawn using this kit.

If more teachers were aware of this kit and promoted its use, blind students would of need alternative or compensator questions in lace of an involve drawing graphs or figures.

TACTILE MAPS

Visually y impaired students are always offered a compensatory question for a map, It that does not reduce for them, the need to know the world around. A map in a graved form can be conveniently used to teach the location and the relief features of the area. It is devised using an embosser. Teachers can also design their own tactile maps, using a thick cardboard, supplemented with thread, cotton or term atoll to highlight the different features such as mountains, plateaus, plains. Drivers, in case an embosser are not available. Remember however, not to make map too complicated. As far as possible, try showing only two to three feature son a single map.

GLOBE

The blind student should not be deprived of the knowledge of the structure of retire earth. The basic concept of its spherical structure and the poles can be easily taught using a globe.

SCIENCE

Science as defined above is sometimes called pure science to differentiate it from applied science, which is the application of research to human needs. Fields of science are commonly classified along two major lines:

1. Natural sciences, the study of the natural world, and
2. Social sciences, the systematic study of human behavior and society.

TYPES OF SCIENCE

Physical Science

1. Physics
2. Chemistry

Earth science

1. Ecology
2. Oceanography
3. Geology
4. Meteorology

Life Science

1. Biology
2. Zoology
3. Human biology
4. Botany

HISTORY OF SCIENCE

Science as inquiry has a long history in science education. Here are a few milestones:

1. 1910: John Dewey writes about the importance of inquiry science.
2. 1927: Gerald Craig writes about the importance of teaching science through investigations.
3. 1947: Natural Sciences and Science Education (NSSE) Yearbook endorses science programs based on features that include problem-solving skills.

4. 1960s: Major revision of science education occurs through development of new science curricula that emphasize inquiry approaches (ESS [Elementary Science Stud)], SAPA [Science-A Process Approach, SCIS [Science Curriculum Improvement Study).
5. 1970s: Science educators question effectiveness of "extreme" version of discovery science, i.e., minimal teacher intervention.
6. 1980s: Growing interest in the nature of science, including its implications for how authentic inquiry can be carried out in science classrooms.
7. 1990s: Domination of constructivist (see Glossary of Terms) learning theory, including emphasis on importance of children's existing ideas and how they affect what is learned during scientific inquiry.
8. 2000: Shift in emphasis in classroom scientific inquiry nom a focus on "science processes" to a focus on evidence, explanation and, current scientific knowledge.
9. (Note: A more detailed history of the inquiry approach can be found in et al., 2006).

These milestones have had an ongoing impact on Alberta elementary science programs (Kamal, 2006).

CHARACTERISTICS OF SCIENCE

A good research question...

1. Answers something new! Replications, by themselves, are not good enough. The point of conducting _research is to advanced knowledge—to test something in a unique way, to test the prediction of a theory, to explore new methodology, etc. It is extremely important to show that a scientific finding can be replicated. Any valid scientific finding needs to be replicable... or in other words, reliable. The best kinds of research studies both replicate previous research while incorporating so1nething new. That's not always possible in a single study; sometimes it takes two or three experiments to accomplish this. (That's why most journal articles will contain a number of research studies rather than a single study).

2. Is based on and builds upon previous research. A good research question trusts the prediction of a theory. A research question that you generate off the top of your head can be useful, but almost always, research questions developed after an understanding of previous research and theory is much stronger and more relevant to science (and will be viewed more favorably by reviewers of your research).

1. Is practical (e.g., Can you really do this study this semester? Do you have the equipment resources to sufficiently answer your question? Will you need a zillion subjects for the study?) .

4. Is often simple. You don't have to answer the "big" questions of psychology -just add a little piece to existing research. A good piece of advice when conducting research is "Keep it Simple" You don't want to be left with a pile of data that you don't know how to interpret. (You'd be surprised at how often that happens!).[2]

5. Is based on primary (not secondary) sources; Primary source basically refers to the original source of research, usually from a publication. A secondary source, on the other hand, is a summary or description of the primary source. Newspapers, magazines, and topic books are secondary sources; journal articles are usually primary sources.'

MAIN FEATURES OF SCIENCE

As diverse as sciences are, all scientific explanations have a lot in common. Psychological research, just like all other scientific research, adheres to these principles.

SCIENTIFIC EXPLANATIONS ARE EMPIRICAL

"Empirical" means "based on the senses." All scientific explanations must be based on empirical observations or experiments (or at the very least, be directly interred when direct observation cannot be achieved).

SCIENTIFIC EXPLANATIONS ARE TENTATIVE

This means that all findings are subject to change should there be enough evidence to necessitate a change. There is always chance that the scientific theory is wrong, no matter how much supporting evidence there is for the theory. In other words, nothing is ever proven in science.

SCIENTIFIC EXPLANATIONS ARE PROBABILISTIC

Nothing can be measured precisely; there is always a degree of uncertainty in one's measurement. This is especially true in psychology because humans are amazingly complex. In psychology, keep in mind that any finding is what's likely to be true but because of the impreciseness and variability in human observation, human behaviour, and measures we say there's only probability of a finding being true.

SCIENTIFIC EXPLANATIONS ARE TESTABLE

There must exit an outcome that does not support the theory. An example of a non-testable theory is Freud's theory of personality. You can't test the id, the ego, or the superego. Thus, Freud's theory is not scientific. (The same applies to dream interpretation — certainly not scientific.)

SCIENTIFIC EXPLANATIONS ARE PARSIMGNIOUS

If' there are multiple theories that explain the data, the simplest one is usually correct. This is sometimes called the principle of simplicity. Here's a silly example that shows the principle: If I put on a blindfold and tell you how many fingers you're holding up, you can either explain this by a) telepathy (i.e., mind-reading), or b) that I cheated and saw your fingers. Which is the most parsimonious explanation? Clearly, the 'cheating' explanation is much simpler and requires the fewest assumptions.

SCIENTIFIC EXPLANATIONS ASSUME CAUSE & EFFECT

For every effect, there is a cause. If we assume no cause, the explanation is not scientific. In fact, much of psychological research is about finding the *Causes* of human behavior.

SCIENTIFIC EXPLANATIONS ARE GENERAL

Scientific findings must be applicable to other situations, to other people, to other scenarios, in other locations, at other times, etc.

This is called "external validity." If the finding only happens once and does not apply to anyone or anything else, it's not scientific.

CONSTRUCTIVIST TEACHING

Learning takes place when there is a change in the learner's existing ideas, either by adding some new knowledge or by reorganizing what is already known. There are three useful approaches to constructive science teaching.

1. Teacher demonstrates the unknown event
2. Teacher leads discussion and identifies examples drawn from student experiences
3. Students conduct the event and discuss the event

Characteristics of constructivist teaching

1. Prior awareness of the ideas that students bring to the learning situation
2. Clearly defined conceptual goals for learners
3. Use of teaching strategies which challenge or develop the initial ideas of students
4. Providing learners with opportunities to use the new ideas
5. Providing a classroom atmosphere that encourages students to suggest and discuss ideas.

BRANCHES OF CHEMISTRY

1. Analytical chemistry	1. Nuclear chemistry
2. Astro chemistry	2. Organic chemistry
3. Bio chemistry	3. Petro chemistry
4. Chemurgy	4. Phono chemistry
5. Cyto chemistry	5. Photo chemistry
6. Electro chemistry	6. Physical chemistry
7. Geo chemistry	7. Phyto chemistry
8. Histo chemistry	8. Radio chemistry
9. Immuno chemistry	9. Stereochemistry
10. Inorganiche chemistry	10. Stoichiometry
11. Kinetics	11. Thermo chemistry

12. Magneto chemistry	12. Zoo chemistry
13. Neuro chemistry	13. Zymurgy

CHEMISTRY TERMS

1. Acid, alcohol, alkali, alkalimetal, alkalineeaithmetal, alkane, allotrope, alloy, amino acid, analysis, anion, anode, ato1n,ato_mic mass, atomic number,
2. base, boiling point, bond, Brownian motion,
3. carbohydrate catalyst cathode,cation chain chainreaction, chromatography, combustion, compound, concentrated, condensation, corrosion, covalentbond, crystal,crystallization,
4. dilute, diffusion, distillation,
5. electrode, electrolysis, electron, electrovalency, element, emulsion, equation, ester, ether, evaporation, fat, fattyacid, fermentation, fission, foam, formula, fuel, fusion,gas, halogen,
6. hydrocarbon, hydrolysis, inert, inorganic, insoluble, ion, ionic bond, ionization, isomer, isotope, lanthanide or rare - earth element, liquid, litmus test,
7. meltingpoint, metal, metalloid, mineral, mixture, molarity, mole, molecule, monomer,
8. neutron, neutral, noble gas or inert gas, nonmetal, nucleus, oil, ore, organic, oxidation,
9. pH, plastic, polymer, precipitate, proton, radioactivity, reaction, reagent, redox reaction, reduction,
10. salt, saponification, saturated, soap, solid, soluble, solution, solvent, sublimation, substitutionreaction, sugar, suspension, synthesis,
11. transition metal, unsaturated valency, van der Waals forces

IMPORTANCE OF CHEMISTRY IN OUR DAILY LIFE

Everything is made of chemicals. Many of the changes we observe in the world around we see that caused by chemical reactions. Chemistry is very important because it helps to know the composition, structure & change of matter. All the matters are made up of chemistry. In our every day like various chemical are being used in various from, some of those are being used as food, some of those used changing etc.

ELEMENT IN THE HUMAN BODY

Body is made of chemical compounds, which are combinations of elements. Probably know body is mostly water, which is hydrogen and oxygen. '

HEALTH CARE AND BEAUTY

The diagnostics tests carried out in laboratories, the prognostics estimations, medical prescriptions, pills, the vaccines, the antibiotics play very vital role in health monitoring, control of diseases and in alleviating the sufferings of the humanity. Right from birth control to enhancement of life expectancy - all have been made possible using the unequivocal services of chemistry. From simple sterilization surgical instruments with antiseptic solution to chemotherapy and Genome sequencing are all nothing but applications of chemistry. Injecting cows, buffaloes, goat and with bovine some towrope Increases milk - producation but it si indiscriminately being used by sport sons to un - ethically enhance performance. Aging - a chemical change can only be checked chemically. Most beauty products are produced through chemical synthesis to clean, nurture and protect skin. However their certain ingredients are hazardous to our health in the long run.

INDUSTRIES ANF TRANSPORT

From cloth mills, lather factories, petro - chemical industries and refineries to metal industries - all use numerous fuels for power generation and chemical products for processing their product and improve the quality and simultaneously produce pollution. Now a day's chemical "effluent treatments plants use chemicals to control or neutralist he hazrdous impact of pollutants produced by the industries. Aviation and shipping industries generate power through power plants which burns fuels. Petrol and diesel amit out green house gases dangerous for ht esurvival on earth which damage the ozone layer that protects us from UV rays. As a result global warming gas taken place which is a destroyer of the planet earth. But again chemistry paves the way with bio - fuels.

FOOD SECURITY AND AGRICULTURE

The famous green revolution to increase agriculture produce so as to ensure food security was triggered by the advent of inorganic fertilizers. Since then fertilizers are extensively used by farmers to restore the ferlity of soil in the fields. Pesticides are used to protect the crop during farming and preserve the grains from pests, rats and mice during storage. Genetically modified seeds which are used to enhance production and earn profits through export food grains are agricultural application of Bio - chemistry. Whereas refrigeration system for cold storage of vegetables. and raw meat uses Poly Urethanes Foam (PUF) and the chemical properties of gases, the preservatives in packaged food products are known to have adverse impact on our body.

SCIENCE AND TECHNOLOGY

The destructive effects of Atom Bombs dropped on Hiroshima and Nagasaki. Generations in japan have suffered the decantation and three has been no solace. The threat of weapons of mass - destruction (WMDs)like Nuclear, chemical and Biological weapons looms large on the Humanity. Terrorists are using RDX and other explosive to run currents of fear 'down the spines scross the globe. Nuclear reactors which are going to serve the future generations through power generation leaves with the problem of Nuclear Waste Management. Whereas the destructive power is generated through chains of chemical reactions, we remain assured that chemistry has facilitated the chain of counter measures too in the form of safety suites and NBC resistant bunkers. Forensic science the comprehensive scientific analysis of material evidence in the context of the law uses principles of chemistry to facilitate crime investigation. Tele - communications, Information Technology and Space Missions - all banks on the chemistry of semi - conductor sand nano -tubes.

COOKING p

Chemistry explains how food changes as we cook it, how to preserve food, how our bosy uses the food eatd, and how ingredients interact to make food.

CLEANING

Part of the importance of chemistry is it explains how cleaning works. We use chemistry to help decide what cleaner is best for dishes, laundry, yourself, and to your home. We use chemistry when use bleaches and disinfectants and even ordinary soap and water. How do they work? That's chemistry.

MEDICINE

It is very need to understand basic chemistry so that we can understand how vitamins, supplements, and drugs can help or harm us. Paint of the importance's of chemistry lies in developing and testing new medical treatments and medicines.

ENVIRONMENTAL ISSUES

Chemistry is at the heart of environmental issues. What makes one chemical a nutrient and another chemical a pollutant? How we can clean up the environment? We're all chemist. We use chemical every day and perform chemical reaction without thinking much about them. Chemistry is important because everything you di is chemistry! Even our body is made of chemicals. Chemical reactions occur when we breathe, eat, or just sit there reading. All matter is made of chemicals, so the importance of chemistry is that it's the study of everything.

IMPORTANCE OF STUDYING CHEMISTRY

Chemists constantly experiment and prepare new substances for use in daily life. The list of the practical uses of chemistry is endless. All aspects of our life- food, clothing, shelter, hygiene, health, transportation, lighting, heating, entertainment, etc, are influenced by chemistry. A few examples are as follows.

1. The tablets, capsules, and injections you take when you are ill are prepared from chemicals.
2. Fertilizers, insecticides and pesticides have been developed by chemists. This has lead to an increase in the production of food. These developments have been responsible, to a large extent, for the success of the Green Revolution in India.

3. Detergents, soaps, cosmetics and perfumes are mostly products of chemistry.
4. Durable and crease-resistant synthetic fibres like nylon, rayon, and terylene have been developed through the processes of chemistry.
5. Plastic products, paints, synthetic rubber, glass and fuels for cars, aeroplanes and rockets are all gilts of chemistry.

CHEMISTRY EQUATIONS

A chemical equation is the symbolic representation of a chemical reaction wherein the reactant entities are given on the left-hand side: _and the product entities on the right-hand side. The coefficients next to the symbols and formulae of entities are the absolute values of the stoichiometric numbers.

A chemical equation consists of the chemical formulas of the reactants (the starting substances) and the chemical formula of the products (substances formed in the chemical reaction). The two are separated by an arrow symbol (usually read as "yields") and each individual substance's chemical formula is separated from others by a plus sign. As an example, the equation for the reaction of hydrochloric acid with sodium can be denoted:

$$2\ HCl + 2\ Na\ 2\ NaCl + H2$$

This equation would be read as "two HCl plus two Na yields two NaCl and H two." But, for equations involving complex chemicals, rather than reading the letter and its subscript, the chemical formulas are read using **IUPAC nomenclature**. Using IUPAC nomenclature, this equation would be read as "hydrochloric acid plus sodium yields **sodium chloride** and **hydrogen** gas."

This equation indicates that sodium and HCl react to form NaCl and H2. It also indicates that two sodium molecules are required for every two hydrochloric acid molecules and the reaction will form two sodium chloride molecules and one **diatomic** molecule of hydrogen gas molecule for every two hydrochloric acid and two sodium molecules that react.

Chemical equations can be defined as symbolic and quantitative representations of the changes that occur in the process of chemical reactions, based on the principle that matter is neither created nor destroyed during chemical reactions. For example the chemical equation $xA + yB \; pC + qD$ shows that A and B are the reactants while C and D are the products. The subscripts x, y, p and q are the stoichiometric coefficients which represent the relative amount of substance of the reactants and products. The single-headed arrow indicates the direction of the reaction and shows that the reaction is an irreversible one. The arrow means "gives", "yields" or "forms" and the plus (+) sign means "and". One of the most important ways in which chemists can communicate information about a reaction is through the writing of chemical equations. These equations enable chemists from different countries to simply and without error communicate with one another.

DIFFICULTIES IN CHEMISTRY EQUATION

According to Johnstone (2006) "Chemistry is a capabilities of human learning as well as in the intrinsic nature of the subject"

According to Johnstone (2006) "Chemistry is a capabilities of human learning as well as in the intrinsic nature of the subject." "Chemistry is a world filled with interesting phenomena, appealing experimental activities, and fruitful know for understanding the natural and manufactured world. However, it is complex nature of chemistry and also the fact that it is one of the most conceptually difficult subjects on the school curriculum; it is of major importance that anyone teaching chemistry is aware of the areas of difficulty in the subject.

The concepts and principles in _chemistry range from concrete to abstract.

Many students of chemistry find certain concepts difficult to comprehend. Their chemistry is traceable to inadequate understanding of the underlying concepts of the atomic model, and how these are used to explain macroscopic properties and laws of chemistry is a world filled with interesting phenomena, appealing experimental activities, and fruitful kno for understanding the natural and manufactured world. However, it is complex nature of chemistry and also the fact that it is one of the most conceptually difficult subjects on the school curriculum; it is of major importance that anyone teaching chemistry is aware of the areas of difficulty in the subject. The concepts and principles in chemistry range from concrete to abstract. Many students of chemistry find certain concepts difficult to comprehend. The chemistry is traceable to inadequate understanding of the underlying concepts of the atomic model, and how these are used to explain macroscopic properties and laws of chemistry.

Many students have a tendency to read a problem, find the relevant section in the book, take the approach the author used and apply it to their problem, quickly write down an answer and think that they are done. Working problems in this manner gets students good at finding answers in the book and perhaps recalling key words or recognizing correct answers when they see them. The problem is that exams do not usually ask you to find a section in the book or relate a few key words. You need to be able to generate the answers on your own.

Again, "how you practice is how you will play the game". Being able to play the chemistry game well, means a student can generate correct answers without assistance. This skill is required on an exam, so you will need to practice it. When you read a problem and you do not immediately know the answer, resist the temptation to look back in the book. Close the book, take a blank piece of paper and write out anything you know about the problem. Try any way you can think of to solve the problem. Many ways may not work, but try something. Some people who are perfectionists have a very difficult time with this. They do not want to write down wrong answers so they don't write down anything at all. By not writing anything down they cannot solve the problem so they get stuck.

When you get stuck, start Writing. When you first try this you may feel like a rat crawling through a maze and you will make a lot of wrong mental turns and bump into a lot of walls. But after going through this maze several times you will be able to travel it rapidly and get back on track even after making a wrong turn. This maze that l am referring to is your thought process and it is different for everyone. Only you can figure out how to get through yours. The sooner you do this the better you will perform.

1. Generally, students found problem solving difficult of the respondents were able to solve the questions correctly.
2. Selecting relevant information from memory and major source of difficulty as 59.7% of the total number of scripts analyzed.
3. Many students did not reach the reasoning stage, because students do not seem to have adequately developed mathematical operations in solving the stoichiometric problems. They do not think chemically about the obtained results in the problem solving process. Scripts or solutions had reasoning, probably because of careless omissions and lack of critical and logical reasoning.
4. Attempted solutions had errors in computation.

NEED AND SIGNIFICANCE OF THE STUDY

Need of the Study

1. To face the students problems in chemistry equations.
2. Studying the chemistry educations is vital for many reasons.
3. It helps to understand the science in which they live to learn how solve the problems in chemistry and improved and developed.
4. Appreciate the values enshrined in the chemistry equation problem solved.
5. To analyse variations in male and female students' problems faced; in solving equations in chemistry. To analyze variations in rural and urban students' problems faced in solving equations in chemistry.
6. To suggest possible strategies to improve the students' problem solving equations in chemistry.

Significant of the Study

1. Teachers, helps their students to improve their solving equation in chemistry.
2. Students should improve solving equation in chemistry by themselves.
3. Students should create new ideas in study on solving equations in chemistry.

STATEMENT OF THE PROBLEM

This is the title of the present study *"Problems Faced Solving Equations in Chemistry among XI The Standard Students".*

OBJECTIVES OF THE STUDY

1. To find out whether there is any significant difference between male and female students in their problems faced in solving equations in chemistry among XI standard students level.
2. To find out whether there is any significant difference between Mathematics group and Science group students in their problems faced in solving equations in chemistry among XI standard students level.
3. To find out whether there is any significant difference between Rural and Urban locality students in their problems faced in solving equations in chemistry among XI standard students level.
4. To find out whether there is any significant difference between Tamil medium and English Medium students in their problems faced in solving equations in chemistry among XI standard students level.
5. To find out whether there is any significant difference between Rural and Urban school students in their problems faced in solving equations in chemistry among XI standard students level.
6. To find out whether there is any significant difference between illiterate and literate parent's students in their problems faced in solving equations in chemistry among XI standard students level.

HYPOTHESIS OF THE STUDY

1. There is no significant difference between male and female students in their problems faced in solving equations in chemistry among XI standard students level.
2. There is no significant difference between Mathematics group and Science group students in their problems faced in solving equations in chemistry among XI standard students level.

3. There is no significant difference between Rural and Urban locality of students in their problems faced in solving equations in chemistry among XI standard students level.
4. There is no significant difference between Tamil medium and English Medium students in their problems faced in solving equations in chemistry among XI standard students level.
5. There is no significant difference between Rural and Urban school students in their problems faced in solving equations in chemistry among XI standard students level.
6. There is no significant difference between illiterate and literate parent's students in their problems faced in solving equations in chemistry among XI standard students level.

LIMITATION OF THE STUDY

1. In this study questionnaire was administrated only for Xl standard students studying at Ramanathapuram District.
2. The present information was collected only from 250 samples.

POPULATION AND SAMPLE

Population

The population is a set the totality of all objects or individuals. A population is by a group of individuals who have are studying in the X1 standard students.

Sample

A sample is a det of item of individuals selected from a larger aggregate or population. The sample selected for the present study consists of 250 Xl standard from different school with the help of stratified random sampling technique.

CONCLUSION

This chapter is deals with a detailed background of the meaning and definition, Importance's types and branches of chemistry are discussed and valuable information about the chemistry equation. It also underlined and highlighted the improved of the students problem faced. Moreover, this chapter helps the investigator to acquaint with related content of chemistry equation. Next chapter deals the review of related literature.

Chapter - II

Review of Related Literature

INTRODUCTION

Review of related literature pertaining to a problem marks the researcher familiar with the summary of previous research, the writings of recognized experts, with what is already known, what is still unknown and untested and thus provides a background for the development of the present study. A review of related literature is an important pre – requisite for the planning and efficient execution of any investigation. The study of related literature gives the investigator an idea of quantum of work done in the field makes him to scrutinize the methodology used and him to work along useful lines. This brings the researchers to the proximity of the solution.

Once a topic has been decided upon, it is essential to review all relevant material which has bearing on the topic. It is necessary to show how the problem under investigation related literature is one of the first steps of the research process. It is a valuable guide to defining the problem, recognizing its significance, suggesting promising data gathering devices, appropriate study design and source of data.

IMPORTANCE OF REVIEW OF RELATED LITERATURE

In the words of Good, "The key to the vast store house of published literature may open doors to sources of significant problems and explanatory hypothesis and provide helpful orientation for definition of the problem, background for selection of procedure, and comparative data for interpretation of results". (John.V.Best., James,V.Khan, 1993, P-155) in order to be truly creative original, one must read extensively and critically, one must read extensively and critically as a stimulus to think. "Besides enlarging the knowledge about the topic, writing a literature review will give the investigators to gain and demonstrate skills two areas.

INFORMATION SEEKING

The ability to scan the literature efficiently using manual or computerized methods, to identify a set of articles and books.

CRITICAL APPRAISAL

The ability to apply principles of analysis to identify unbiased and valid studies.

It enables the researchers to define his problem. The knowledge of related literature brings the researcher up-to-date on the work which others have done and thus to state the objective clearly used concisely.

It helps the researcher to avoid unfruitful and useless problem area.

It helps the researcher to avoid duplications of well established facts.

It helps the researcher to understand the research methodology which refers to the way; the study is to be conducted.

It helps the researchers to know about tool and instruments which proved to be useful in these previous studies.

The final and important specific reason for reviewing the related literature is to know about the recommendations of previous researchers listed in their studies for further research.

One of the essential aspects of research process is the review of related literature. It plays a crucial role in planning of the study.

Review of the related literature, besides, allowing the researcher to acquaint himself with current knowledge in the field or are in which he is going to conduct his research serves the following specific purpose.

I. By reviewing the related literature the researcher can avoid unfruitful and useless problem areas. He can select those areas in which positive finding are very, likely to result and his endeavors would be likely to add to the knowledge in a meaningful way.

II. Through the review of related literature the researcher can avoid unintentional duplication of well established findings. It is no use to replicate a study when the stability and validity of its results have been clearly established.

III. The review of related literature gives the researcher an understanding of the research methodology which refers to the way the study is to be conducted. It helps the researcher to know about the tools and instruments which proved to be useful and promising the previous studies. The advantages of the related literature are also to provide insight into the statistical methods through which validity of results is to be established.

IV. The final and important specific reason for reviewing the related literature is to know about the recommendations of previous researchers listed in their studies for further research.

NEED OF REVIEW OF RELATED LITERATURE

The review of literature is essential due to the following reasons:

1. One of the early steps I planning a research work is to review research done previously in the particular area of interest and relevant are quantitative and quantitative analysis of this research usually gives the worker an indication of the direction.

2. It is very essential for every investigator to be up-to-date in his information about the literature, related to his own problem

already done by others. It is considered the most important pre-requisite to actual planning and conducting the study.

3. It avoids the replication of the study of findings to take an advantage from similar of related literature and regards to methodology, technique of data collection procedure adopted and conclusions drawn. He can justify his own endeavor in the field.
4. It provides as source of problem of study, an analogy may be drawn for identifying and selecting the problem of research. The researchers formulate his hypothesis on the basis of review of literature. It also provides the rationale for the study. The results and findings of the study can also discuss at length. The review of literature indicates the clear picture of the problem to be solved. The scholarship in the field can be developed by reviewing the literature of the field.

OBJECTIVE REVIEW OF LITERATURE

The review of literature serves the following purpose in conducting research work.

1. It provides theories, ideas, explanations or hypothesis which may prove useful in the formulating of a new problem.
2. It indicates whether the evidence already available solves the problem adequately without requiring further investigation. It avoids the application.
3. It provides the sources for hypothesis. The researcher can formulate research hypothesis on the basis of available studies.
4. It suggests method, procedure, source of data and statistical techniques appropriate to the solution of the problem.
5. It locates comparative data and findings useful in the interpretation and discussion of results. The conclusions drawn in the related studies may be significally compared and may be used as the subject for the findings of the study.
6. It helps in developing experts and general scholarship of the investigator in the area investigated.
7. It contributes towards the accurate knowledge of the evidence or the literature.

8. It one's area of activity is a good avenue towards marking oneself. This knowledge is an institution of higher learning or a research organization.

SOURCES OF REVIEW OF LITERATURE

There are several of literatures which may be used for this purpose. These services can be broadly classified into these heads.

1. Books and Text Books materials
2. The Periodical Literature and
3. General References.

1. BOOKS AND TEXT - BOOKS MATERIALS

The most useful lift of books published in the English language is the cumulative book index and book review index, books review digest, subject guide to books indicates that books are in print or press or forthcoming books, National union catalogue is also useful for this purpose. There are a number of publications that locate specific references that cover particular are o knowledge. The cumulative book index is published in the English language.

Sources f information in the social sciences 'organized' by subject area and indexed by author and title, this work contains comprehensive list of reference books and monographs.

2. PERIODICALS

A periodical is defined as a publication issued in successive parts, usually at regular intervals, and as a rule, intended to be continued indefinitely. These include yearbooks, documents, Almanacs, the cumulative book index, international abstracts, journals, newspapers, magazines, international index to periodicals.

Periodicals generally placed in open shelves in the periodical room. Their effective use is predicted on the use of an index to identify the articles on subject matter under the study.

3. ABSTRACTS

Other types of reference guide is the abstracts, review, or digest. In addition to provide a systematized list of reference sources, it includes a summary of the contents, usually the brief summaries of research studies are given form the abstract educational abstracts in humanities.

PURPOSES OF REVIEW OF LITERATURE

The Purpose of review of literature are given below:

Discovering important variable

Distinguishing what has been done from what needs to be done.

Synthesizing the available studies to have perspective.

Determining meanings, relevance of the study and relationship with the study and its deviation from the available studies.

The main purpose of this reviews is to put of the report are to provide readers with guidelines regarding where they can look to find more information and to establish the author's credential by letting readers know that the researcher is aware of what has been going on with regard to the current and related topics.

Principles and procedures for the review of Literature

The Principles and procedures for the review of literature are given below:

It is generally advisable to get first and over all view by consulting general source, such as a text-book which is more likely to provide the meaning and nature of the concepts and variables or theoretical framework of the field. The logical starting point is to get a clear picture of the problem to be solved. A text – book usually provides the theoretical aspects of the problem. It is very essential to develop deep understanding about the variables and the field.

After developing the about the general of his problem. The investigator should review the empirical researches of the area. The best reference for this phase is the handbook of research. Encyclopedia of Educational research, the review of Educational research and international abstracts for more up to – date findings.

The research for library material must be systematic and through. The investigator generally should by collecting his reference from the educational index. When a large number of references are to be copied, they should be typed because precision is required here.

The researchers should take note systematically in the light of such criteria as uniformity, accuracy and ease of assembly. The notes should be taken on the card.

Each entry should be made separately; references should be recorded with complete bibliographic data. It should be recorded on front side of the card and content should be taken below and reverse side of it. Each note should be recorded carefully and accurately.

The investigator should take as complete notes as he might need. On the other hand, taking unnecessary notes in wasteful. The useful and necessary material should be recorder precisely. It would be better that similar sources are gathered. It is necessary that a general education of each source, rather than simply a summary of its content be made. Such evaluation is necessary both in presenting the study in the review of literature, and in using the study as background for the interpretation of the findings of the study.

The actual note – taking process is always a difficult task for the researcher. He has to spend long hours in the library taking notes by hand. It is a very tedious job and leads to importance to carelessness and illegibility. He should make use of the facilities available in the library for this purpose.

Review of related literature allows the researcher to acquaint himself with current Knowledge in the field or area in which he is going to conduct his research./ It also serves the following specific purposes.

1. The review of related literature anables the researches to define the limits of his field. It helps the researcher to delimit and define his problem. The knowledge of related literature brings the researcher up - to - data on the work. Which others have done and to state the objectives clearly and concisely.
2. By reviewing the related literature the research can avoid in fruitful and unless problem areas. He can 'select those areas in which positive findings are likely to research and his endeavors would be likely to add to the knowledge in meaningful way.

3. Through the review of related literature, the research can avoid .an unintentional duplication of well established findings. There is no use to replicate a study when the stability and validity of its result have been clearly established.
4. The review of related literature gives the research understandings of the research methodology which refers to the way study is to be conducted. It helps the research to know about the books arid instruments" which proved to be useful and promising the previous studies. The advantage of the related literature is also to provide insight into statistical methods through which validity of is to be established and
5. The final and important specific reason for reviewing the related literature is to know about the recommendations of previous research for further research which they have listed in their studies.

VALUE OF THE REVIEW OF RELATED LITERATURE

It is a valuable guide to define the problem and recognize its significance. It helps in suggesting, promising data - gathering devices, appropriate study design and sources of data. It provides suggestions for possible modifications in the research to avoid unanticipated difficulties. it unfolds a backdrop of interpreting the results of the research study.

SOURCES OF RELATED LITERATURE

The investigator identified several sources of related literature. They included,

1. Articles of Newspaper
2. Surveys of research in Education ,
3. Dissertation abstracts
4. Internet
5. Journals
6. E - Journals

7. E - Test books
8. Encyclopedia
9. Textbooks
10. Unpublished theses.

RESEARCH STUDIES DONE IN INDIA ANI) ABROAD

Rickey and Stacy (2000) in this study "The role of metacogntion in learning chemistry" discussed metacognition and its role in conceptual change and problem solving in chemistry. They argued that promoting metacognition in the science classroom prompts students to refine their ideas about scientific concepts and improves their problem solving success.

Fleming, Greg and Paul (2000) conducted a study to find out the effectiveness of molecular orbital animations for organic chemistry. The study revealed that using this theme allowed students to better understand the 'whys' and 'hows' of organic chemistry.

Fleming, Greg and Paul (2000) conducted a study to find out the effectiveness of molecular orbital animations for organic chemistry. The study revealed that using this theme allowed students to better understand the 'whys' and "hows' of organic chemistry.

Kozma and Russel (2000) conducted a historic and observational; study describing how scientists use representations and tools in the chemistry laboratory and derived its implications for the design of educational environments. They found that chemists use representations and tools to mediate between the physical substances that they study and the chemical entities and processes that underlie and account for the material qualities of these physical substances. One of the key implications arising from this study was the need for designing learning environments and symbol systems that can support the use of representations by students to understand the structures and processes that underlie their scientific investigations.

Hollingworth and McLoughlin (2001) conducted a study in developing chemistry student's metacognitive problem solving skills online. The study conducted that met cognition can be developed in contexts that engage students in self-monitoring their own problem solving approaches, in scenarios where they can ultimately use that knowledge. This requires creating real life anchors for the development of problem solving skills and enabling students to explore. test and review their own strategies. The study also anticipated that the research will result in significant changes to the way teaching in the sciences is currently conceptualised. While maximising the potential of online technologies.

Zinberg (2001) conducted a study to understand the factors that affect the decision to study chemistry at the college level. She analyzed the attitudes of' the students and the faculty towards the department, towards science in general, and towards chemistry in particular and discussed the disparity between what is valued by the students and by the faculty. One of the outcomes of the study was the conclusion that the faculty plays an important role in shaping the :social-psychological and intellectual development of its students, in part, by creating an environment within which formal learning takes place, and where the student can see an adult professional-academic chemist at work. The study concluded that the initial period of study of the subject and the interaction with the faculty is crucial for developing a positive attitude towards the subject.

Hollingworth (2001) conducted a study on the role of computers in teaching chemistry problem solving. In this study the ways in which computers and LCT used in chemistry problem solving were reviewed and details were presented of an on-line tutorial developed for enhancing the problem solving skills of science students. The research emphasized the strategic use, rather than the mere possession of knowledge that improves learning and reflective thinking required tire student to organize monitor and evaluate their thinking and learning to come to a deeper understanding of their own processes of learning.

Adesoji and Raimi (2004) examined the effect of supplementing laboratory instruction with problem solving strategy and/or practical skills teaching on student's attitude toward chemistry.

Treagusta (2004) in a study on capitalizing university student's metacognitive qualities of first year university non-major chemistry students found that many students expressed an understanding and awareness of their own learning. The students in this study, some with no chemical background were confronted with learning basic chemistry when chemistry was not necessarily their greatest passion. The results of the research provided an insight into students opinions about what and how they were learning.

Surif and Li (2004) conducted a study to find oat relationship between cognitive styles, levels of cognitive thinking and chemistry achievement among form four science students. The results revealed that the student's cognitive styles and the level of cognitive thinking should be taken into account in the teaching and learning of chemistry. Teaching styles that matched the student's cognitive styles could enhance the students learning. The study concluded that the teachers should reflect on their current teaching practices and match the needs of the students.

Danili and Reid (2004) in their research study suggested some strategies to improve performance in school chemistry, based on two cognitive factors such as working memory space and extent of field dependency. The use of the new materials was compared to the normal teaching process Working with 210 pupils aged 15 tol6. It was found that there was a significant difference in the average improvement of the experimental group and the control group, in favour of the experimental group. This result was independent of the effect of the teacher, and of the interaction of teaching method and teacher. It is suggested that approaches to learning must take into account cognitive factors in the learners in the context of information processing understandings of learning.

House (2005) tried to identify the non cognitive predictors of achievement in introductory college chemistry. The purpose of this study was to investigate the predictive relationship between initial student attitudes, admissions test scores, years of high school math taken, and subsequent achievement in introductory college chemistry. The sample consisted of l'/9 students who began as new freshmen during the same fall semester and took an introductory chemistry course daring their first year of college. The results of this study indicated that non cognitive variables were significant predictors of student performance. These findings also indicated that, for some types of academic outcomes, non cognitive variables may be better predictors of achievement than traditional measures such as admissions test scores. I

Hofstein et al (2005) studied the ability of high – school Chemistry students, who learn Chemistry through the inquiry approach, to ask meaningful and scientifically sound questions. The three common features investigated were the number of questions that were asked by each of the students, the cognitive level of the questions, and the nature of the questions that were chosen by the students, for the purpose of further investigation. It was found that students in the inquiry group who had experience in asking questions in the Chemistry laboratory outperformed the control group in their ability to ask more and better questions.

Danili and Reid (2006) analyzed the cognitive factors that can potentially affect pupil's test performance. The two cognitive styles, 'field dependent/field independent' and 'convergent/ divergent', were explored in relation to three formats of assessment (multiple choice, short answer and structural communication grid) in five classroom chemistry tests.

Liu (2006) conducted a study' to test the hypothesis that computer modeling enhanced hands-on chemistry laboratories are more effective than hands- on laboratories or computer modeling laboratories alone in facilitating high school student's understanding of chemistry concepts. Thirty-three high school chemistry students from a private all-girl high school in northeastern United States were selected as the sample. The combined computer modeling and hands-on laboratories were more effective than either computer simulations or hands-on laboratory alone in promoting student's conceptual understanding of chemistry concepts. The study revealed that coupling computer modeling with traditional chemistry laboratory activities can be effective in facilitating chemistry learning.

Frailich, Kesner and Hofstein (2007) investigated the influence of Web based chemistry learning on student's perceptions of the classroom learning environment, attitudes their attitudes regarding the relevance of chemistry and achievements. The experimental group was treated with four relevant activities from the Website that was developed, all dealing with the concept of chemical bonding. It was found that the experimental group outperformed the comparison group significantly in most of the research categories. The study concluded that the web-based learning environment has potential to enhance the comprehension of chemistry concepts, student's attitudes and interests and to increase student's and /ai'eliess regarding the relevant aspects of chemistry to daily life.

Sirhan (2007) in his study tried to find out the key reasons for the difficulty in learning Chemistry at school level. The problems identified were related to understandings of attitudes and motivation as Well as the psychological understandings. The common problems were working memory overload, language and communication, lack of motivation and difficulty in concept formation. The study also emphasised the need for motivation and development of positive attitude in effective chemistry learning.

Bassey, Umoren and Udida (2007) investigated the influence of cognitive styles and attitude on the academic performance of 200 senior secondary students in chemistry in Akwa lbom State. The study revealed that there was a significant difference in student academic performance in chemistry due to their cognitive styles; students with analytic cognitive styles performed significantly higher than relational and inferential. There was a significant positive relationship between student's attitude to chemistry and their performance in chemistry.

Uzuntiryaki (2007) conducted a study on learning styles and high school student's chemistry achievement. Two hundred and sixty five tenth grade students enrolled in chemistry course and seven chemistry teachers were participated in the study. Results showed that there was a statistically significant difference among students with different learning styles with respect to chemistry achievement. But there was no statistically significant effect of matching between student's learning styles and teacher's learning styles on student's chemistry' achievement.

Rahmawati (2008) conducted a study on utilizing metacognitive skills and green chemistry for self reflection: An auto ethnographic research. The study revealed that the metacognitive skills and green chemistry approaches are powerful for creating meaningful learning experiences for students and sustainability in education. Thereby empowering the students to participate actively in society. The green chemistry approaches not only promote the idea of sustainability. but also the student's empowerment.

Neerinck and Palmer (2009) comprehensive analysis of the attitudes of Belgian chemistry students, who had chosen their specialist study area for their final of chemistry studies, towards organic chemistry, physical chemistry, inorganic chemistry, biochemistry and analytical chemistry, The aim of the study was to examine how the student attitudes towards that science relate to the student's development within that science after having taken the decision to pursue physical sciences. The study found that if attitude-behaviour congruency is relevant in determining course selection, then choice of course is not so much determined by the evaluative and potency attitudes of the students by, their activity attitudes.

Hussein and Reid (2009) analysed working memory and difficulties in school chemistry. The study involved various diagnostic surveys of areas of difficulties, 'followed by the redesign of several large portions of the curriculum presentation. The paper focused on the outcomes in terms of understanding. The new teaching materials were designed explicitly in such a way that the working memory demand was lowered. To develop more positive attitudes, applications were stressed. The curriculum content was not changed, teachers were not trained in any way in the use of the materials, and the time allocation remained the same.

Alavi and Hoseini (2009) in their study identified the effect of the educational factors on the academic performance in chemistry of Shahid Bahonar University students. "General Chemistry" in of Kerman was chosen as one of the subsets of chemistry and students were randomly selected the research sample. For data analysis, 't' test and one-sided variance analysis were used. The results of the research showed that motivation, previous experiences, emotional conditions, instructor, valuation procedures, academic records, and age had a positive effect the university student's academic performance. The student's age had effect on their performance in chemistry. The physical environment, the student's parent's educational level and job and the student's gender; had not a meaningful effect on the student's performance.

Furlan and Bell-Loncella (2010) studied the effects of integrating computation and visualization in a general chemistry laboratory module to enhance learning of IR spectroscopy. The effectiveness of the computation—visualization component was measured by pre- and post quizzes, a survey, and I correct interpretation_ of experimental IR spectra. The assessment results showed that the student's conceptual understanding of IR spectroscopy was enhanced and that their ability to interpret IR spectra improved. Students learned the basics of the software package, gained invaluable introductory skills in molecular modeling and computational chemistry, and enjoyed the experience.

Kind and Kind (2011) conducted a study among 150 pre-service science teachers (PST's) to compare individual academic and personal characteristics with their misconceptions about basic chemical ideas taught to 1 l-16 year-olds, such as particle theory, change of state, conservation of mass, chemical bonding, mole calculations, and combustion reactions. Data, collected by questionnaire, indicated that despite all PSTS being regarded technically as 'academically well-qualified' for science teaching, biology and physics specialists have more extensive misconceptions than chemists. Samuel (2012) in his study on Remediation of student's weakness for enhanced achievement in chemistry investigated the effectiveness of Diagnostic Remedial Teaching (DRT) strategy (referred to as Component Task Analysis Model of instruction, CUTAM) in enhancing student's achievement in Chemistry.

Ali (2612) conducted a case study of the common difficulties experienced by high school students in chemistry classroom, the possible reasons for these difficulties, and the Ways in which teachers help students overcome these difficulties in Gilgit-Baltistan (Pakistan). A qualitative case study method was used to investigate the questions, which used in-depth interviews with teachers, classroom observation, and post observation, discussion with the teachers, as main data collection tools.

CONCLUSION

This chapter review of related literature discussed about the importance of the related studies. More which also discussed about the studies done in India and abroad connected with the present study. The third chapter will present the research methodology of the present study.

Chapter -III

Methodology

INTRODUCTION

Research is considered to be format, systematic and intensive process of carrying on a scientific method of analysis (Best and khan, 1992). It requires careful enquiry and application of various techniques of thinking, employing validated tools and instruments and systematic procedures in order to understand a problem.

Research is directed towards the solution of a problem through planned and systematic procedures. The success of any research programme largely depends on the suitability of the method and the tools and techniques used to collect reliable and valuable data.

"Method or methodology refers to the way the study is to be conducted. It refers to design through which validity of results is to be established" (Heyman, 1968).The selection of appropriate methods depends upon the nature of the problem selected. Hence, methodology occupies a prominent place in any kind of research. The method selected should always be appropriate to problem under investigation, feasible, preplanned and well understood. Wastage of time, energy and money could be averted and efficiency of the research could be raised by the appropriate application of methodology. In research, varieties of methods and techniques have been developed to obtain relevant data for analysis and interpretation of data. Researchers point out that a method selected for the investigation should always be relevant and appropriate to the said that wastage of energy, money and time can be easily averted by choosing appropriate methodology for an investigation. Thus methodology plays an important position in many type of research.

In this chapter, the detailed methodology followed for studying the present study is explained. The general aim of the study is to find out the problems faced in solving equations in chemistry among IX std Students. The objectives of the study, assumptions of the study, hypotheses of the study, research strategy, tools and sample and data collection procedures are outlined in this chapter.

STATEMENT OF THE PROBLEM

The title of the present study is precisely stated below: *"A Study on Impact of Teaching the Epic Silappathikaram in Dramatization among IX th Standard Students".*

DEFINITION OF KEY TERMS

The key terms used in the present study are conceptualized in order to facilitate objective collection and measurement of data.

Chemistry

Chemistry is one of the most important branches of science; it enables learners to understand what happened around them. Because chemistry topics are generally related to or based on the structure of matter, chemistry proves a difficult subject for many students. Chemistry curricula commonly incorporate many abstract concepts, which are central to further learning in both chemistry and other sciences.

Problem

Equations of chemistry

Student

Person who is studying for a XI standard Ramanathapuram District Hr. Secondary school as students.

OBJECTIVE OF THE STUDY

1. To find out whether there is any significant difference between male and female students in their problems faced in solving equations in chemistry among XI standard students level.
2. To find out whether there is any significant difference between Mathematics group and Science group students in their problems faced in solving equations in chemistry among XI standard students level.
3. To find out whether there is any significant difference between Rural and Urban locality of students in their problems faced in solving equations in chemistry among XI standard students level.
4. To find out whether there is any significant difference between Tamil medium and English Medium students in their problems faced in solving equations in chemistry among XI standard students level.
5. To find out whether there is any significant difference between Rural and Urban school students in their problems faced in solving equations in chemistry among XI standard students level.
6. To find out whether there is any significant difference between illiterate and literate parent's students in their problems faced in solving equations in chemistry among XI standard students level.

HYPOTHESIS OF THE STUDY

1. There is no significant difference between male and female students in their problems faced in solving equations in chemistry among XI standard students level.
2. There is no significant difference between Mathematics group and Science group students in their problems faced in solving equations in chemistry among XI standard students level.
3. There is no significant difference between Rural and Urban locality of students in their problems faced in solving equations in chemistry among XI standard students level.
4. There is no significant difference between Tamil medium and English Medium students in their problems faced in solving

equations in chemistry among XI standard students level.

5. There is no significant difference between Rural and Urban school students in their problems faced in solving equations in chemistry among XI standard students level.

6. There is no significant difference between illiterate and literate parent's students in their problems faced in solving equations in chemistry among XI standard students level.

RESEARCH METHOD

Research method is a systematic procedure in which the desired outcomes are achieved by setting up situation in such a form that the investigator gathers information and draws conclusions on the basis of the collected data. In this study, survey method is considered as the appropriate method to study the Problem solving equations in chemistry among XI Std Students. The general type of data gathering instrument used in survey research is called questionnaire through which respondents respond to from the target population. Investigators consider four basic standards of questionnaire, 2) common questions for all individual respondent, 3) ability to respond the item by the respondents and 4) Willing to respond the items in the questionnaire.

In the present study, questionnaires are selected due to the following reasons:

1. In survey, the investigator may directly meet the respondents and has an opportunity to establish a rapport with them. This kind of rapport motivates the respondents to respond all the items in the questionnaire in an enthusiastic way.

2. There is an opportunity for the investigator to explain the purpose of the study, so that the respondents could respond promptly and objectively.

3. Sometimes the respondents may not be in a position to understand the meaning of the items given in the questionnaire. At that time, the investigator may explain the real meaning of the items so as to help the respondents to have clarity about the concept.

4. The use of questionnaires in Survey research helps in saving money, time and energy by convering a large number of respondents at a given time.
5. Normally, the respondents do not like to indicate their names and feel free to express their views and options. Questionnaire helps the researchers collect data in a confidential way and even the researcher does not know from whom she has collected a particular response. the anonymity ensures frank response and leads to objective collection of data.
6. It is understood that the questionnaire reduces the burden of the respondents and permits to get immediate and proper response.
7. Questionnaires are the most flexible tools which posses' unique advantages over other kind of tools in collecting both quantitative and qualitative data.
8. The data obtained from the questionnaire could be easily scored, tabulated and analyzed, when compared with other research tools.

STAGES OF RESEARCH

The present study involves the following research steps:

Stage 1:

Clarity of problem

In order to ensure the clarity of the problem, the review of related literature is done.

Stage 2:

Selection of research method At the second step of research, appropriate research method is identified.

Stage 3:

Identification of research tools.

At this stage relevant tools for collection of data are identified.

Stage 4:

Selection of Sample

The size of the sample and the appropriate sampling technique are decided at this stage.

Stage 5:

Tool administration and data collection

This stage involves the administration of tools to the subjects and the collection of relevant data from the sample.

Stage 6:

Data analysis.

The collected data are classified and tabulated. they are further analysed by using appropriate statistical techniques.

Stage 7:

Presentation of findings

The data analysis as a result of the application of statistical techniques are presented as findings

RESEARCH TOOLS

The following tools are used to collect relevant data from the respondents. Personal Data Sheet (PDS) Problems faced in solving equations in chemistry developed by the investigator, which consists of 46 questions.

PROBLEM SCALE

This scale was developed and validated by Researcher. The tool was systematically developed by following pre- pilot stage, pilot stage and post-pilot stage. In the pre-pilot stage a total of 50 items was collected. Then the items were presented to the experts in the field to seek their opinion regarding suitability and clarity of items. On the basis of suggestions provided by experts, some items were discarded. Finally 46 items were retained for inclusion in the questionnaire.

SCORING PROCEDURE OF PROBLEM FACED EQUATIONS CHEMISTRY PROBLEM SCALE

This tool is made up of two alternatives – Yes or No

1) A score of 1 is assigned to 'Yes' response.

2) A Score of 0 is assigned to 'No' response.

RELIABILITY AND VALIDITY OF THE SCALE

The author of the tool used rational equivalence method to calculate the co-efficient of reliability. The correlation co-efficient of 0.77 was calculated. This indicates high reliability of the scale. Regarding validity, the author established face validity and content validity of the scale. Based on the systematic procedure followed in developing the tool, it is confidently said that the tool has sufficient content validity.

STUDENT INFORMATION BLANK (PDS)

In the present study, the questionnaire known as 'Student information Blank' was used to collect certain data related to higher Secondary XI students. The Student information Blank aims at collecting information regarding the following:

1)	Gender	:	Male / Female
2)	Age	:	
3)	Group	:	Mathematics/ Science Group
4)	Locality of Student	:	Rural / Urban
5)	Medium	:	Tamil/ English
1)	Locality School	:	Rural / Urban
2)	Parent's Qualification	:	Illiterate / literate

SAMPLE FOR THE STUDY

In the present study, 12 schools in the Ramanathapuram Dt. were selected by means of stratified random sampling technique. From the 12 Schools, a sample of 250 students was selected by means of stratified random sampling technique. the students were stratified on the basis of their gender, Group, locality of school, medium, Locality of School and parent Qualification. The School wise distribution of the sample is given below:

TABLE 2

SCHOOL -WISE DISTRIBUTION OF SAMPLE

S.NO	School	N
1	Govt. Boys Hr. Sec. School – Thiruvadanai	22
2	Syed Ammal Hr. Sec. School - Ramanathapuram	21
3	Govt. Girls Hr. Sec. School – R.S. Mangalam	20
4	St. Arulanthar Hr. Sec. School – Ooriyur	22
5	St. Andrews Girls Hr. Sec. School – Ramanathapuram	20
6	Govt. Girls Hr. Sec. School – Thiruvandanai	22
7	Govt. Hr. Sec. School – Sanaveli	20
8	Municipality Girls Hr. Sec. School – Ramanathapuram	21
9	Govt. Boys Hr. Sec. School - R.S. Mangalam	21
10	Swartzs Boys Hr. Sec. School- Ramanathapuram	19
11	AVMS Hr. Sec. School – Ramanathapuram	19
12	St. Francies Hr. Sec. School – C.K. Mangalam	23
	Total	250

DATA COLLECTION

In the present study, the two questionnaires were directly administered to the higher Secondary students in order to ensure objective collection of data. This is preferred because it enhances high response rate her has an opportunity to clarity the doubts raised by the respondents.

Before the administration of tools, necessary permission was obtained from the Heads master. Having obtained permission from the questionnaires was administered to the students who are pursuing their courses of study in the 12 school. Prior to the tool administration, proper explanations were given by the investigator about the present investigation and the mode of responding the items in the questionnaires. The respondents were informed that the data collected would be utilized for statistical analysis and interpretation only and not other purposes. A close rapport was maintained with the respondents in order to create an open and friendly environment: The friendly approach in the data collection procedures would help to collect objective and valid data from the student respondents. No time limit was fixed white responding the items. The respondents were asked to respond all the items in the questionnaires. Thus attempts were made to collect objective data from the XI students of Ramanathapuram(dt).

DATA ANALYSIS

In the present study, the collected data are analyzed by using appropriate statistical techniques. The data collected are analyzed at two levels-descriptive and differential.

For descriptive analysis of data, mean and SD scores are calculated.

For differential analysis, 't' test is applied in order to find out the significance of difference between means.

DELIMITATIONS OF THE STUDY

Following are the delimitations of the study:

1) The study was confined to twelve schools which are under the Control of Ramanathapuram (Dt)
2) Only the XI students are included within the purview of the study.
3) Among the different facets of Chemistry Equations only the problems faced that are found
4) The data for studying the chemistry Equation problem faced are collected only through questionnaire.
5) Even though many methods are available, only survey method is selected because of its suitability.

CONCLUSION

In this chapter, the systematic plan and procedure followed for studying in the present investigation is described in detail. Appropriate Hypotheses are formulated to set the research in right direction. the research strategy followed is explained. The selection of tools and the mode of scoring are elaborated. The sampling technique, the data collection procedures and data analysis are also discussed. Finally, the delimitations of the study are also explained. The next chapter deals with the analysis and interpretation of the collected data.

Chapter-IV

Analysis of Data

INTRODUCTION

This chapter deals with the statistical analysis of the data with reference to the hypotheses. Interpretation is also made to account for the result. The choice of statistical techniques for data analysis is largely determined by the research hypothesis to be tested.

Analysis and interpretation of data collected are the two major steps in the process at research. For a good research work, a systematic organization, classification and tabulation of the data are essential. The data collected through the administration of the tools or any other manner need to be systemized, organized and analyzed in other to determine the inherent meaning.

MEANING

The analysis and interpretation of data involves the objective material in the possession of the research and his subjective reactions and desire to derive from the data, the inherent meaning in their reactions to the problem.

NEEDS FOR ANALYSIS

In the present study, we have obtained a series of paired data which are to be analysis because these are correlated. The nature and extent of relation is essential to make decisions, formulate policies and estimate future. The study of relations makes decision making more effective and useful. The provide valuable information which analyst can employ to support a judgment concerning the existence of a cause effect relationship between the variable selected for analysis.

STATISTICAL TECHNIQUES APPLIED IN DATA ANALYSIS

The following statistical techniques were applied to analyses and interpret the collected data.

1. Descriptive Analysis
2. Differential Analysis
3. Descriptive Analysis

In order to find out whether the problem faced in solve equations in chemistry mean and SD course of calculated and values presented in the tabular form

Variable	max scores	mean value	mean	SD
Problem faced equations chemistry	46	23	26.33	5.29

1. DIFFERENTIAL ANALYSIS

In the present study attempt made to find out whether problem faced in solve equations in chemistry among eleven standard student the variables classified or the follows

1.	Gender	:	Male/Female
2.	Group	:	Mathematics /Science
3.	Locality of student	:	Rural /Urban
4.	Medium of Instruction	:	Tamil/English
5.	Locality of school	:	Rural/Urban
6.	Parent's qualification	:	Illiterate / Literate

In order to find out significance of difference between the groups which are classified on the basis of the above categories 't' test is employer This sun section deals with the application of 't' test interpretation of result.

HYPOTHESES -I

GENDER

There is no significance difference between male and female students on the problems faced in solving equations in chemistry among XI standard students level.

Table 1

Significance of difference between male and female students problems faced in solving equations in chemistry among XI standard students level.

Gender	Mean	SD	N	't' Value	Significance
Male	26.60	5.59	88		Level 0.05
Female	26.06	5.00	162	0.71	Accepted

Table value: 1.96

The above table reveals the following conclusions

The male and female XI standard students do not differ in problems faced in solving equations in chemistry testified by the't' value 0.71 which is not significant at 0.05 level of confidence.

From the table it is found that gender of students is not a variable influencing problem faced in solving equations in chemistry hence the Hypotheses is accepted.

HYPOTHESES -II

GROUP

There is no significance difference between mathematics group and science group students on the problems faced in solving equations in chemistry among XI standard students level.

Table 2

Significance of difference between mathematics group and science group students problems faced in solving equations in chemistry among XI standard students level.

Group	Mean	SD	N	't' Value	Significance Level 0.05
Mathematics	26.21	5.71	118		
Science	26.28	4.77	132	0.10	Accepted

Table value: 1.96

The above table reveals the following conclusions

The male and female XI standard students do not differ in problem faced in solving equations in chemistry testified by the't' value 0.10 which is not significant at 0.05 level of confidence.

From the table it is found that subject of students is not a variable influencing problems faced in solving equations in chemistry hence the Hypotheses is accepted.

HYPOTHESES -III

Locality of student

There is no significance difference between Rural and Urban locality of students on the problems faced in solving equations in chemistry among XI standard students level.

Table 3

Significance of difference between Rural and Urban locality of students problems faced in solving equations in chemistry among XI standard students level.

Locality of student	Mean	SD	N	't' Value	Significance Level 0.05
Rural	25.86	4.82	155		
Urban	26.88	5.77	95	1.44	Accepted

The above table reveals the following conclusions

The Rural and urban XI standard students do not differ in problem faced in solving equations in chemistry testified by the't' value 1.44which is not significant at 0.05 level of confidence. From the table it is found that of Locality of students is not a variable influencing problems faced in solving equations in chemistry hence the Hypotheses is accepted.

HYPOTHESES -IV

Medium of Instruction

There is no significance difference between Tamil and English medium students on the problems faced in solving equations in chemistry among XI standard students level.

Table 4

Significance of difference between Tamil and English medium students problems faced in solving equations in chemistry among XI standard students level.

Medium of Instruction	Mean	SD	N	't' Value	Significance Level 0.05
Tamil	26.01	5.07	139		
English	26.54	5.39	111	0.79	Accepted

Table value : 1.96

The above table reveals the following conclusions

The Tamil and English XI standard students do not differ in problems faced in solving equations in chemistry testified by the 't' value 0.79 which is not significant at 0.05 level of confidence.

From the table it is found that of Medium of Instruction students is not a variable influencing problems faced in solving equations in chemistry hence the Hypotheses is accepted.

HYPOTHESES -V

Locality of school

There is no significance difference between Rural and Urban school students on the problems faced in solving equations in chemistry among XI standard students level.

Table 5

Significance of difference between Rural and Urban students problems faced in solving equations in chemistry among XI standard students level.

Locality of student	Mean	SD	N	't' Value	Significance Level 0.05
Rural	24.86	4.92	101		
Urban	27.19	5.21	149	3.59	Rejected

Table value : 1.96

The above table reveals the following conclusions

The Rural and urban XI standard students do not differ in problems faced in solving equations in chemistry testified by the't' value 3.59 which is not significant at 0.05 level of confidence.

From the table it is found that of Locality of school **students** is not a variable influencing problems faced in solving equations in chemistry hence the Hypotheses is rejected.

HYPOTHESES -VI

Parent qualification

There is no significance difference between Illiterate/Literate Parent's students on the problems faced in solving equations in chemistry among XI standard students level.

Table 6

Significance of difference between Illiterate /Literate Parent's students problems faced in solving equations in chemistry among XI standard students level.

Parent Qualification	Mean	SD	N	't' Value	Significance Level 0.05
Illiterate	29.34	5.35	32		
Literate	25.79	5.05	218	3.53	Rejected

Table value : 1.96

The above table reveals the following conclusions

The Illiterate/ Literate XI standard Parent's students do not differ in problems faced in solving equations in chemistry testified by the 't' value 3.53 which is not significant at 0.05 level of confidence.

From the table it is found that of Parent qualification **students** is not a variable influencing problems faced in solving equations in chemistry hence the Hypotheses is rejected.

RESULT OF HYPOTHESES TEST

In the present study, six hypotheses are formulated to testing. The result of hypotheses testing is presented below.

HYPOTHESES - I

There is no significance difference between male and female students on the problem faced in solving equations in chemistry among XI standard students level. The calculated t = 0.071 reveals no significant difference between the group against the hypotheses accepted.

HYPOTHESES – II

There is no significance difference between mathematics group and science group students on the problem faced in solving equations in chemistry among XI standard students level. The calculated t = 0.010 reveals no significant difference between the group against the hypotheses accepted.

HYPOTHESES – III

There is no significance difference between Rural and Urban locality of students on the problem faced in solving equations in chemistry among XI standard students level. The calculated t = 1.44 reveals no significant difference between the group against the hypotheses accepted.

HYPOTHESES – IV

There is no significance difference between Tamil and English medium students on the problem faced in solving equations in chemistry among XI standard students level. The calculated t = 0.79 reveals no significant difference between the group against the hypotheses accepted.

HYPOTHESES - V

There is no significance difference between Rural and Urban School students on the problem faced in solving equations in chemistry among XI standard students level. The calculated t = 3.59 reveals significant difference between the group against the hypotheses rejected.

HYPOTHESES - VI

There is no significance difference between Illiterate/Literate Parent's students on the problem faced in solving equations in chemistry among XI standard students level. The calculated t = 3.53. Reveals significant difference between the groups against the hypotheses rejected.

CONCLUSION

Analysis and Interpretation of the Hypothesis are given in this chapter. In the upcoming chapter summary and conclusion of the study will be given.

Chapter - V

Summary and Conclusion

INTRODUCTION

Chemistry is one of the most important branches of science; it enables learners to understand what happened around them. Because chemistry topics are generally related to or based on the structure of matter, chemistry proves a difficult subject for many students. Chemistry curricula commonly incorporate many abstract concepts, which are central to further learning in both chemistry and other sciences. The branch of science concerned with the substances of which matter is composed, the investigation of their properties and reactions, and the use of such reactions to form new substances.

Chemistry is often regarded as a difficult subject, an observation that sometimes repels learners from continuing with studies in chemistry. With the establishment of new syllabuses in chemistry for secondary schools in different countries in the last decayed. One of the essential characteristics of chemistry is the constant interplay between the macroscopic and microscopic levels of thought, and it is this aspect of chemistry (and physics) learning that represents a significant challenge to novices.

STATEMENT OF THE PROBLEM

The title of the present study is precisely stated below: "*Problems Faced Solving Equations In Chemistry Among XI The Standard Students*".

NEED AND SIGNIFICANCE OF THE STUDY

1. To improve the students attitude of creatively in science.
2. To analyse variations in male and female students 'attitude of creativity in science.
3. To analyse variations in government and government aided and self finance students' attitude of creativity in science.

Significance of the study

1. Teachers, helps their students to improve their attitude and creativity
2. Students should improve attitude and creativity by themselves.
3. Students should create new ideas in science.

OBJECTIVE OF THE STUDY

1. To find out whether there is any significant difference between male and female students in their problems faced in solving equations in chemistry among XI standard students level.
2. To find out whether there is any significant difference between Mathematics group and Science group students in their problems faced in solving equations in chemistry among XI standard students level.
3. To find out whether there is any significant difference between Rural and Urban locality of students in their problems faced in solving equations in chemistry among XI standard students level.
4. To find out whether there is any significant difference between Tamil medium and English Medium students in their problems faced in solving equations in chemistry among XI standard students level.

5. To find out whether there is any significant difference between Rural and Urban school students in their problems faced in solving equations in chemistry among XI standard students level.
6. To find out whether there is any significant difference between illiterate and literate Parent's students in their problems faced in solving equations in chemistry among XI standard students level.

HYPOTHESIS OF THE STUDY

1. There is no significant difference between male and female students in their problems faced in solving equations in chemistry among XI standard students level.
2. There is no significant difference between Mathematics group and Science group students in their problems faced in solving equations in chemistry among XI standard students level.
3. There is no significant difference between Rural and Urban locality of students in their problems faced in solving equations in chemistry among XI standard students level.
4. There is no significant difference between Tamil medium and English Medium students in their problems faced in solving equations in chemistry among XI standard students level.
5. There is no significant difference between Rural and Urban School students in their problems faced in solving equations in chemistry among XI standard students level.
6. There is no significant difference between illiterate and literate Parent's students in their problems faced in solving equations in chemistry among XI standard students level.

RESEARCH METHOD

Research method is a systematic procedure in which the desired outcomes are achieved by setting up situation in such a form that the investigator gathers information and draws conclusions on the basis of the collected data (Good, 1945). In this study, survey method is considered as the appropriate method to problem faced in solving equations chemistry among XI Std students. The general type of data gathering instrument used in survey research is called questionnaire through which respondents respond to from the target population. Investigators consider four basic standards of questionnaire, 2) common questions for all individual respondent, 3) ability to respond the item by the respondents and 4) willing to respond the items in the questionnaire (Floyd Flower, 1984).

In the present study, questionnaires are selected due to the following reasons:

1. In survey, the investigator may directly meet the respondents and has an opportunity to establish a rapport with them. this kind of rapport motivates the respondents to respond all the items in the questionnaire in an enthusiastic way.
2. There is an opportunity for the investigator to explain the purpose of the study, so that the respondents could respond promptly and objectively.
3. Sometimes the respondents may not be in a position to understand the meaning of the items given in the questionnaire. At that time, the investigator may explain the real meaning of the items so as to help the respondents to have clarity about the concept.
4. The use of questionnaires in Survey research helps in saving money, time and energy by convering a large number of respondents at a given time.
5. Normally, the respondents do not like to indicate their names and feel free to express their views and options. Questionnaire helps the researchers collect data in a confidential way and even the researcher does not know from whom she has collected a particular response. the anonymity ensures frank response and leads to objective collection of data.
6. It is understood that the questionnaire reduces the burden of the respondents and permits to get immediate and proper response.
7. Questionnaires are the most flexible tools which posses' unique advantages over other kind of tools in collecting both quantitative and qualitative data.

8. The data obtained from the questionnaire could be easily scored, tabulated and analyzed, when compared with other research tools.

RESEARCH TOOLS

The following tools are used to collect relevant data from the respondents. Personal Data Sheet (PDS)

Problem faced in solving equations in chemistry develop by the investigator

SAMPLE

The following tools are used to collect relevant data from the respondents.

Personal Data Sheet (PDS)

Problem faced in solving equations in chemistry develop by the investigator

PROBLEM SCALE

This scale was developed and validated by Researcher. The tool was systematically developed by following pre- pilot stage, pilot stage and post-pilot stage. In the pre-pilot stage a total of 50 items was collected. Then the items were presented to the experts in the field to seek their opinion regarding suitability and clarity of items. On the basis of suggestions provided by experts, some items were discarded. Finally 46 items were retained for inclusion in the questionnaire.

SCORING PROCEDURE OF PROBLEM FACED EQUATION CHEMISTRY PROBLEM SCALE

This tool is made up of two alternatives – Yes or No

1) A score of 1 is assigned to 'Yes' response.

2) A Score of 0 is assigned to 'No' response.

RELIABILITY AND VALIDITY OF THE SCALE

The author of the tool used rational equivalence method to

calculate the co-efficient of reliability. The correlation co-efficient of 0.77 was calculated. This indicates high reliability of the scale. Regarding validity, the author established face validity and content validity of the scale.

Based on the systematic procedure followed in developing the tool, it is confidently said that the tool has sufficient content validity.

STUDENT INFORMATION BLANK (PDS)

In the present study, the questionnaire known as 'Student information Blank' was used to collect certain data related to higher Secondary XI students. The Student information Blank aims at collecting information regarding the following:

1) Gender : Male / Female
2) Age :
3) Group : Mathematics/ Science Group
4) Locality of Student : Rural / Urban
5) Medium : Tamil/ English
6) Locality School : Rural / Urban
7) Parent's Qualification : Illiterate / literate

DATA COLLECTION

In the present study, the two questionnaires were directly administered to the higher Secondary students in order to ensure objective collection of data. This is preferred because it enhances high response rate her has an opportunity to clarity the doubts raised by the respondents.

Before the administration of tools, necessary permission was obtained from the Heads master. Having obtained permission from the questionnaires was administered to the students who are pursuing their courses of study in the 12 school. Prior to the tool administration, proper explanations were given by the investigator about the present investigation and the mode of responding the items in the questionnaires. The respondents were informed that the data collected would be utilized for statistical analysis and interpretation only and not other purposes. A close rapport was maintained with the respondents in order to create an open and friendly environment: The friendly approach in the data collection procedures would help to collect objective and valid data from the student respondents. No time limit was fixed white responding the items. The respondents were asked to respond all the items in the questionnaires. Thus attempts were made to collect objective data from the XI students of Ramanathapuram District.

APPLICATION OF STATISTICAL TECHNIQUES

In the present study, the collected data are analyzed by using appropriate statistical techniques. The data collected are analyzed at two levels-descriptive and differential.

For descriptive analysis of data, mean and SD scores are calculated. For differential analysis, 't' test is applied in order to find out the significance of difference between means.

DELIMITATIONS OF THE STUDY

Following are the delimitations of the study:

1. The study was confined to twelve departments which are under the Control of Ramanathapuram (Dt)
2. Only the XI students are included within the purview of the study.
3. Among the different facets of Chemistry Equations only the problems faced that are found
4. The data for studying the chemistry Equation problem faced are collected only through questionnaire.
5. Even though many methods are available, only survey method is selected because of its suitability.

MAJOR FINDINGS

In the present study, six hypotheses are formulated to testing. The result of hypotheses testing is presented below.

Hypotheses-I There is no significance difference between male and female students on the problems faced in solving equations in chemistry among XI standard students level. The calculated t = 0.071 reveals no significant difference between the group against the hypotheses accepted.

Hypotheses -II There is no significance difference between mathematics group and science group students on the problems faced in solving equations in chemistry among XI standard students level. The calculated t = 0.010 reveals no significant difference between the group against the hypotheses accepted.

Hypotheses -III There is no significance difference between Rural and Urban locality of students on the problems faced in solving equations in chemistry among XI standard students level. The calculated t = 1.44 reveals no significant difference between the group against the hypotheses accepted.

Hypotheses -IV There is no significance difference between Tamil and English medium students on the problems faced in solving equations in chemistry among XI standard students level. The calculated t = 0.79 reveals no significant difference between the group against the hypotheses accepted.

Hypotheses -V There is no significance difference between Rural and Urban School students on the problems faced in solving equations in chemistry among XI standard students level. The calculated t = 3.59 reveals significant difference between the group against the hypotheses rejected.

Hypotheses -VI There is no significance difference between Illiterate/Literate Parent's students on the problems faced in solving equations in chemistry among XI standard students level. The calculated t = 3.53. reveals significant difference between the groups against the hypotheses rejected.

IMPLICATION OF THE STUDY

1. Research study may be conducted on the development of problem faced in solving equations in chemistry to all level students.
2. Research study may be conducted to village students.
3. Research study may be conduct to Tamilnadu chemistry research centres.

SUGGESTION FOR FURTHER RESEARCH

1. The following research topics are suggested for further research in this area.
2. Every institution should take care and motivate the student's problem solving chemistry equation.
3. The same study may be conducted and developed students problem faced in solving equations in chemistry.
4. Some variables may also be taken for further study.
5. The investigation may be extended to higher secondary level for find out problem faced in solving equations in chemistry.
6. The investigation area may be extended to some more districts, state and national level.
7. Furthermore this study can be extended at research and developed level (M.Phil and Ph.D.) to find out the efficacy.

CONCLUSION

In the present study that the Conclusion, attempts are made to find out the problems faced solving equations in chemistry among at XI standard students. The study also reveals that the four hypothesis research there are no significance difference between the boys and girls students science & Maths group students, locality of rural &urban students, Tamil and English medium students. It is based in the findings, the last two hypothesis research students there is significance difference between rural &urban school students literate parent's students& Illiterate parent's students on the problems faced in solving equations in chemistry among at XI standard students level. Further study of the research the investigation will be conducted at higher level to find out the students level. It is also reveals that will be extended in future level.

BIBLIOGRAPHY

1. Adeyegbe, S. O. (1989). Emphasizing meaningful learning in Chemistry. *Association of Nigeria 26(1),* 130-135.
2. Ashmore, A. D., Frazer, M. J., & Casey, R. J. (1979). Problem solving network in Chemistry. *Chemistry Education. 56*(6), 377-379.

3. Bello, O. O. (1990). A preliminary study of chemistry students' errors in stoichiometric prob *Science Teachers' Association of Nigeria.*

4. Boujaoude S. & Barakat H., (2000), Secondary school students' difficulties with stoichiometry,*Review,* 81 (296), 91-98.

5. BouJaoude, S. & Barakat, H. (2003). Students' PRelationships to Conceptual Understanding and Learning Approaches. *7, March 2003.*

6. Chandrasegaran, A. L.; Treagust, D. F. ; Waldrip, B. G. & Chandrasegaran, A. (2011). Students' dilemmas in reaction stoichiometry problem solving: deducing the limiting reagent in chemical reactions.*Pract.,* DOI: 10.1039/B901456J. Retrieved on 10 December 2011 from:

7. Chiu, M. H. (2005). A national survey of students' conceptions in chemistry in Taiwan,

8. Dahsan, C. & Coll, R. K., (2007). Thai Grade 10 and 11 students' understanding of stoichiometry and related concepts, *Int. J. Sci. Math. Educ.*

9. Eniayeju, P. A. (1990). Seeking meaning in mole ratio instruction. *Nigeria, 26*(2), 93-100.

10. Goering-Boone, V., & Rayner-Canham, G. (2001). Stoichiometric problem s *CHEM 13 News, 293,* 10-11.

11. Hackling, M. W., & Garnett, P. J. (1985). Misconceptions in chemical equilibrium. European Journal of Science Education, 7, 205-214.

12. Johnstone, A. (2006). Chemical education research in Glasgow in pers 63.

13. Mulford D. R. & Robinson W. R., (2002). An inventory of alternate conceptions among first semester general chemistry students, *J. Chem. Educ.,*

14. Olmsted, J. (1999). Amount tables as a diagnostic tool for *Education, 76*(1), 52-54.

15. Onwu, G. O., & Moneme, C. O. (1986). A network analysis of students' problem solving difficulties in electrolysis. *Journal of Science Teachers Association of Nigeria,*

16. Perera, J. S. H. Q. & Wijeratne, W. D. H. M. (2006). A comparative study of students' achievement in chemistry, mathematics skills and numerical problem solving skills. *technical education* (pp. 52 – 61). Gadong. Brunei Darussalam To´th, E. & Sebestye´n, A. (2009). Relationship between students' knowledge structure and problem strategy in stoichiometric problems based on the chemical equation, Eur. J. Phys. Chem. Educ., 1(1), 8

17. West Africa Examination Council (May/June, 2010). Senior School Certificate Examination (O' Level) Chief Examiner's Report: Lagos Office, Nigeria.

18. West Africa Examination Council (May/June, 2011). Senior School Certificate Examination (O' Level) Chief Examiner's Report: Lagos Office, Nigeria. ntq;fNl];

Effectiveness of Intervention strategies in Learning

Chapter-I

INTRODUCTION

Mathematics is very broadly divided into four foundations, algebra, analysis, geometry, and applied mathematics, which includes theoretical computer science. Historically, algebra is the study of solutions of one or several algebraical equations involving the polynomial functions of one or several variables. The case where all the polynomial s has degree one leads to linear algebra. The case of a single equation, in which one studies the roots of one polynomial and that leads to field theory (Galois Theory).The general case of several equations of high degree leads to algebraical geometry, so named because the sets of solutions of such systems are often studied by geometric methods. According to National Education policy (1986),"Mathematical should be the mean to develop the child for thinking analytically with consciousness reasoning".

The learning of a process or concept in algebra is never complete until it is seen in its relationships to other processes and concepts in the fields Thus each new experience should broader the pupils understanding of the number systems and processes of mathematics learning in a developmental process given time and guidance, algebra should eventually appear as a logical manner.

Since Algebraical calculation are very needed in the subject of the physical and social science .without algebra students may feel very difficult in their progress. Secondary school education will remain to teach Algebra secondary stage of education. While solving algebraically problem students commit lit of errors in calculations. Commitment of these errors reduces their marks into exam. At the same time they develop hatred towards Algebraical calculations in mathematics area. In order to change and avoid this temperature the investigator made an attempt to conduct the study of Errors Committed by secondary school students in Algebra.

Meaning and definition of mathematics

Mathematics is the tool specially suited for dealing with abstract concepts of any kind and there is no limit to its power in this field. In other words as in mathematics we find results at the abstract level with the help of process of reasoning therefore mathematics may be regarded as science of abstract form.

1. Mathematics has its own language-sign symbols, terms and operation etc.
2. Mathematics involves man's high cognitive powers.

Meaning of education

The act or process of education and the result of education, as determined by the knowledge, skill or discipline of character is acquired and the process is unending. The act or process or training by prescribed or customary course of study or discipline-as, an education for the bar or the pulpit-has a finishing point and we say the student has finished his education.

The Destiny of India is now being shaped in her classrooms (Kothari-1966). Education is the most essential human value. Knowledge is developed through literacy education.

Education being a most important social activity, its meanings has been changing through the ages due to changes in social and physical conditions as well as philosophical outlook of people towards life.

Meaning and definition of mathematics

Mathematics is the tool specially suited for dealing with abstract concepts of any kind and there is no its power in this field. In other words as in mathematics we find results at the abstract level with the help of process of reasoning therefore mathematics may be regarded as science of abstract form.

1. Mathematics has its own language-sign symbols, terms and operation etc.
2. Mathematics involves man's high cognitive powers.

Meaning of education

The act or process of education and the result of educational, as determined by the knowledge, skill or discipline of character is acquired and the process is unending. The act or process or training by prescribed or customary course of study or discipline-as, an education for the bar or the pulpit-has a finishing point and we say the student has finished his education.

The Destiny of India is now being shaped in her classrooms (Kothari-1966). Education is the most essential human value. Knowledge is developed through literacy education.

Definition of education

According to J.C. AGGARWAL (1987), Education aims to seek and cultivate new knowledge, to engage vigorously and fearlessly in the pursuit of truth and to interpret old knowledge and benefits in the light of new needs and discoveries-**JOHN DEWEY** writes the Education is the process of living through a continuous reconstruction of experience. It is the development of all these capacities in the individual, which will enable him to control his environment and fulfil his responsibilities.

Education meets the immediate needs of a child and also prepares him for his future life. It develops all his intellectual and emotional powers, so that he is able to meet the problems of life squarely and solve them successfully. It also develops the social qualities of service, tolerance, co-operation and fellow feeling.

"Education is a key that open the eyes of a person towards the brightness of the world" -**Dr. Radhakrishnan**.

One of the most popular definitions, given by our ancient Indian Educational thinker Rabindranath Tagore is given below:

"Education means enabling the mind to find out the ultimate truth which emancipates us form the bondage of the lust and gives us the wealth, not of things but of inner light, not power but of love, making this truth of its own and living expression to it".

"The Central task of education is to implant a will and facility for learning; it should produce not learned but learning people. The truly human society is a learning society, where grandparents, parents and children are students together - **Eric Hoffer.**

No one has yet realized the wealth of sympathy, the kindness and generosity hidden in the soul of a child. The effort of every true education should be to unlock that treasure- **Emma Goldman.**

"The only purpose of education is to teach a student how to live his life-by developing his mind and equipping him to deal with reality. The training he needs is theoretical, i.e., conceptual. He has to be taught to think, to understand, to integrate, to provide. He has to be taught the essentials of the knowledge discovered in the past and he has to be equipped to acquire further knowledge by his own effort"- **Ayn Rand.**

ARISTOTLE

"Education is the creation of sound mind in a sound body. It develops man's faculty, especially his mind so that he may be able to enjoy the contemplation of supreme truth, goodness and beauty of which perfect happiness essentially consists".

The concept of education

The word education derived from two Latin words. They are Edure and Educere. Educere means to bring up and to nourish. Educere means to bring forth and propulsion from internal to external. The term education in the widest sense may be held to include the whole process of development through which a human being passes from infancy to maturity.

Education is the aggregate of all the processes by means of which a person develops abilities, attitudes and other forms of behaviour of positive value in the society in which he lives.

Gandhiji defined education in the following quote. "By Education I mean an all round drawing out of the, best in child and man; body, mind and spirit.

Need of education

Across countries, education plays a vital role not only in acquiring knowledge but also inculcating social, ethical, moral and spiritual values. In our model, schooling teaches people to interact with others and raises the benefits of civic participation including voting and organizing. Education raises the benefits of civic participation. Education is able to install in the child a sense of maturity and responsibility in bringing in him the desired changes. According to this needs and demands of ever changing society of which he is an integral part.

Importance of education

The importance of education is quite clear. Education is the knowledge of putting one's potentials to maximum use. One can safely say that a human being is not in the proper sense complete till he is educated.

The second reason for the importance of education is that only through the attainment of education, man is enabled to receive information from the external world; to acquaint himself with past history and receive all necessary information regarding the present. Without education, main is as though in a closed room and with education he finds himself in room with all its windows open towards outside world.

Meaning of algebra

Algebra from Arabic (al u gabr) is a branch of mathematics concerning the study of structure, relation and quantity. Elementary algebra is often taught in high schools and gives an instruction to the basic ideas.

The name algebra comes from the name of the treatise first written by Al-Khwarizmi who is the founder as we know it today titled kitab-al-Mukhtasar filt – is ab Al-Jabrwa-al-Moghabalah meaning the book of summary Concerning calculating by transposition and reduction; the word Al-jabs which algebra is derived from meaning "Deunion" "Connection or completion".

Definition of algebra

A branch of mathematics that substitutes letters for numbers. An algebraic equation represents a scale, what is done on one side of the scale with a number is also done to the other side of scale. The numbers are the constants. Algebra can include real numbers, complex numbers, matrices, vectors etc. moving from arithmetic to Algebra will look something like this: Arithmetic: 5+3= 3+5 in Algebra it would look like: a+b = b+a.

1. Ultimately the overall aim of teaching mathematics is to ensure alround and harmonious development of the personality of the child.
2. To prepare them for higher education in sciences, Engineering, Technology, etc.
3. To enable the student to solve the mathematical problems of his daily life.
4. To develop the power of logical thinking.
5. To promote the power of concentration in students.
6. To develop the ability to analyze and to generalize
7. To develop speed and accuracy in performing arithmetical computations and operations.
8. To provide opportunities for aesthetic enjoyment and recreation.
9. To inculcate the habit of working systematically.

Objectives of teaching mathematics in secondary stage

"Knowledge for knowledge sake" is a noble ideal, but most students simply cannot afford to follow it. This ideal may be pursued in college education but not in school education. In school education the major objectives of teaching mathematics are:

1. To understand the interrelationship of mathematical facts, formulae, principles and processes.
2. To understand the theoretical and abstracts of mathematics.
3. To develop skill in solving the same problem by various possible methods.
4. To learn the application of mathematics in his day-to-day social, vocational, occupational and recreational life.
5. To gain confidence and competence in the learning of mathematics.
6. To enjoy solving mathematical problems of every type.
7. To stress problem solving techniques through abstract formulae and theorems.

Formulation of objectives

The objectives of teaching mathematics at the entire school stage or secondary stage may be classified as under:

Objectives have to be formulated in respect of Algebra we are going to teach. These objectives provide a definite direction to the teacher for the planning of his work. They help him to determine what to teach, how to teach, hoe to illustrate and how to test.

The objectives have to be properly described and expressed in terms of the expected behavioural changes or the learning outcomes. They should not appear do general and vague .They should indicate clearly what the student is expected to achieve through the learning of a unit They should also fulfill the specific purposes of learning that particular unit. They should be testable so that the teacher can have proper assignment of the learning out comes.

The objectives of teaching mathematics at the entire school stage or secondary stage may be classified as under:

Now we illustrate this procedure with the help of Algebra,

$$(a+b)^2 = a^2 + b^2 + 2ab$$

IMPORTANCE OF MATHEMETICS EDUCATION

In this world of today nobody can live without mathematics for a single day. Mathematics is intimately involved in every moment of everyone's life. Right from human existence of earth, it has been a faithful companion.

Mathematics is an indispensable part of education, not only because of its great disciplinary value, but also because of its many other educational values. Mathematics is a science of all sciences and an art of all arts.

Mathematics provides us inductive and deductive knowledge to enrich our imagination and modes of thinking and even behaviour to excel in life. The material progress of the present day world is the work of our mathematicians to improve the quality of life by reducing time, distance and human effect.

Mathematics forms the vase of all essential knowledge and progress in science and technology. Bacon is right when he says, "Mathematics is the gate and key of all sciences".

Mathematics is a subject which is of great importance for the personal development of a student, in a general and for the development of the power of logical reasoning. It is a universal language.

Any person ignorant of mathematics will be at the mercy of others and will be easily cheated. Even Napolean said, "The progress and the improvement of mathematics are linked to the prosperity of the state".

METHODS OF ALGEBRA

1. Directed Numbers and their operations.
2. Algebraic graph
3. Solving system of equations
4. Partial Fractions
5. Factorization
6. Synthetic Division
7. Square root
8. Logrithms

SOME STANDARD RESULTS OF ALGEBRA

$(a+b)^2 = a^2 + 2ab + b^2$

$(a-b)^2 = a^2 - 2ab + b^2$

$(a^2-b^2) = (a+b)(a-b)$

$(a+b)^3 = a^3 + 3a^2b + 3ab^2 + b^3$

$(a-b)^3 = a^3 - 3a^2b + 3ab^2 - b^3$

$(a^3+b^3) = (a+b)(a^2-ab+b^2)$

$(a^3-b^3) = (a-b)(a^2+ab+b^2)$

$(a+b+c)^2 = a^2+b^2+c^2+2(ab+bc+ca)$

Where a and b are two variables.

LEARNING

Hilgard considers learning as 'the process by which an activity originates or is changed through reacting to an encountered situation provided that characteristics of the change in activity cannot be explained on the basis of native responses, tendencies, maturity or temporary status of the organism.

MEANINGFUL LEARNING

Before we try to understand the concept of meaningful learning, it will be better here to know once again what learning stands for. The definition given by R.S.Woodworth, appears befitting, which runs as "An activity may be called learning in so far it develops the individual in any way good or bad and makes his environment and experiences different from what it would otherwise have been".

Learning can produce both good and bad developments in the learner. But the learner, his guardians, his teachers and the society in general want the process of learning to lead to good results and healthy outcomes. That learning is to be avoided, curbed or replaced which is likely prove harmful in any way. Not only informal learning, but even formal learning can be injurious to the learner and his well wishers in some way. Child comes to school for better experiences, were the situations should not be worse for him. Every activity for the process of learning should be governed by certain aims and objectives. There cannot be anything of wasteful, useless, aimless or meaningless nature.

Meaningful learning is therefore that learning which is oriented towards good experiences and outcomes. In it there is no place for meaningless and harmful experiences. It must ensure posited results. It is constructive, productive, purposeful and progressive in nature.

PRINCIPLES OF MEANINGFUL LEARNING

There are many principles of meaningful learning in general and in mathematics in particular which are being discussed here:

1. Interest and Attention
2. Definite Aim
3. Principle of Utility
4. Importance of Learning Activities
5. Motivation
6. Proper Attitude
7. Proper Methods
8. Correlation
9. Proper Use of Mental faculties
10. Laws of Exercise

PRESENT STATUS OF TEACHING MATHEMATICS

Now mathematics is considered problematic subject by many students. Mathematics is disliked by students in general. It is also not taught effectively by teachers in the class room. Student's achievement

Level is very low in mathematics. Also majority of students feel that mathematics is a difficult subject and it can be understood and followed only by exceptionally intelligent students.

There are many problems that affect mathematics teaching and result learners are not attracted to the subject mathematics.

About the mathematics teaching, teacher complains of excessive workload of facilities. Head masters and management complain about the teachers. The mathematics teacher point out the following problems:

1. Teacher burden
2. Teacher attitude
3. Lack of purpose
4. Method of teaching
5. Large classes
6. The student disinterest
7. Heavy syllabus.

What is emphasized here is that there are many problems that affect mathematics teaching in schools. Since India's scientific and technological development largely depend on mathematical ability of learners. It is essential to identify these problems and initiate appropriate measure for the elimination of such problems.

DEFINITION OF THE KEY TERM

ALGEBRA

The word Algebra is distortion of the word 'A1 – Jebr'. In this al means 'the' and jebr refers to the operation of transferring a quantity from one side of equation to another.

In Algebra we generally denote numbers by letters. The two main characteristics of algebra are symbolism and genaralizations.

In arithmetic we write,

Area of rectangle = Length X Breath

But in Algebra, it is written as

A = L X B

Where A stands for area, L for length and B for breath.

NEED FOR THE STUDY

1. There are practically very few researches in this topic. It is a thrust area.

2. 40% of the students cannot involve deeply, because algebra requires more attention and interest.
3. Many of the students do not have practice in algebraical problems.
4. Review of the study revealed that very few have done the study in helping learners in Algebraical learning.

SCOPE OF THE STUDY

1. The study is restricted to IX standard students.
2. The study is focused on the topic Algebraical.

STATEMENT OF THE PROBLEM

Problem of the present research is to study the "*Effectiveness of certain Intervention Strategies in Achieving Algebraical learning Among IX standard students.*"

OBJECTIVES OF THE STUDY

1. To find out whether there is any significant difference between the mean scores of boys and girls in pre-test of control group in achieving Algebraical learning among IX standard students.
2. To find out whether there is any significant difference between the mean scores of boys and girls in pre-test of Experimental group in achieving Algebraical learning among IX standard students.
3. To find out whether there is any significant difference between the mean scores of boys in pre-test of control group and Experimental group in achieving Algebraical learning among IX standard students.
4. To find out whether there is any significant difference between the mean scores of girls in pre-test of Control group and Experimental group in achieving Algebraical learning among IX standard students.
5. To find out whether there is any significant difference between the mean scores of boys and girls in post-test of control group in achieving Algebraical learning among IX standard students.

6. To find out whether there is any significant difference between the mean scores of boys and girls in post-test of Experimental group in achieving Algebraical learning among IX standard students.
7. To find out whether there is any significant difference between the mean scores of boys in post-test of control group and Experimental group in achieving Algebraical learning among IX standard students.
8. To find out whether there is any significant difference between the mean scores of girls in post-test of control group and Experimental group in achieving Algebraical learning among IX standard students.
9. To find out whether there is any significant difference between the mean scores of control group and Experimental group of pre-test performance in achieving Algebraical learning among IX standard students.
10. To find out whether there is any significant difference between the mean scores of control group and Experimental group of post-test performance in achieving Algebraical learning among IX standard students.
11. To find out whether there is any significant difference between the mean scores of control group of pre-test and post-test performance in achieving Algebraical learning among IX standard students.
12. To find out whether there is any significant difference between the mean scores of Experimental group of pre-test and post-test performance in achieving Algebraical learning among IX standard students.

HYPOTHESES

1. There is no significant difference between the mean scores of boys and girls in pre-test of control group in achieving Algebraical learning among IX standard students.
2. There is no significant difference between the mean scores of

boys and girls in pre-test of Experimental group in achieving Algebraical learning among IX standard students.

3. There is no significant difference between the mean scores of boys in pre-test of control group and Experimental group in achieving Algebraical learning among IX standard students.
4. There is no significant difference between the mean scores of girls in pre-test of Control group and Experimental group in achieving Algebraical learning among IX standard students.
5. There is no significant difference between the mean scores of boys and girls in post-test of control group in achieving Algebraical learning among IX standard students.
6. There is no significant difference between the mean scores of boys and girls in post-test of Experimental group in achieving Algebraical learning among IX standard students.
7. There is no significant difference between the mean scores of boys in post-test of control group and Experimental group in achieving Algebraical learning among IX standard students.
8. There is no significant difference between the mean scores of girls in post-test of control group and Experimental group in achieving Algebraical learning among IX standard students.
9. There is no significant difference between the mean scores of control group and Experimental group of pre-test performance in achieving Algebraical learning among IX standard students.
10. There is no significant difference between the mean scores of control group and Experimental group of post-test performance in achieving Algebraical learning among IX standard students.
11. There is no significant difference between the mean scores of control group of pre-test and post-test performance in achieving Algebraical learning among IX standard students.
12. There is no significant difference between the mean scores of Experimental group of pre-test and post-test performance in achieving Algebraical learning among IX standard students.

LIMITATIONS OF THE STUDY

1. The researcher conducted the experiment only in the school located in urban area
2. This study was conducted in only one chapter of the maths syllabus for secondary school students
3. This study was conducted to IX standard students particularly in government Modern Higher Secondary School, Machuvadi, Pudukkottai.
4. The experimental treatment was given with duration of one month only
5. The sample consist of 80 students

CONCLUSION

In this chapter we discuss about overview of the problem and significance, its needs and objectives of the study. The next chapter deals with the review of related literature.

Chapter - II

Review of Related Literature

INTRODUCTION

This chapter reveals the previous related research studies in India and Abroad. The main purpose of reviewing the literatures is to understand the previous work done in the relevant field of human errors committed by students in Algebra, Further, the related literatures help the researcher to thoroughly analyze and scrutinize the methodological perspectives used in the previous studies and this work may offer relevant ideas to prefer appropriate methodological procedure for the present study. At the same time, reviewing the previous studies may avoid unnecessary duplication of research work and help in focusing the entire present study in a right direction. In this chapter, the investigator reviewed, the related literature in the areas of human errors committed by students in Algebra with the available resources the investigator collected some related studies and present in this chapter. The previous studies are given below.

IMPORTANCE OF REVIEW

Significant of review of literature task that continues throughout the duration of the basis. It being with a search for a suitable topic, since a thesis intends to be a contribution in the field of knowledge. Although completely new and original problems are rare .A previous study should not be exactly replicated unless the technique used has been discovered faulty or the findings and conclusions become doubtful or unless some new sources of information have been discovered to shed new light on the problem. A good test is one which still requires solution.

Once a topic has been described upon, it is essential to review all relevant material which has a bearing on the topic .This Review of literature is included in the final report of the thesis as a key section or chapter. It is necessary to show how the problem under investigation related to previous research studies. In somehow the problem under investigation relates to previous research studies. In some subject areas it is important to locate the problem within a theoretical frame work and in such cases the underlying theory needed to be reviewed as well.

REVIEW OF RELATED STUDIES

The review of related literature is an essential aspect of research project. Such a review represents the third step of the scientific method outlined by Dewey and other social philosophers. It is an indispensable stop in the solution of any research problem. Good, Barr and Scats have analysed the purpose of review of related literature as follows:

1. To slow whether the evidence already available, solves the problems adequately without further investing action and this to avoid the risk of duplication.
2. To provide ideas, theories, explanation or hypotheses valuables in formulating the problems.
3. To suggest method of research appropriate to the problems.
4. To locate comparative data useful in the interpretation of result, and
5. To contribute to the general Scholarship of the investigator.
6. It provides the sources for hypotheses. The researcher can formulate research hypotheses on the basis of available studies.

7. It contributes towards the accurate knowledge of the evidence or literature in one's area of activity is a good avenue towards making oneself. Whether one is almost all students with mathematics difficulties demonstrate problems with accurate and automatic retrieval of basic arithmetic combinations.

The intervention strategies like home work, assignments, arithmetic calculation and speed calculations are followed as valid and reliable indicators of potential mathematics difficulties.

STUDIES CONDUCTED IN INDIA

Blanc D (2012), conducted a research on " the realization space of a pi-algebra; a module problem in algebraic topology". In this study seems clear that the deformations theory can be applied with little change to study other module problems in algebra and topology.

Alsina Claudi (2012), Did a study on "Teaching math's through useful applications with local and Global perspective" in this study they explored that the appropriate quantitative literacy in learning alone applied to learners Math's problem.

Schliemann (2012), conducted a research on "Constraint and Co- operation in algebraic problem solving". In this proposes that neither the individual nor the set of individuals modify individual mental process social interactions based on constraint only provide the individual with superficial notions, while co-operation as a system of interpersonal actions governed by the law of equilibrium and organized into reversible systems, allows for the development objective and coherent system of operations.

Ganesan (2012), conducted a study on "The effect of problem solving modelling in enhancing students achievement in mathematics "In this study found that the control group and the experimental group were homogenous with regret to this achievement motivation, anxiety, inventory, attitude, forwards mathematics and have environment.

Kong (2011), Conducted a study on "students engagement in the process of mathematics learning and its effect on learning out comes." In this results indicated that students learning outcomes were not only quantitatively but also quantitatively.

Ramamoorthy (2011), Conducted a study on "common spelling errors in English committed by standard VI Students". Major finding of the study, i) Matriculation students improved in their learning of spelling after the remedial teaching programme. ii) A remedial teaching programme involving the techniques such as oral drill, intensive writing practice, correlation mimicry, and phonetic methods, was found effective in teaching commonly miss pelt words. iii) The common caused for poor spelling were the length of the word, word with silent letters of the word, word with similar sounds and words with consonant clusters.

Vasanthal (2011), Conducted a study on "Developing problem solving strategies in learning Mathematics among IX STD students. In this study that the students mean achievement in the post test has been achievement in the post test has been increased and the errors were considerably reduced in the post test. The level of performance of the experimental group students is found to be high after the implementation of the remedial programme.

Sarala (2010), Conducted a study on "conceptual errors of secondary school pupils in learning select areas in modern mathematics." Major findings of the study were i) The number of conceptual errors committed by secondary school pupils in the areas selected for study was very high ii) conceptual errors in mathematics were seen to be influenced by sex, locality of school, management of school, intelligence, study habits, socio economic status and caste V) Interest in Mathematics was been to have no influence on errors.

Marria Cardella and Elaver (2010), conducted a study on "meta cognitive instruction in mathematics on low ability students". The findings i) Understanding how to approach a problem ii) Identifying the appropriate scheme for organizing the information iii) Recognizing there may be more than one right way to solve the problem Vi) Verifying their solution.

Raman (2009), Conducted a study on "Impact remedial teaching programmes for the common errors committed by students of standard IX". In this study, major findings of the study students committed more conceptual errors, followed by computational errors, entry behaviour errors and perceptual errors.

Rathy (2008), Has done study on "Error analysis of written mathematical tasks at primary stage". In this study, her findings are I) Low achievers commit many errors than average achievers. II)Average achievers commit many errors in encoding as low achievers stopped at transformation stage.

Patel (2008), conducted a study on "Mathematical ability", In this study pupils possessing high reasoning ability were found to be better in Mathematical ability than the pupils with low reasoning ability. The pupils possessing a favourable attitude towards mathematics were found better in mathematical ability than those with a lesser favourable attitude. The pupils possessing high anxiety were inferior in mathematical ability to pupils having low anxiety.

Iyer (2007), conducted a research on 'some factors related to under achievement in Mathematics of secondary school students". The study revealed that 1) out of the personality variables selected, 10 variables were most effective in discriminating between all the achievements pairs. 2) There was significantly a greater number of over achievers among the high intelligence group than among the low intelligence group.

Toppino and Kaserman (1991) had done an experimental research on memory and attention. They found that recall is improved when learning is spaced rather than presented all at once.

Pellagrin and Davis (1993) found that elementary school children became progressively inattentive when recess was delayed, resulting in more active play when recess occurred.

Rskes, Christopher R.; Valentine, Jeffrey C. And McGatha, Maggie B. (2010) investigated Methods of Instructional Improvement in Algebra: A Systematic Review and Meta – Analysis.

Banda, Devender R.; Matuszny, Rose Marie and Therrien, William J. (2009) did an experiment in Enhancing Motivation to Complete Math Tasks Using the High – Preference Strategy

Vasanthal (1991) in her study developed problem solving strategies in learning mathematics among IX standard students.

The study was done with the objectives of developing the problem solving strategies in doing problems in Geometry, Mensuration and

Algebra. The study suggests some remedial programmes to the students of IX standard, in order to facilitate adoption of the problem solving strategies in learning mathematics. The findings of the study showed that the problem solving strategies developed by the researcher have significantly improved.

Bhirud (2007), conducted study on "Diagnostic Test in Algebra". In this study, Findings revealed that in the higher classes the topics are of complex nature, still it was found that the learning objectives, the content in units and the errors could be co-ordinate and a test not only with vertical but also with transversal division could be constructed.

Sharma (2006), conducted a study on "Diagnostic test related to the use of algebra for the students of grade VIII of Allahabad in Uttar Pradesh". He found that the high scoring students failed in mathematics at the upper class. Further, it could be said that the better group had not much benefit from its two years school in the same class.

STUDIES CONDUCTED IN ABROAD

Zhang et. al (2012), conducted a research on "bootstrap standard Error". In this study formulate for standard errors of parameter estimates are more difficult to obtain than in the usual inter subject factor analysis because of the independence of successive observations. The standard bootstrap of individual time points is not appropriate because it destroys their order in time and consequently gives incorrect standard errors estimates.

Cotic et. al (2012), conducted a study on "problem based instruction in mathematics and its impact on the cognitive results of the students and on affective motivational aspects." In this research findings are great value in the undergraduate education of teachers as well as for qualified and practising teachers and their further and regular professional training.

Zollman and Alan (2011), conducted a study on "Students use Graphic organizes to improve mathematical problem solving Communications." In this study discusses graphic organizes and their potential benefit for both students and teachers, describe the specific graphic organizer adaptations they created for mathematical problem solving and discusses some of their results of using the "for corners and a diamond"graphic organizer.

Ozgun – Kuca et.al (2011), conducted a study on "Algebra 2.0". The study found that can play a meaningful role in the problem solving experiences of students. By providing learners with multiple ways to look at problems, and multiple ways to explore possible solutions, students, using technology engage in tasks in a way that sustains their curiosity while allowing them to explore problems in collaborative settings.

Star et. al (2010), conducted a research on, instructional strategies that Deleon student understanding, within and between Algebraic Representations", In this study who complete a mathematics course beyond the level of Algebra II more than double the odd of pursuing and completing post secondary education. Many districts now require completion of an Algebra I course prior to completion of 9th grade. Regrettably, student's difficulties in Algebra have been well documented in national and international assessments.

Rossi and Paul (2010) conducted a research on An Uncommon Approach to a common Algebraic Error". In this study a result intended to help students achieve a greater understanding of a familiar algebraic error. The basic rules of documentary algebra can often appear beyond the grasp of many students.

Audry Williams (2010), Conducted a research on "Teaching research, and service by the numbers at Boise state". This study discuses the new work load policy at Boise state University which gives professors remarkable flexibility in their teaching, research, and service. Boise state has described its goal as redefining itself as a "metropolitan research university of distinction". The policy measures out in 30 "units" the teaching, Scholarship, and services that faculty members are supposed to do in an academic year.

Potgieter et. al (2009), Conducted a research on "transfer of algebraic and graphical thinking between mathematic and chemistry". In this study found that we exposed a group of students to a chemistry instrument based on the Nernst equation in electro

Chemistry, and an equivalent group of students to a similar mathematics instrument, in which the questions were stripped of all chemistry contexts. Both tests contained items requiring algebraic questions in both the chemistry and mathematic tests.

Caballero and Gil (2009), Conducted a research on "A Crypto logical way of teaching mathematics". In this study gives special attention is paid here to the concepts of proof and verification through the definition of Zero-Knowledge Crypto logical protocols. Many other different Cryptographic and cryptanalytic activities and modern Cryptographic applications such as resources for motivations mathematics learning and for achieving a significant important in student understanding of several algebraic, analytical and statistical concepts.

Mitchell and Sarah (2008), conducted a research on "Year 7 Algebra". In this study describes the both groups were introduced to algebra over five lesions and given test and an attitude questionnaire before and after the lessons. Students in the focus group were asked to respond to writing prompts for their homework after each lesson. A selection of students from both groups was interviewed on the basis of test and questionnaire response.

CONCLUSION

A review of related research showed that there were many studies on the intervention strategies in specific topic such as algebra found to be difficult by the students have not been explored. Therefore an investigation is necessary to find out certain strategies to improve the IX standard students in Algebra.

Once the review of related literature is over, the next step on the part of the researcher is to plan for the investigation. This is precisely elaborated in the next chapter.

Methodology

INTRODUCTION

This chapter deals with the methodological procedure used in this study. The methodological procedure includes Research methods, research tool, sampling, validity, Reliability, Data collection, Data analysis etc., adopted in the present study. The methodology considered as a "Blue print" for research. In this study the relevant data is collected by it investigator and analyzed by making appropriate statistical technique.

RESEARCH DESIGN

In an experimental design, the researcher actively tries to change the situation, circumstances, or experience of participants (manipulation), which may lead to change in behaviour or outcomes of randomly assigned to different conditions and variables of interest are measured. The researcher tries to control the other variable in order to avoid confounds to causality. Therefore experiments are often highly fixed in the natural situation even before the data collection starts. It is also called "Empirical Research "or "Cause and effect Method". It is data based research. Coming up with conclusions which are capable of being verified with experiment. It is appropriate when proof is sought that certain variables affect other variables.

Selection of control and experimental group

A control group in a scientific experiment is a group separated from the rest of the experiments where the independent variable being tested cannot influence the results. This isolates the independent variables effect on the experiment and it rules out the alternated explanation of the experimental results.

An experimental group is the group of scientific experiments where the experimental procedure is performed. This group is exposed to the independent variable being tested and the changes observed and recorded.

Steps involved in the experimental process

1. Selecting the standard
2. Assessing the entry behaviour of the children by conducting a pre test
3. Selection of control and Experimental group based on the students marks
4. Teaching children through traditional method for control group
5. Teaching children through using algebrical learning method in teaching maths concepts
6. The treatment effect was given for four weeks
7. Administering the post-test for the children of control group and experimental group
8. Entering the scores of the post test of the students
9. Categorizing and analyzing the pre and post-test scores
10. Identifying the impact of the both traditional method and achieving method of experimental group in teaching concepts of maths subject.

Variables controlled in the experimental study

Researcher point out that certain intervening variable that appear in the experiment failure to control such variable may affect the outcome of the experiment. The following variables are controlled in the experimental study.

1. Time factor

2. Maturation
3. Pattern of the test.

Time factor

Time is one of the variables. It is controlled during the study. The time variable is controlled by prescribing equal time limit to the group in teaching the concept of Maths as well as the duration of times of the test.

Maturation

Maturation means number of students in each group. In this study equal numbers of students are selected for the control and Experimental group. This study consist 40 students per in each group.

Conducting a criterion test for pre-test control and experimental group

The criterion test was administrated and developed for collecting data in pre-test control and experimental group. This pre-test is used to assess the entry behaviour of the student. The criterion test score identified the basic knowledge of the students in the relevant field.

For the effective administration of the test following suggestions/ directions given by the **Dececco abd Crawford (1977) was carefully followed.**

1. Careful organization and efficient distribution of all the test material.
2. Brief directions and brief answers raised by students.
3. A record of time and chalk board to help the students pace their efforts.

OBJECTIVES OF THE STUDY

1. To find out whether there is any significant difference between the mean scores of boys and girls in pre-test of control group in achieving Algebraical learning among IX standard students.
2. To find out whether there is any significant difference between the mean scores of boys and girls in pre-test of Experimental

group in achieving Algebraical learning among IX standard students.

3. To find out whether there is any significant difference between the mean scores of boys in pre-test of control group and Experimental group in achieving Algebraical learning among IX standard students.
4. To find out whether there is any significant difference between the mean scores of girls in pre-test of Control group and Experimental group in achieving Algebraical learning among IX standard students.
5. To find out whether there is any significant difference between the mean scores of boys and girls in post-test of control group in achieving Algebraical learning among IX standard students.
6. To find out whether there is any significant difference between the mean scores of boys and girls in post-test of Experimental group in achieving Algebraical learning among IX standard students.
7. To find out whether there is any significant difference between the mean scores of boys in post-test of control group and Experimental group in achieving Algebraical learning among IX standard students.
8. To find out whether there is any significant difference between the mean scores of girls in post-test of control group and Experimental group in achieving Algebraical learning among IX standard students.
9. To find out whether there is any significant difference between the mean scores of control group and Experimental group of pre-test performance in achieving Algebraical learning among IX standard students.
10. To find out whether there is any significant difference between the mean scores of control group and Experimental group of post-test performance in achieving Algebraical learning among IX standard students.
11. To find out whether there is any significant difference between the mean scores of control group of pre-test and post-test

performance in achieving Algebraical learning among IX standard students.

12. To find out whether there is any significant difference between the mean scores of Experimental group of pre-test and post-test performance in achieving Algebraical learning among IX standard students.

HYPOTHESIS OF THE STUDY

1. There is no significant difference between the mean scores of boys and girls in pre-test of control group in achieving Algebraical learning among IX standard students.
2. There is no significant difference between the mean scores of boys and girls in pre-test of Experimental group in achieving Algebraical learning among IX standard students.
3. There is no significant difference between the mean scores of boys in pre-test of control group and Experimental group in achieving Algebraical learning among IX standard students.
4. There is no significant difference between the mean scores of girls in pre-test of Control group and Experimental group in achieving Algebraical learning among IX standard students.
5. There is no significant difference between the mean scores of boys and girls in post-test of control group in achieving Algebraical learning among IX standard students.
6. There is no significant difference between the mean scores of boys and girls in post-test of Experimental group in achieving Algebraical learning among IX standard students.
7. There is no significant difference between the mean scores of boys in post-test of control group and Experimental group in achieving Algebraical learning among IX standard students.
8. There is no significant difference between the mean scores of girls in post-test of control group and Experimental group in achieving Algebraical learning among IX standard students.
9. There is no significant difference between the mean scores of control group and Experimental group of pre-test performance in achieving Algebraical learning among IX standard students.

10. There is no significant difference between the mean scores of control group and Experimental group of post-test performance in achieving Algebraical learning among IX standard students.
11. There is no significant difference between the mean scores of control group of pre-test and post-test performance in achieving Algebraical learning among IX standard students.
12. There is no significant difference between the mean scores of Experimental group of pre-test and post-test performance in achieving Algebraical learning among IX standard students.

LIMITATIONS OF THE STUDY

1. The researcher conducted the experiment only in the school located in urban area
2. This study was conducted in only one chapter of the maths syllabus for secondary school students
3. This study was conducted to IX standard students particularly in government Modern Higher Secondary School, Machuvadi, Pudukkottai District.
4. The experimental treatment was given with duration of one month only
5. The sample consist of 80 students

RESEARCH METHOD

The researcher adopted Experimental method for this research. The researcher conducted the experiment for IX standard students in Government Modern Higher Secondary School, Machuvadi, Pudukkottai.

RESEARCH TOOL

The investigator himself developed a research tool which is indicated below.

A questioner on co-ordination maths was taken by the researcher. The researcher conducted pre-test at the beginning of the study and Post-test after providing a suitable teaching learning experience.

Construction of research tool

The pattern of the test is same as the control and Experimental group. The test consists of fifty marks. All the Questions are objective type. The question paper consists of three levels. They are knowledge, understanding and application levels. In this study control and experimental group of the students are treated equally, without any partially based on the understanding the concept of the topic.

Samples of the study

80 students of male and female studying in class IX STD of Government Modern Higher Secondary School, Machuvadi, Pudukkottai District were taken as the sample for analysis.

Description of the research tool and scoring procedure

The researcher has taken only objective type questions. The test paper consist of choose the best answer. Each question carries one mark. If the answer is correct one mark will be given if not zero.

PILOT STUDY

A pilot study is an initial investigation to give information that will be necessary when designing a future trial or study. For example a pilot may be used to:

1. Assess the time required to examine each patient,
2. To determine the quality of a proposed questionnaire
3. To estimate the variability of key variables.

Hence the investigator conducted the pilot study in the experiment to determine the quality of the question paper.

VALIDITY OF THE TOOL

Validity is the extent to which a test is measured what it claims to measure. It is vital for a test to be valid in order for the results to be accurately applied and interpreted. Validity is not determined by a single statistics, but by a body of research that demonstrates the relation between the test and the behaviour it is intended to measure.

There are three types of validity:

1. Content Validity
2. Criterion Validity
3. Construct Validity

In the present study Content Validity was used

Content validity

When a test has content validity, the items on the test represent the entire range of possible items the test should cover

RELIABILITY OF THE TOOL

Reliability refers to the consistency of a measure. A test is considered reliable if we get the consistency of scores repeatedly. It can be estimated in a number of different ways.

1. Test – Retest Reliability
2. Inter – Rater Reliability
3. Parallel – Forms Reliability
4. Inter – Consistency Reliability

Test-retest reliability

To guage test-retest reliability, the test is administrated twice at two different points in time. This kind of reliability is used to access the consistency of a test across time. This type of reliability assumes that there will be no change in the quality or construct being measured. Test-Retest reliability is the best method used for things that are stable over time. Generally, reliability will be higher when little time has passed between tests.

SAMPLING TECHNIQUE USED

80 students have been taken as sample for present study IX standard A section boys and girls are Control groups. And B section IX standard students boys and girls are Experimental groups.

COLLECTION OF DATA

The investigator collected the data from the selected control group and experimental group. The pre-test and post-test was conducted using the criterion test. The investigator himself taught maths to the control group by using traditional method. The experimental method was taught through the algebraically learning concepts in Govt. Modern. Hr. Sec. School, Machuvadi, Pudukkottai. After completion of the treatment the post-test was conducted to measure the understanding ability of learning in various concepts of the maths in both groups. Thus all the data were collected systematically for the analysis in the present study.

ANALYSIS OF THE DATA

In the present study, the relevant data obtained from the test scores in the pre-test and the post-test were analyzed using different statistical techniques.

Descriptive analysis

It provides information about the nature of a particular group of individuals. Mean and standard deviation were calculated to determine the central tendencies and dispersion variables to describe the properties of the sample.

Differential analysis

It provides inference involving determination of statistical significance of difference between groups with reference to the selected variables. To compare the difference between the mean scores of the sample can be calculated by using the T" test.

Relational analysis

Correlation refers to the relationship between two or more paired variables or more sets of data. The degree of relationship is measured and represented by co-efficient of correlation. This coefficient may be identified either the letter.

STATISTICAL TECHNIQUES USED

Standard deviation

Standard deviation is the average or mean of all the averages for multiple sets of data. Scientists and statisticians use the standard deviation to determine how closely sets of data are to the mean of all the sets. Standard deviation is an easy calculation to perform.

't' TEST

A **'t'-test** is any statistical hypothesis test in which the test statistic follows a student's **'t'** distribution if the null hypothesis is supported. It can be used to determine if two sets of data are significantly different from each other, and is most commonly applied when the test statistic would follow a normal distribution if the value of a scaling term in the test statistic were known. When the scaling term is unknown and is replaced by an estimate based on the data, the test statistic (under certain conditions) follows a Student's *t* distribution.

CONCLUSION

The researcher carried out the study of *Effectiveness of certain Intervention Strategies in Achieving Algebraical learning Among IX standard students.*"The pre test performance of the control group and experimental group level is minimum, when compared to the post test performance of control and experimental group. The experimental group having high level of performance in post test, when introducing the algebraically learning. Both boys and girls performance is better in experimental group of the post test. The present research revealed that teacher should always teach maths concepts by using novel method algebraically learning for easy understanding of mathematics.

Chapter IV

Analysis and Interpretation of Data

INTRODUCTION

This chapter deals with the statistical analysis of data collected for the study. The Hypothesis formulated for the study was verified. The analysis of date is done for each hypothesis and the findings concerned are presented.

In the present study, the following pre-requisites are kept in mind for the scientific interpretation of data collected through relevant tools.

SYSTEM OF DATA ANALYSIS

The purpose of the present study is to find out the achieving algebraical learning at secondary level. In this Study, the test of significance (t-test) was used to test the Research Hypothesis and the computation of t-value was identified by the investigator using the Mean and Standard Deviation. Since the total number of students selected for the present study is forty, the investigator used the formula of t-test related to correlated and un-correlated group.

HYPOTHESIS TESTING

HYPOTHESIS - 1

There is no significant difference between the mean scores of boys and girls in pre-test of control group in achieving algebraical learning among IX standard students.

TABLE 1

S. No	Gender	N	Mean	Standard Deviation	t – value	Level of significance at 0.05 level
1	Boys	18	29.44	6.87		
2	Girls	22	30	7.83	0.2410	No significant

NULL HYPOTHESIS

Since our obtained 't' – value (0.2410) is less than the table value (2.03), with degree of freedom 38, there is no significance difference between the mean scores of boys and girls in pre-test of control group and therefore the hypothesis is accepted.

FINDING

There is no significance difference between the mean scores of boys and girls in pre-test of control group and therefore the **hypothesis is accepted.**

HYPOTHESIS - 2

There is no significant difference between the mean scores of boys and girls in pre-test of Experimental group in achieving algebraical learning among IX standard students.

TABLE 2

S. No	Gender	N	Mean	Standard Deviation	t – value	Level of significance at 0.05 level
1	Boys	25	30.2	7.54		
2	Girls	15	31.66	7.91	0.5753	No significant

NULL HYPOTHESIS

Since our obtained 't' – value (0.5753) is less than the table value (2.03), with degree of freedom 38, there is no significance difference between the mean scores of boys and girls in pre-test of Experimental group and therefore the hypothesis is accepted.

FINDING

There is no significance difference between the mean scores of boys and girls in pre-test of Experimental group and therefore the **hypothesis is accepted.**

HYPOTHESIS - 3

There is no significant difference between the mean scores of boys in pre-test of control group and Experimental group in achieving algebracial learning among IX standard students.

TABLE 3

S. No	Gender	N	Mean	Standard Deviation	t – value	Level of significance at 0.05 level
1	Control Group Boys	18	29.44	6.87		
2	Experimental Group Boys	25	30.2	7.54	0.3440	No significant

NULL HYPOTHESIS

Since our obtained 't' – value (0.3440) is less than the table value (2.02), with degree of freedom 41, there is no significance difference between the mean scores of pre-test in control group boys and Experimental group boys. Therefore the hypothesis is accepted.

FINDING

There is no significance difference between the mean scores of pre-test in control group boys and Experimental group boys. Therefore the **hypothesis is accepted.**

HYPOTHESIS – 4

There is no significant difference between the mean scores of Girls in pre-test of control group and Experimental group in achieving algebracial learning among IX standard students.

TABLE 4

S. No	Gender	N	Mean	Standard Deviation	t – value	Level of significance at 0.05 level
1	Control Group Girls	22	30	7.83		
2	Experimental Group Girls	15	31.66	7.91	0.6295	No significant

NULL HYPOTHESIS

Since our obtained 't' – value (0.6295) is less than the table value (2.03), with degree of freedom 35, there is no significance difference between the mean scores of pre-test in control group girls and Experimental group girls. Therefore the hypothesis is accepted.

FINDING

There is no significance difference between the mean scores of pre-test in control group girls and Experimental group girls. Therefore **the hypothesis is accepted.**

HYPOTHESIS – 5

There is no significant difference between the mean scores of boys and girls in post-test of control group in achieving algebraical learning among IX standard students.

TABLE 5

S. No	Gender	N	Mean	Standard Deviation	t – value	Level of significance at 0.05 level
1	Boys	18	33.33	7.65		
2	Girls	22	32.27	7.51	0.4398	No significant

NULL HYPOTHESIS

Since our obtained 't' – value (0.4398) is less than the table value (2.03), with degree of freedom 38, there is no significance difference between the mean scores of boys and girls in post-test of control group and therefore the hypothesis is accepted.

FINDING

There is no significance difference between the mean scores of boys and girls in post-test of control group and therefore the **hypothesis is accepted.**

HYPOTHESIS – 6

There is no significant difference between the mean scores of boys and girls in post-test of Experimental group in achieving algebraical learning among IX standard students.

TABLE 6

S. No	Gender	N	Mean	Standard Deviation	t – value	Level of significance at 0.05 level
1	Boys	25	37	5.65		
2	Girls	15	37.66	5.77	0.3531	No significant

NULL HYPOTHESIS

Since our obtained 't' – value (0.3531) is less than the table value (2.03), with degree of freedom 38, there is no significance difference between the mean scores of boys and girls in post-test of experimental group and therefore the hypothesis is accepted.

FINDING

There is no significance difference between the mean scores of boys and girls in post-test of experimental group and therefore the **hypothesis is accepted.**

HYPOTHESIS – 7

There is no significant difference between the mean scores of boys in post-test of control group and Experimental group in achieving algebracial learning among IX standard students.

TABLE 7

S. No	Gender	N	Mean	Standard Deviation	t – value	Level of significance at 0.05 level
1	Control Group Boys	18	33.33	7.65		
2	Experimental Group Boys	25	37	5.65	1.7262	No significant

NULL HYPOTHESIS

Since our obtained 't' – value (1.7262) is less than the table value (2.02), with degree of freedom 41, there is no significance difference between the mean scores of pre-test in control group boys and Experimental group boys. Therefore the hypothesis is accepted.

FINDING

There is no significance difference between the mean scores of pre-test in control group boys and Experimental group boys. Therefore the **Hypothesis is accepted.**

HYPOTHESIS – 8

There is no significant difference between the mean scores of Girls in post-test of control group and Experimental group in achieving algebracial learning among IX standard students.

TABLE 8

S. No	Gender	N	Mean	Standard Deviation	t – value	Level of significance at 0.05 level
1	Control Group Girls	22	32.27	7.51		
2	Experimental Group Girls	15	37.66	5.77	2.4679	significant

NULL HYPOTHESIS

Since our obtained 't' – value (2.4679) is greater than the table value (2.03), with degree of freedom 35, there is significance difference between the mean scores of post-test in control group girls and Experimental group girls. Therefore the hypothesis is rejected.

FINDING

There is significance difference between the mean scores of post-test in control group girls and Experimental group girls. Therefore the **hypothesis is rejected.**

HYPOTHESIS – 9

There is no significant difference between the mean scores of Control and Experimental group students of pre-test performance in achieving algebracial learning among IX standard students.

TABLE 9

S. No	Gender	N	Mean	Standard Deviation	t – value	Level of significance at 0.05 level
1	Control Group pre test	40	29.72	7.35		
2	Experimental Group pre test	40	30.93	7.72	0.7189	No significant

NULL HYPOTHESIS

Since our obtained 't' – value (0.7189) is less than the table value (1.96) at 0.05% level degree of freedom 78, there is no significance difference between the mean scores of control group and experimental group pre-test performance and therefore the hypothesis is accepted.

FINDING

There is no significance difference between the mean scores of control group and experimental group pre-test performance and therefore the **hypothesis is accepted** .

HYPOTHESIS – 10

There is no significant difference between the mean scores of Control and Experimental group students of post-test performance in achieving algebraical learning among IX standard students.

TABLE 10

S. No	Gender	N	Mean	Standard Deviation	t – value	Level of significance at 0.05 level
1	Control Group post test	40	32.8	7.58		
2	Experimental Group post test	40	37.33	5.71	2.012	significant

NULL HYPOTHESIS

Since our obtained 't' – value (2.012) is greater than the table value (1.96) at 0.05% level degree of freedom 78, there is significance difference between the mean scores of control group and experimental group post-test performance and therefore the hypothesis is rejected.

FINDING

There is significance difference between the mean scores of control group and experimental group post-test performance and therefore the **hypothesis is rejected.**

HYPOTHESIS – 11

There is no significant difference between the mean scores of Control group students of pre-test and post-test performance in achieving algebraical learning among IX standard students.

TABLE 11

S. No	Control Group	N	Mean	Standard Deviation	t – value	Level of significance at 0.05 level
1	Pre - test	40	29.72	7.35		
2	Post - test	40	32.8	7.58	1.855	No significant

NULL HYPOTHESIS

Since our obtained 't' – value (1.855) is less than the table value (1.96) at 0.05% level degree of freedom 78, there is no significance difference between the mean scores of control group of pre-test and post-test performance and therefore the hypothesis is accepted.

FINDING

There is no significance difference between the mean scores of control group of pre-test and post-test performance and therefore the **hypothesis is accepted.**

HYPOTHESIS – 12

There is no significant difference between the mean scores of Experimental group students of pre-test and post-test performance in achieving algebraical learning among IX standard students.

TABLE12

S. No	Experimental Group	N	Mean	Standard Deviation	t – value	Level of significance at 0.05 level
1	Pre - test	40	30.93	7.72		
2	Post – test	40	37.33	5.71	4.218	significant

NULL HYPOTHESIS

Since our obtained 't' – value (4.218) is less than the table value (1.96) at 0.05% level degree of freedom 78, there is significance difference between the mean scores of pre-test and post-test performances. Therefore the hypothesis is rejected.

FINDING

There is significance difference between the mean scores of pre-test and post-test performances. Therefore the **hypothesis is rejected**.

Chapter V

Summary of Findings and Conclusion

INTRODUCTION

Research methods are utmost importance in a research process. They describe the various steps of the plan of attack to be adopted in solving problems. The present problem comes under experimental research as the study deals with the existing or present condition of IX standard students.

Though the data are valid, reliable and adequate, they do not serve any useful purpose unless they are carefully processed, systematically classified and tabulated, scientifically analyzed, intelligently interpreted and rationally concluded.

According to Best (1977), "Statistical data describe group behaviours or group characteristics abstracted from a number of individual observation which are combined to make generalization possible. The data after collection have to be processed and analyzed in accordance with the outline laid down for the purpose at the time of developing the research plan. Analysis of data is thus considered as an important awareness of any type of research. It needs high level of judgement skill, thorough knowledge and technical ability of generalization.

Interpretation of data is an extremely important and useful branch of important and useful branch of science of statistics. Statistical facts by themselves have no utility, but interpretation makes it possible to utilize the collected data in various fields of activity. The usefulness of collected data lies in its proper interpretation.

STATEMENT OF THE PROBLEM

Problem of the present research is to study the *Effectiveness of certain Intervention Strategies in Achieving Algebraical learning Among IX standard students.*"

OBJECTIVES OF THE STUDY

1. To find out whether there is any significant difference between the mean scores of boys and girls in pre-test of control group in achieving Algebraical learning among IX standard students.
2. To find out whether there is any significant difference between the mean scores of boys and girls in pre-test of Experimental group in achieving Algebraical learning among IX standard students.
3. To find out whether there is any significant difference between the mean scores of boys in pre-test of control group and Experimental group in achieving Algebraical learning among IX standard students.
4. To find out whether there is any significant difference between the mean scores of girls in pre-test of Control group and Experimental group in achieving Algebraical learning among IX standard students.
5. To find out whether there is any significant difference between the mean scores of boys and girls in post-test of control group in achieving Algebraical learning among IX standard students.
6. To find out whether there is any significant difference between the mean scores of boys and girls in post-test of Experimental group in achieving Algebraical learning among IX standard students.

7. To find out whether there is any significant difference between the mean scores of boys in post-test of control group and Experimental group in achieving Algebraical learning among IX standard students.
8. To find out whether there is any significant difference between the mean scores of girls in post-test of control group and Experimental group in achieving Algebraical learning among IX standard students.
9. To find out whether there is any significant difference between the mean scores of control group and Experimental group of pre-test performance in achieving Algebraical learning among IX standard students.
10. To find out whether there is any significant difference between the mean scores of control group and Experimental group of post-test performance in achieving Algebraical learning among IX standard students.
11. To find out whether there is any significant difference between the mean scores of control group of pre-test and post-test performance in achieving Algebraical learning among IX standard students.
12. To find out whether there is any significant difference between the mean scores of Experimental group of pre-test and post-test performance in achieving Algebraical learning among IX standard students.

SUMMARY OF FINDINGS

1. There is no significance difference between the mean scores of boys and girls in pre-test of control group and therefore the **hypothesis is accepted**.
2. There is no significance difference between the mean scores of boys and girls in pre-test of Experimental group and therefore the **hypothesis is accepted**.
3. There is no significance difference between the mean scores of pre-test in control group boys and Experimental group boys. Therefore the **hypothesis is accepted.**

4. There is no significance difference between the mean scores of pre-test in control group girls and Experimental group girls. Therefore the **hypothesis is accepted**.
5. There is no significance difference between the mean scores of boys and girls in post-test of control group and therefore the **hypothesis is accepted**.
6. There is no significance difference between the mean scores of boys and girls in post-test of experimental group and therefore the **hypothesis is accepted**.
7. There is no significance difference between the mean scores of pre-test in control group boys and Experimental group boys. Therefore the **hypothesis is accepted**.
8. There is significance difference between the mean scores of post-test in control group girls and Experimental group girls. Therefore the **hypothesis is rejected**.
9. There is no significance difference between the mean scores of control group and experimental group pre-test performance and therefore the **hypothesis is accepted**
10. There is significance difference between the mean scores of control group and experimental group post-test performance and therefore the **hypothesis is rejected**.
11. There is no significance difference between the mean scores of control group of pre-test and post-test performance and therefore the **hypothesis is accepted**.
12. There is significance difference between the mean scores of pre-test and post-test performances. Therefore the **hypothesis is rejected**.

EDUCATIONAL IMPLICATIONS OF THE STUDY

Teacher using selected strategies during the problem solving session will help the students in solving the problem accurately; teachers can also develop creativity and self confidence among students in solving problems mentally. Teachers can assist in optimizing then the learning potentialities as problem solvers. In class room, teacher need to be problem solvers, they should emulate the examples of good problem solvers; they should also make the students think deeply so as to enable them to solve problems methodically. Therefore it is of the greatest importance that problem solving should become one of the primary functions in the elementary, high and higher secondary schools, while teaching mathematics.

SUGGESTIONS FOR THE FUTHRER STUDY

1. The present study was confined to only one school. The same study may be executed to a large number of schools combining these located both in rural and urban areas.
2. The study was conducted on the chapter "Algebra" the study may be conducted on other mathematical concepts also.
3. The study has been limited to IX standard and this may be extended to XII standard to find out the further impact of this strategy.
4. The study may be conducted in other matriculation schools of Tamil Nadu.
5. Separate studies may be carried out for boys and girls to find out gender differences.
6. The investigations may be extended to graduate and post graduate levels to find out the effectiveness of the approach at the tertiary level.

CONCLUSION

Though the strategies, the mathematics algebriacial achieving of students has increased and comparably the student's score on the strategy has also increased. From this, it is evident that problem solving skill could be increased if we are able to train the students to use strategies.

BIBILIOGRAPHY

1. Aggarwal (1990), "Statistical Methods, Concepts, Application and Computation", Sterling Publications, New Delhi.
2. Awasthy (1965), "Teaching Techniques in India" Allied Publishers Pvt. (Ltd), Bombay.

3. Dar (1965), "Science Teaching in Schools", Jallandhar – Sterling Publishers, Banglore.
4. Falk (1965), "Biology Teaching Methods", Johnwiley Publishers, London.
5. Herr, Norm and James Cunnigham (1999), "Hands – On Chemistry Activities with Real-Life Applications". John wiely/ Jossey-Bass, Publishers Northridge, California.
6. Jevons (1965), "The Teaching of Science", Allen and Unwin Ltd, Bombay.
7. Karmer (1975), "Teaching the Life Science", Macmilliam Publication, London.
8. Kiran Lata Pangwal and Shireesh Pal Singh (2011), "Emerging Trends in Education", A.P.H. Publishing Corporation, New Delhi.
9. Nair (1971), "Teaching Science in our Schools", S. Chand and Co. Pvt. Ltd., New Delhi.
10. Sharma (1992), "Modern Science Teaching", Dhanpat Rai & Sons Publishers, Delhi.
11. Sik. Gupta (1978), "Teaching Physical Sciences in Secondary Schools", Sterling Publishers Pvt. Ltd, New Delhi.
12. Vaidya, Narendera (1968), "Problem Solving in Science", S.Chand and Co. Pvt. Ltd., New Delhi.
13. Vaidya, Narendera (1970), "Some Aspects of Piaget's Work and Science Teaching", S.Chand and Co. Pvt. Ltd, New Delhi.
14. Schmalz, M.S. (2008). "IT/CS Workshop in Multimedia Courseware". Journal of Teaching Technical Concepts. 15. 23-30.
15. Johnstone, A.H. (1993). The development of Chemistry teaching. Journal of Chemical Education, 70(9), 701 ± 705.
16. Halimah (1999). "Multimedia Learning in Computer Science". Journal Pendidikan.2.1-5.
17. Gabel, D. (1998). The complexity of chemistry and implications for teaching. In B.J. Fraser & K.G. Tobin (Eds.), International

handbook of science education (pp. 233 ± 248). Boston, MA: Kluwer Academic Publishers.

18. Krajcik, J.S. (1991). Developing students' understanding of chemical concepts. In S.M. Glynn, R.H. Yeany, & B.K. Britton (Eds.), the psychology of learning science: International perspective on the psychological foundations of technology-based learning environments (pp. 117 ± 145). Hillsdale, NJ: Erlbaum.

19. Kozma, R.B., Russell, J., Jones, T., Marx, N., & Davis, J. (1996). The use of multiple, linked representations to facilitate science understanding. In R.G.S. Vosniadou, E. Decorte, & H. Mandel (Eds.), International perspective on the psychological foundations of technology-based learning environments (pp. 41 ± 60). Hillsdale, NJ: Erlbaum

20. Schmalz, M.S. (2008). "IT/CS Workshop in Multimedia Courseware". Journal of Teaching Technical Concepts. 15. 23-30.

21. Halimah (1999). "Multimedia Learning in Computer Science". Jurnal Pendidikan. 2. 1-5.

22. Johnstone, A.H. (1993). The development of chemistry teaching. Journal of Chemical Education, 70(9), 701 ± 705.

23. Griffths, A.K., & Preston, K.R. (1992). Grade-12 students' misconceptions relating to fundamental characteristics of atoms and molecules. Journal of Research in Science Teaching, 29(6), 611 ± 628.

24. Williamson, V.M., & Abraham, M.R. (1995). The effects of computer animation on the particulate mental models of college chemistry students. Journal of Research in Science Teaching, 32, 521 ± 534.

25. Hoffmann, R., & Laszlo, R. (1991). Representation in chemistry. Angewandte Chemie, 30, 1 ± 16.

26. Kozma, R.B., Chin, E., Russell, J., & Marx, N. (2000). The roles of representations and tools in the chemistry laboratory and their implications for chemistry instruction. Journal of the Learning Sciences, 9(2), 105 ± 143.

27. Gabel, D.L., Samuel, K.V., & Hunn, D. (1987). Understanding the particulate nature of matter. Journal of Chemical Education, 64, 695 ± 697.

28. Copolo, C.F., & Hounshell, P.B. (1995). Using three-dimensional models to teach molecular structures in high school chemistry. Journal of Science Education and Technology, 4(4), 295 ± 305.

29. Gabel, D., & Sherwood, R. (1980). The effect of student manipulation of molecular models on chemistry achievement according to Piagetian level. Journal of Research in Science Teaching, 17(1), 75 ± 81.

30. Barnea (2010), "Journal of Chemistry Education Research and Practice", Vol. 11, P-218.

31. Briggs (2011), "Journal of Chemistry Education", Vol. 88, P-1034.

32. Carrio (2011), "Journal of Biological Education", Vol. 45, P-29.

33. Charles (2001), "Journal of Science Scope", Vol. 25, P-27.

34. Goodwin (2011), "Journal of School Science Review", Vol.92,P-49.

35. Leopold (2012), "Journal Learning and Instruction", Vol.7, P106.

36. Loverude (2011), "Journal of Physics Education Research", Vol 7, P106.

37. Lyon (2011), "Journal of Natural Resources and Life Sciences Education", Vol. 40, P199.

38. Roberto (2011), "Journal of College Science Teaching", Vol 40, P85.

39. Rahayu (2011), "Journal of Research in Science and Technological Education", Vol. 29, P 169.